HEBREW
in 10 minutes a day®

by Kristine Kershul, M.A., University of California, Santa Barbara

Consultant: Daphna Donyets

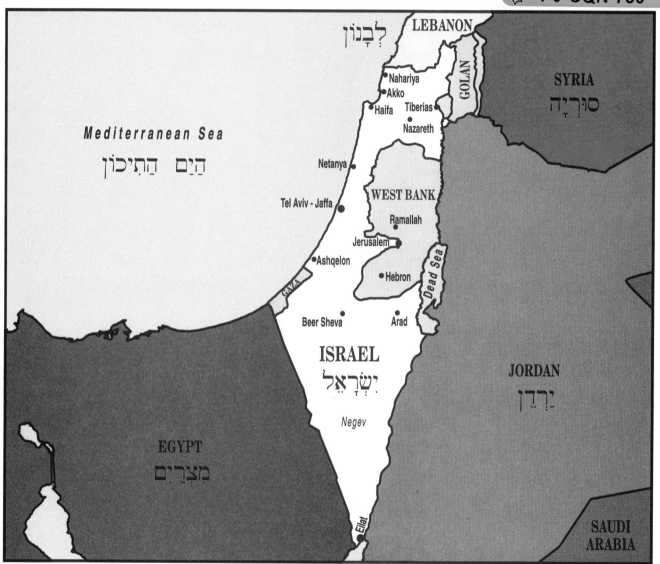

Bilingual Books, Inc.

1719 West Nickerson Street, Seattle, WA 98119
Tel: (206) 284-4211 Fax: (206) 284-3660
www.10minutesaday.com

ISBN-13: 978-0-944502-25-9   ISBN-10: 0-944502-25-3   Third printing, July 2006

Can you say this?

(zeh) *(mah)*
מַה זֶה ? ←
is it · what

(sef-air) *(zeh)*
זֶה סֵפֶר ? ←
a book · it is

(sef-air) *(roht-seh)* *(ah-nee)*
אֲנִי רוֹצֶה סֵפֶר . ←
want · I

If you can say this, you can learn to speak Hebrew. You will be able to easily order meals, concert tickets, pastry, or anything else you wish. With your best Hebrew accent you simply ask "← זֶה *(zeh)* מַה *(mah)*?" and, upon learning what it is, you can order it with "← אֲנִי *(ah-nee)* רוֹצֶה *(roht-seh)* אֶת *(et)* זֶה *(zeh)*." Sounds easy, doesn't it?

The purpose of this book is to give you an **immediate** speaking ability in Hebrew. Using the acclaimed "*10 minutes a day®*" methodology, you will acquire a large working vocabulary that will suit your needs, and you will acquire it almost automatically. To aid you, this book offers a unique and easy system of pronunciation above each word which walks you through learning Hebrew. Just remember, you read Hebrew from right to left. Look for the blue arrows (←) as they will help you develop this habit.

If you are planning a trip or moving to where Hebrew is spoken, you will be leaps ahead of everyone if you take just a few minutes a day to learn the easy key words that this book offers. Start with Step 1 and don't skip around. Each day work as far as you can comfortably go in those 10 minutes. Don't overdo it. Some days you might want to just review. If you forget a word, you can always look it up in the glossary. Spend your first 10 minutes studying the map on the previous page. And yes, have fun learning your new language.

As you work through the Steps, always use the special features which only this series offers. This book includes sticky labels and flash cards, free words, puzzles and quizzes. When you have completed the book, cut out the menu guide and take it along on your trip.

When you first see words like מַה and סֵפֶר Hebrew can appear forbidding. However, Hebrew is a logical language once you learn how to decode these letters. You will see different types of Hebrew: printed as in this book; cursive which looks different from the printed form; Hebrew with or without the vowel signs; Hebrew with additional dots inside many of the letters as an indication of stress and Hebrew with an additional י or ו to make reading easier. Step one, decode the alphabet. Hebrew is written from right to left which takes some getting used to, but just practice, practice, practice!

These Hebrew letters sound alike but do not look alike. Practice writing all these letters.

(t)	*(t)*		*(s)*	*(s)*		*(k)*	*(k)*		*(H)*	*(H)*		*(v)*	*(v)*
ת	ט		שׂ	ס		ק	כּ		כ	ח		ו	ב

In these letters, the dot, called a "dagesh," is the only way to differentiate one from another.

(sh)	*(s)*		*(f)*	*(p)*		*(H)*	*(k)*		*(v)*	*(b)*
שׁ	שׂ		פ	פּ		כ	כּ		ב	בּ

When printing carefully distinguish between the following letters as the differences are slight.

(n)	*(g)*		*(n)*	*(v)*		*(t)*	*(H)*		*(h)*	*(H)*		*(r)*	*(d)*
נ	ג		נ	ב		ת	ח		ה	ח		ר	ד

Some letters also change their appearance when they are at the end of a word.

(ts)	*(ts)*		*(m)*	*(m)*		*(n)*	*(n)*		*(f)*	*(f)*		*(H)*	*(H)*
ץ ← צ			ם ← מ			ן ← נ			ף ← פ			ך ← כ	

Vowels in Hebrew look like dots and dashes below, above or next to the Hebrew letters. These dots and dashes make it easier for you to learn to pronounce Hebrew. Later, when you are more comfortable with the language, you will not need them anymore. Here are some examples.

(uh) or silent	*(oo) as in boo!*	*(ee) or (ih) as in sit*	*(oh)*	*(eh) as in let*	*(ay) as in day or (eh) as in let*	*(ah)*
אְ	וּ	יִ	וֹ	אֶ	אֵ	אַ אָ
אְ	אֻ	אִ	אֹ	אֶ	אֵ	אָ

Sometimes the phonetics may seem to contradict your pronunciation guide. Don't panic. The easiest and best possible phonetics have been chosen for each individual word. Pronounce the phonetics just as you see them. Don't over-analyze them. Speak with a Hebrew accent and, above all, enjoy yourself.

On the next page you will find a listing of all Hebrew letters in Hebrew alphabetical order. Practice these new letters and sounds with the examples given which are Hebrew first names.

English Sound	Hebrew Letter	Write it here	English Sound	Hebrew Name	Write it here
(silent, takes its sound from the vowel)	א		(ah-hah-rohn)	אַהֲרֹן	
b	בּ		(ben)	בֶּן	
v	ב		(reh-oo-ven)	רְאוּבֵן	
g (as in good)	ג		(gahd)	גַּד	
d	ד		(dahn)	דָּן	
h	ה		(hil-el)	הִלֵּל	
v	ו		(veh-red)	וֶרֶד	
z	ז		(zee-vah)	זִיוָה	
H=hk (breathe hard)	ח		(Hah-nah)	חַנָּה	
t	ט		(toh-vah)	טוֹבָה	
y	י		(yah-ah-kohv)	יַעֲקֹב	
k	כּ		(kee-nair-et)	כִּנֶּרֶת	
H=hk (breathe hard)	כ		(mee-Hahl)	מִיכַל	
l	ל		(lay-ah)	לֵאָה	
m	מ		(may-rahv)	מֵרַב	
n	נ		(nah-tahn)	נָתָן	
s	ס		(sahv-yohn)	סַבְיוֹן	
(silent, takes its sound from the vowel)	ע		(ah-mohs)	עָמוֹס	
p	פּ		(p'nee-nah)	פְּנִינָה	
f	פ		(free-dah)	פְּרִידָה	
ts (as in cats)	צ		(ts'vee)	צְבִי	
k	ק		(kair-ren)	קֶרֶן	
r	ר		(root)	רוּת	
sh	שׁ		(shmoo-el)	שְׁמוּאֵל	
s	שׂ		(sah-rah)	שָׂרָה	
t	ת		(tah-mar)	תָּמָר	

4

When you arrive in יִשְׂרָאֵל *(yiss-rah-el)* **Israel** ← the very first thing you will need to do is ask questions —

"Where is the bus stop?" "Where can I exchange money?" "Where (אֵיפֹה) *(ay-foh)* **where** ← is the lavatory?"

"אֵיפֹה *(ay-foh)* **where** ← is a restaurant?" "אֵיפֹה *(ay-foh)* **where** ← do I catch a taxi?" "אֵיפֹה *(ay-foh)* **where** ← is a good hotel?" "אֵיפֹה *(ay-foh)* ← is

my luggage?" and the list will go on and on for the entire length of your visit. In Hebrew, there

are SEVEN KEY QUESTION WORDS to learn. For example, the seven key question words

will help you find out exactly what you are ordering in a restaurant before you order it — and not

after the surprise (or shock!) arrives. Notice that the words for "what," "who," and "when" all

begin with the same letter — "מ" (which is pronounced like "m"). Take a few minutes to study

and practice saying the seven key question words listed below. Then cover the עִבְרִית *(eev-reet)* **Hebrew** ← with

your hand and fill in each of the blanks with the matching עִבְרִית *(eev-reet)* **Hebrew** ← word.

_____ אֵיפֹה WHERE = אֵיפֹה ← *(ay-foh)*

_____ WHAT = מַה ← *(mah)*

_____ WHO = מִי ← *(me)*

_____ מָתַי WHEN = מָתַי ← *(mah-tie)*

_____ HOW = אֵיךְ ← *(ayH)*

_____ לָמָה WHY = לָמָה ← *(lah-mah)*

_____ HOW MUCH = כַּמָה ← *(kah-mah)*

5

Now test yourself to see if you really can keep these *(mih-lim)* מִלִּים ← straight in your mind. Draw

lines between the *(eev-reet)* עִבְרִית ← and English equivalents below.

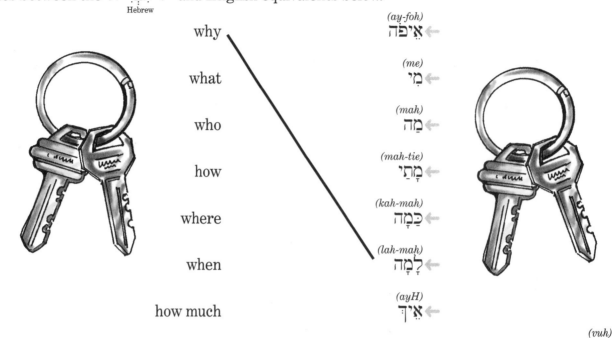

why		*(ay-foh)* אֵיפֹה ←
what		*(me)* מִי ←
who		*(mah)* מָה ←
how		*(mah-tie)* מָתַי ←
where		*(kah-mah)* כַּמָּה ←
when		*(lah-mah)* לָמָּה ←
how much		*(ayH)* אֵיךְ ←

Examine the following questions containing these words. Practice the sentences out loud *(vuh)* וְ and

then practice by copying the Hebrew in the blanks underneath each question.

(zeh) (mah)
מָה זֶה ?
is it   what?
_____

(zeh) (ayH)
אֵיךְ זֶה ?
is it   how
_____

(zeh) (ay-foh)
אֵיפֹה זֶה ?
is it   where?
_____

(zeh)(mah-tie)
מָתַי זֶה ?
is it   when
_____

(zeh) (kah-mah)
כַּמָּה זֶה ?
is it   how much
_____

(zeh) (me)
מִי זֶה ?
is it   who
_____

(ay-foh)
"אֵיפֹה" ← will be your most used question *(mih-lah)* מִלָּה . Say each of the following *(eev-reet)* עִבְרִית ←
where   word   Hebrew

sentences aloud. Then write out each sentence without looking at the example. If you don't

succeed on the first try, don't give up. Just practice each sentence until you are able to do it

easily. The blue arrows are there to remind you to read and write from right to left!

(shay-roo-teem) *(yesh)* *(ay-foh)*
אֵיפֹה יֵשׁ שֵׁירוּתִים ?
where (is) there toilet

(tahk-see)
טַקְסִי ?
taxi
(yesh) *(ay-foh)*
אֵיפֹה יֵשׁ
(moh-neet)
מוֹנִית ?
taxi

(oh-toh-boos) *(yesh)* *(ay-foh)*
אֵיפֹה יֵשׁ אוֹטוֹבּוּס ?
where (is) there (a) bus

_____   _____   אֵיפֹה יֵשׁ אוֹטוֹבּוּס ?

(mees-ah-dah) *(yesh)* *(ay-foh)*
אֵיפֹה יֵשׁ מִסְעָדָה ?
(a) restaurant

(bahnk) *(yesh)* *(ay-foh)*
אֵיפֹה יֵשׁ בַּנְק ?
(a) bank

(mah-lohn) *(yesh)* *(ay-foh)*
אֵיפֹה יֵשׁ מָלוֹן ?
where (is) there (a) hotel

_____   _____   _____

(ken)
כֵּן , you can see similarities between *(eev-reet)* עֲבְרִית and *(ahn-gleet)* אַנְגְּלִית , if you look closely. Don't let
yes   Hebrew   English

the Hebrew alphabet confuse you. The many similarities in pronunciation will surprise you and

make your work here easier. Listed below are five "free" words beginning with "א" (aleph) to

help you get started. Be sure to say each *(mih-lah)* מִלָה aloud *(vuh)* וְ then write out the *(eev-reet)* עֲבְרִית word
word   and   Hebrew

in the blank to the left.

אֲגַם, אֲגַם, אֲגַם, אֲגַם, אֲגַם	lake............(ah-gahm)............ אֲגַם ← ☑
_____	autograph.........(oh-toh-grahf)....... אוֹטוֹגְרָף ☐
א	vending machine ....(oh-toh-maht)....... אוֹטוֹמָט ☐
_____	Australia.........(oh-strahl-yah)..... אוֹסְטְרַלְיָה ☐
_____	opera..........(oh-peh-rah)........ אוֹפֶּרָה ☐

(mih-lim)
Free מִלִים like these will appear at the bottom of the following pages in a yellow color band.
words

They are easy — enjoy them! Don't forget that in modern Hebrew both "א" and "ע" are silent.

Hebrew does not have words for "a" or "an," which makes things easier for you. The letter "ה" with a vowel in front of a Hebrew word (on the right) means "the." If you do not see "ה" in front of a Hebrew word, "a" or "an" is assumed. Here are some examples.

(tahk-see)
טַקְסִי ←
taxi

(hah-tahk-see)
הַטַקְסִי ←
the taxi

(shay-roo-teem)
שֵׁירוּתִים ←
toilet

(hah-shay-roo-tim)
הַשֵׁירוּתִים ←
the toilet

(bahnk)
בַּנְק ←
bank

(hah-bahnk)
הַבַּנְק ←
the bank

(mah-lohn)
מָלוֹן ←
hotel

(hah-mah-lohn)
הַמָלוֹן ←
the hotel

(oh-toh-boos)
אוֹטוֹבּוּס ←
bus

(hah-oh-toh-boos)
הָאוֹטוֹבּוּס ←
the bus

(mees-ah-dah)
מִסְעָדָה ←
restaurant

(hah-mees-ah-dah)
הַמִסְעָדָה ←
the restaurant

This only appears difficult because it is different from English. Just remember the core of the

(mih-lah)
מִלָה ←
word

doesn't change, so you should always be able to recognize it. For instance, you will be

understood whether you say

(bahnk)
בַּנְק ←
bank

or

(hah-bahnk)
הַבַּנְק ←
the bank

. Learn to look and listen for the core of the word, and remember to read from right to left — the blue arrows are there to help you.

In Step 2 you were introduced to the Seven Key QuestionWords. These seven words are the basics, the most essential building blocks for learning Hebrew. Throughout this book you will come across keys asking you to fill in the missing question word. Use this opportunity not only to fill in the blank on that key, but to review all your question words. Play with the new sounds, speak slowly and have fun.

baker	*(oh-feh)*	אוֹפֶּה ←	☐
nurse	*(ah-Hoht*	אָחוֹת	☐
Italy	*(ee-tahl-yah)*	אִיטַלְיָה	☐
Europe	*(ay-roh-pah)*	אֵירוֹפָּה	☐
European	*(ay-roh-pee)*	אֵירוֹפִּי	☐

א

Before you proceed עִם *(eem)* ← *with* this Step, situate yourself comfortably in your living room. Now look

around you. Can you name the things that you see in this חֶדֶר *(Hed-air)* ← *room* in עִבְרִית *(eev-reet)* ← *Hebrew* ? After

practicing these מִלִים *(mih-lim)* ← *words* out loud, write them in the blanks below וְ *(vuh)* ← *and* on the next page.

_____ מְנוֹרָה *(mnoh-rah)*
lamp

_____ סַפָּה *(sah-pah)*
sofa

_____ כִּסֵא *(kis-eh)*
chair

_____ שָׁטִיחַ *(shah-tee-aH)*
carpet

_____ שׁוּלְחָן *(shool-Hahn)*
table

דלת דלת דלת דלת ← דֶּלֶת *(deh-let)*
door

_____ שָׁעוֹן *(shah-ohn)*
clock

_____ וִילוֹן *(vee-lohn)*
curtain

_____ טֶלֶפוֹן *(teh-leh-fohn)*
telephone

חַלוֹן *(Hah-lohn)*
window

_____

תְּמוּנָה *(tmoo-nah)*
picture

_____

In Step 3, you learned עִבְרִית *(eev-reet)* ← *Hebrew* has no words for "a" or "an," and that the pronunciation of the

עִבְרִית *(eev-reet)* ← *Hebrew* word for "the" ה varies. Now open your סֵפֶר *(sef-air)* ← *book* to the sticky labels on page 17 and

later on page 35. Peel off the first 11 labels וְ *(vuh)* ← *and* proceed around your room labeling these

items in your home. This will help to increase your עִבְרִית *(eev-reet)* ← *Hebrew* word power easily. Don't forget to

say הַמִלָה *(hah-mih-lah)* ← *the word* as you attach each label. Now ask yourself, "אֵיפֹה יֵשׁ תְּמוּנָה?" *(ay-foh) (yesh) (tmoo-nah)* *picture* and point

at it while you answer, "שָׁם יֵשׁ תְּמוּנָה." *(shahm) (yesh) (tmoo-nah)* *there* *picture* Continue on down the list above until you feel

comfortable with these new מִלִים *(mih-lim)* ← *words* .

_____
_____
_____
_____

א

Ireland	*(eer-lahnd)*	אִירְלַנְד ←	☐
farmer	*(ee-kar)*	אִיכָּר	☐
algebra	*(ahl-geh-brah)*	אַלְגֶבְרָה	☐
elegant	*(eh-leh-gahn-tee)*	אֶלֶגַנְטִי	☐
alcohol	*(ahl-koh-hohl)*	אַלְכּוֹהוֹל	☐

(hah-bite)
the house = הַבַּיִת ←

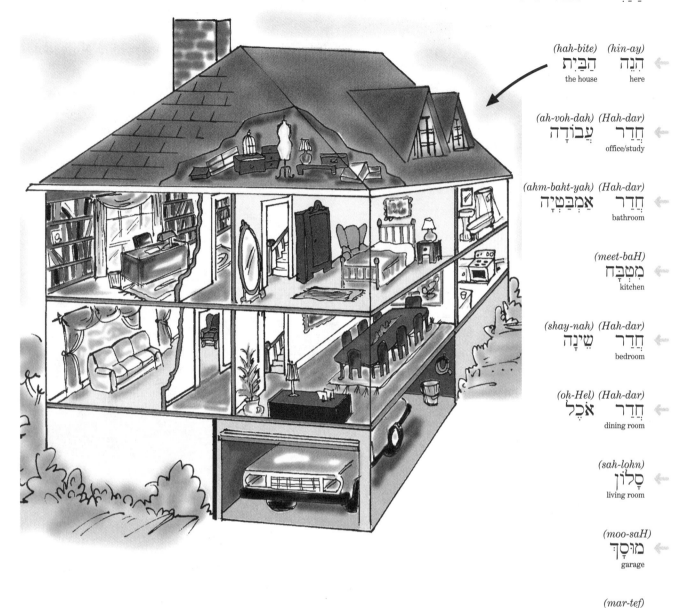

(hah-bite) *(hin-ay)*
הַבַּיִת הִנֵּה ←
the house   here

(ah-voh-dah) *(Hah-dar)*
חֶדֶר עֲבוֹדָה ←
office/study

(ahm-baht-yah) *(Hah-dar)*
חֲדַר אַמְבַּטְיָה ←
bathroom

(meet-baH)
מִטְבָּח ←
kitchen

(shay-nah) *(Hah-dar)*
חֲדַר שֵׁנָה ←
bedroom

(oh-Hel) *(Hah-dar)*
חֲדַר אֹכֶל ←
dining room

(sah-lohn)
סָלוֹן ←
living room

(moo-saH)
מוּסָךְ ←
garage

(mar-tef)
מַרְתֵּף ←
basement

(mih-lim)
While learning these new מִלִּים ←, let's not forget:
         words

(may-Hoh-neet)
מְכוֹנִית ←
car

(oh-fah-noh-ah)
אוֹפַנּוֹעַ ←
motorcycle

(oh-fah-nah-yeem)
אוֹפַנַּיִם ←
bicycle

electronic	*(eh-lek-troh-nee)*	אֶלֶקְטְרוֹנִי ← ☐
ambulance	*(ahm-boo-lahns)*	אַמְבּוּלַנְס ☐
artist	*(oh-mahn)*	אָמָן ☐
England	*(ahn-glee-yah)*	אַנְגְלִיָה ☐
antibiotic	*(ahn-tee-bee-oh-tee-kah)*	אַנְטִיבִּיוֹטִיקָה ☐

א

(Hah-tool)
חָתוּל
cat

(gahn)
גַן
garden

(prah-Heem)
פְּרָחִים
flowers

(kel-ev)
כֶּלֶב
dog

(doh-ar) (tay-vaht)
תֵּיבַת דוֹאַר
mailbox

(doh-ar)
דוֹאַר
mail

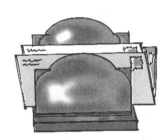

Peel off the next set of labels *(vuh)* וְ wander through your *(bite)* בַּיִת ← house learning these new *(mih-lim)* מִלִּים ← words . It will be somewhat difficult to label your *(kel-ev)* כֶּלֶב ← dog , *(Hah-tool)* חָתוּל ← cat or *(prah-Heem)* פְּרָחִים ← flowers , but be creative. Practice by asking yourself, *(gahn) (yesh) (ay-foh)* "אֵיפֹה יֵשׁ גַן ← garden ?" and reply, *(gahn) (yesh) (shahm)* "שָׁם יֵשׁ גַן ← garden ." *(bite) (yesh) (ay-foh)* "אֵיפֹה יֵשׁ בַּיִת ← house ?"

(shah-lohsh) *(shtah-yeem)* *(aH-aht)*
אַחַת, שְׁתַּיִם, שָׁלוֹשׁ ←
three two one

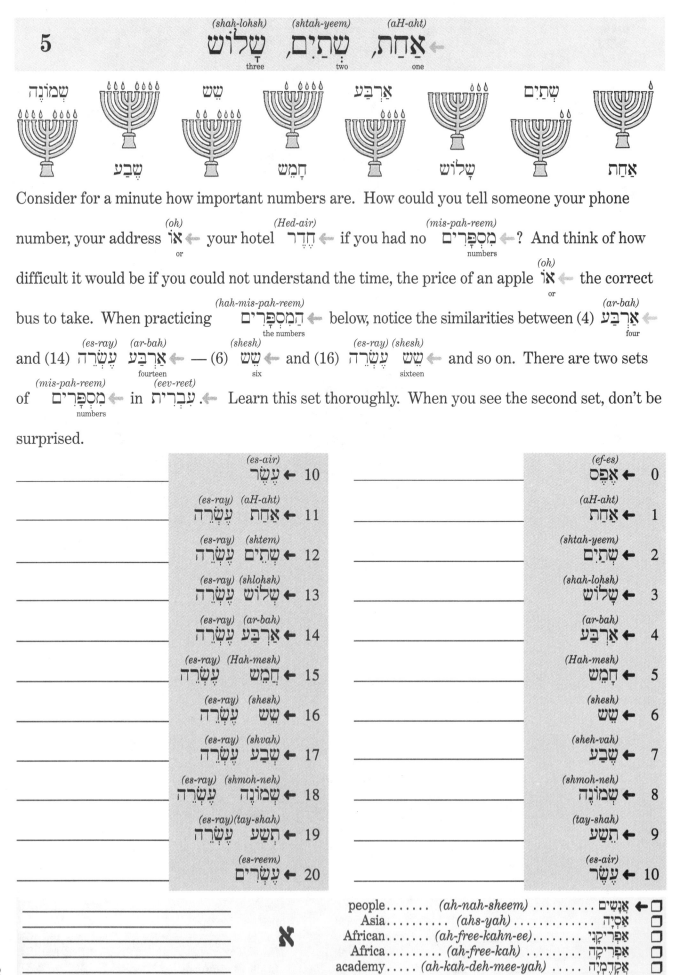

שְׁמוֹנֶה ... שֵׁשׁ ... אַרְבַּע ... שְׁתַּיִם ...

שֶׁבַע ... שָׁלוֹשׁ ... חָמֵשׁ ... אַחַת

Consider for a minute how important numbers are. How could you tell someone your phone

number, your address *(oh)* אוֹ ← your hotel *(Hed-air)* חֶדֶר ← if you had no *(mis-pah-reem)* מִסְפָּרִים ←? And think of how
or numbers

difficult it would be if you could not understand the time, the price of an apple *(oh)* אוֹ ← the correct
or

bus to take. When practicing *(hah-mis-pah-reem)* הַמִּסְפָּרִים ← below, notice the similarities between (4) *(ar-bah)* אַרְבַּע ←
the numbers four

and (14) *(es-ray)* *(ar-bah)* אַרְבַּע עֶשְׂרֵה ← — (6) *(shesh)* שֵׁשׁ ← and (16) *(es-ray)* *(shesh)* שֵׁשׁ עֶשְׂרֵה ← and so on. There are two sets
fourteen six sixteen

of *(mis-pah-reem)* מִסְפָּרִים ← in *(eev-reet)* עִבְרִית ←. Learn this set thoroughly. When you see the second set, don't be
numbers

surprised.

(es-air) עֶשֶׂר ← 10	*(ef-es)* אֶפֶס ← 0
(es-ray) *(aH-aht)* אַחַת עֶשְׂרֵה ← 11	*(aH-aht)* אַחַת ← 1
(es-ray) *(shtem)* שְׁתֵּים עֶשְׂרֵה ← 12	*(shtah-yeem)* שְׁתַּיִם ← 2
(es-ray) *(shlohsh)* שְׁלוֹשׁ עֶשְׂרֵה ← 13	*(shah-lohsh)* שָׁלוֹשׁ ← 3
(es-ray) *(ar-bah)* אַרְבַּע עֶשְׂרֵה ← 14	*(ar-bah)* אַרְבַּע ← 4
(es-ray) *(Hah-mesh)* חָמֵשׁ עֶשְׂרֵה ← 15	*(Hah-mesh)* חָמֵשׁ ← 5
(es-ray) *(shesh)* שֵׁשׁ עֶשְׂרֵה ← 16	*(shesh)* שֵׁשׁ ← 6
(es-ray) *(shvah)* שְׁבַע עֶשְׂרֵה ← 17	*(sheh-vah)* שֶׁבַע ← 7
(es-ray) *(shmoh-neh)* שְׁמוֹנֶה עֶשְׂרֵה ← 18	*(shmoh-neh)* שְׁמוֹנֶה ← 8
*(es-ray)**(tay-shah)* תְּשַׁע עֶשְׂרֵה ← 19	*(tay-shah)* תְּשַׁע ← 9
(es-reem) עֶשְׂרִים ← 20	*(es-air)* עֶשֶׂר ← 10

אָ

people.......	*(ah-nah-sheem)*	אֲנָשִׁים ← ☐
Asia.........	*(ahs-yah)*	אַסְיָה ☐
African......	*(ah-free-kahn-ee)*	אַפְרִיקָנִי ☐
Africa......	*(ah-free-kah)*	אַפְרִיקָה ☐
academy.....	*(ah-kah-deh-mee-yah)*	אָקָדֶמְיָה ☐

Use these *(mis-pah-reem)* מִסְפָּרִים ← on a daily basis. Count to yourself *(beev-reet)* בְּעִבְרִית ← when you brush your teeth,

numbers   *in Hebrew*

exercise *(oh)* אוֹ ← commute to work. Fill in the blanks below according to *(hah-mis-pah-reem)* הַמִסְפָּרִים ← given in

or   *the numbers*

parentheses. Now is also a good time to learn these two very important phrases.

_____ *(bay-vah-kah-shah)* בְּבַקָשָׁה ... *(roht-seh)* רוֹצֶה *(ah-nee)* אֲנִי ←

                                                              please   *want*   *I*

_____ *(bay-vah-kah-shah)* בְּבַקָשָׁה ... *(roht-sim)* רוֹצִים *(ah-naH-noo)* אֲנַחְנוּ ←

                                                              please   *want*   *we*

_____ *(kah-mah)* כַּמָה ? ←   *(bay-vah-kah-shah)* בְּבַקָשָׁה . _____ (5) _____ *(roht-seh)* רוֹצֶה *(ah-nee)* אֲנִי ←

(5) *how many*   *please*   *want*   *I*

_____ *(kah-mah)* כַּמָה ? ←   *(bay-vah-kah-shah)* בְּבַקָשָׁה . _____ (9) _____ *(roht-seh)* רוֹצֶה *(ah-nee)* אֲנִי ←

(9) *how many*   *please*   *want*   *I*

_____ *(kah-mah)* כַּמָה ? ←   *(bay-vah-kah-shah)* בְּבַקָשָׁה . _____ (2) _____ *(roht-seh)* רוֹצֶה *(ah-nee)* אֲנִי ←

(2) *how many*   *please*

_____ כַּמָה ? ←   *(bay-vah-kah-shah)* בְּבַקָשָׁה . _____ (4) _____ *(roht-seh)* רוֹצֶה *(ah-nee)* אֲנִי ←

(4)   *please*

_____ *(kah-mah)* כַּמָה ? ←   *(bay-vah-kah-shah)* בְּבַקָשָׁה . _____ (7) _____ אֲנִי רוֹצֶה ←

(7) *how many*   *please*

_____ כַּמָה ? ←   *(bay-vah-kah-shah)* בְּבַקָשָׁה . _____ (10) _____ *(roht-sim)* רוֹצִים *(ah-naH-noo)* אֲנַחְנוּ ←

(10)   *please*   *want*   *we*

אַחַת אַחַת כַּמָה ? ←   *(bay-vah-kah-shah)* בְּבַקָשָׁה . _____ (1) _____ *(roht-sim)* רוֹצִים *(ah-naH-noo)* אֲנַחְנוּ ←

(1)   *please*   *want*   *we*

_____ כַּמָה ? ←   *(bay-vah-kah-shah)* בְּבַקָשָׁה . _____ (8) _____ *(roht-sim)* רוֹצִים אֲנַחְנוּ

(8)   *please*

_____ כַּמָה ? ←   *(kar-tih-seem)* כַּרְטִיסִים בְּבַקָשָׁה . _____ (3) _____ *(roht-seh)* רוֹצֶה *(ah-nee)* אֲנִי ←

(3)   *tickets*   *want*   *I*

_____ כַּמָה ? ←   *(gloo-yoht)* גְלוּיוֹת בְּבַקָשָׁה . _____ (6) _____ *(roht-sim)* רוֹצִים *(ah-naH-noo)* אֲנַחְנוּ ←

(6)   *postcards*   *want*   *we*

_____ *(how many)*   *(boo-leem)* בּוּלִים בְּבַקָשָׁה . _____ (5) _____ רוֹצִים אֲנַחְנוּ

(5)   *stamps*

_____

_____   ב

_____

ballet .... *(bah-let)* .... בַּלֶט ← ☐

bar .... *(bar)* .... בַּר ☐

bedouin .... *(bed-oo-ee)* .... בֶּדוּאִי ☐

Bulgaria ...... *(bool-gah-ree-yah)* ..... בּוּלְגָרְיָה ☐

boss .... *(bohs)* .... בּוֹס ☐

13

Now see if you can translate the following thoughts *(beev-reet)* בְּעִבְרִית ← . *(hah-t'shoo-voht)* הַתְּשׁוּבוֹת ← are provided at the answers

the bottom of *(hah-ah-mood)* הָעַמּוּד ← . the page

1. I want seven postcards please.

_____

2. I want four stamps please.

_____

3. We want two please.

_____

4. We want three please.

_____

Review *(hah-mis-pah-reem)* הַמִּסְפָּרִים ← 1 through 20. Write out your telephone number, fax number, and the numbers

cellular number. Then write out a friend's telephone number and then a relative's telephone

number. In Hebrew, numbers are written as in English from left to right.

(2   0   6)   3   4   0   —   4   4   2   2

_____

(____   ____   ____) ____ ____ ____ — ____ ____ ____ ____

_____

(____   ____   ____) ____ ____ ____ — ____ ____ ____ ____

_____

(ts'vah-eem)

צְבָעִים ← are the same in *(yiss-rah-el)* יִשְׂרָאֵל ← as they are in *(ah-meh-ree-kah)* אֲמֶרִיקָה ← — they just have different

colors   Israel   America

(sheh-moht) שֵׁמוֹת ← . The flag of *(yiss-rah-el)* יִשְׂרָאֵל ← is not only blue and while but also *(kah-Hohl)* כָּחֹל ← and *(lah-vahn)* לָבָן ← .

names   Israel   blue   white

The flag was created by taking the *(kah-Hohl)* כָּחֹל ← and *(lah-vahn)* לָבָן ← background of the traditional

blue   white

prayer shawl וְ adding the Star of David.

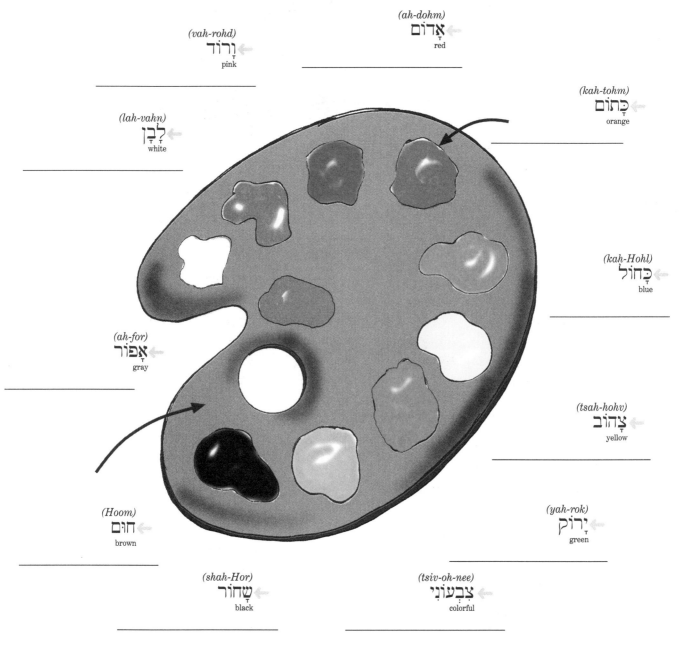

(vah-rohd) וָרֹד ← pink

(ah-dohm) אָדֹם ← red

(kah-tohm) כָּתֹם ← orange

(lah-vahn) לָבָן ← white

(kah-Hohl) כָּחֹל ← blue

(ah-for) אָפֹר ← gray

(tsah-hohv) צָהֹב ← yellow

(Hoom) חוּם ← brown

(yah-rok) יָרֹק ← green

(shah-Hor) שָׁחֹר ← black

(tsiv-oh-nee) צִבְעוֹנִי ← colorful

hospital......	*(bait-Hoh-leem)*	בֵּית חוֹלִים ← ☐
factory.....	*(bait-Hah-roh-shet)*	בֵּית חֲרֹשֶׁת ☐
synagogue........	*(bait-kness-et)*	בֵּית כְּנֶסֶת ☐
Bethlehem.......	*(bait-leh-Hem)*	בֵּית לֶחֶם ☐
workshop.....	*(bait-muh-lah-Hah)*	בֵּית מְלָאכָה ☐

בּ

Peel off the next group of labels וְ proceed to label these *(ts'vah-eem)* צְבָעִים ← (colors) in your *(bite)* בַּיִת. ← Identify the two or three dominant colors in the flags below.

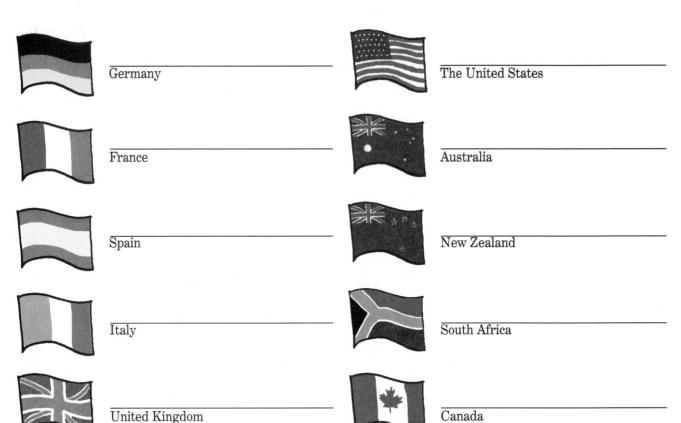

Germany _____

The United States _____

France _____

Australia _____

Spain _____

New Zealand _____

Italy _____

South Africa _____

United Kingdom _____

Canada _____

Keep a close eye on these five *(eev-reet)* עִבְרִית ← letters: כ פ נ מ צ . Notice how they change at the end of a word.

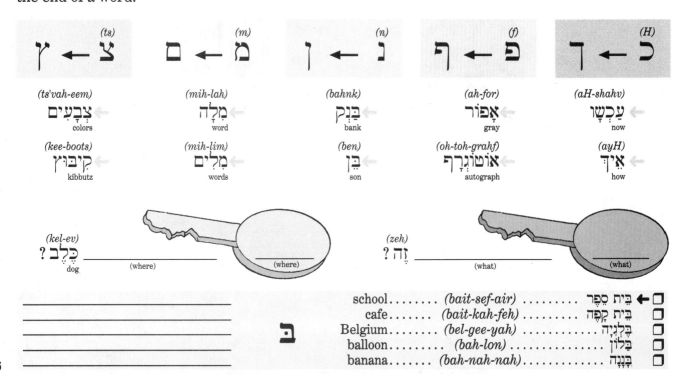

(ts)
ץ ← צ

(m)
ם ← מ

(n)
ן ← נ

(f)
ף ← פ

(H)
ך ← כ

(ts'vah-eem)
צְבָעִים ←
colors

(mih-lah)
מִלָה ←
word

(bahnk)
בַּנְק ←
bank

(ah-for)
אָפוֹר ←
gray

(aH-shahv)
עַכְשָׁו ←
now

(kee-boots)
קִיבּוּץ ←
kibbutz

(mih-lim)
מִלִים ←
words

(ben)
בֵּן ←
son

(oh-toh-grahf)
אוֹטוֹגְרָף ←
autograph

(ayH)
אֵיךְ ←
how

(kel-ev)
? כֶּלֶב
dog
_____ (where) _____ (where)

(zeh)
? זֶה
_____ (what) _____ (what)

_____
_____
_____
_____

ב

☐ ← בֵּית סֵפֶר .... *(bait-sef-air)* .... school
☐ בֵּית קָפֶה .... *(bait-kah-feh)* .... cafe
☐ בֶּלְגְיָה .... *(bel-gee-yah)* .... Belgium
☐ בַּלוֹן .... *(bah-lon)* .... balloon
☐ בַּנָנָה .... *(bah-nah-nah)* .... banana

(mnoh-rah) מְנוֹרָה	*(may-Hoh-neet)* מְכוֹנִית	*(Hoom)* חוּם	*(Hah-lahv)* חָלָב
(sah-pah) סַפָּה	*(oh-fah-noh-ah)* אוֹפַנוֹעַ	*(ah-dohm)* אָדוֹם	*(Hem-ah)* חֶמְאָה
(kis-eh) כִּסֵּא	*(oh-fah-nah-yeem)* אוֹפַנַיִם	*(vah-rohd)* וָרוֹד	*(mel-aH)* מֶלַח
(shah-tee-aH) שָׁטִיחַ	*(Hah-tool)* חָתוּל	*(kah-tohm)* כָּתוֹם	*(pil-pel)* פִּלְפֵּל
(shool-Hahn) שׁוּלְחָן	*(gahn)* גַן	*(lah-vahn)* לָבָן	*(yah-yeen) (kohs)* כּוֹס יַיִן
(deh-let) דֶּלֶת	*(prah-Heem)* פְּרָחִים	*(tsah-hohv)* צָהוֹב	*(kohs)* כּוֹס
(shah-ohn) שָׁעוֹן	*(kel-ev)* כֶּלֶב	*(ah-for)* אָפוֹר	*(it-tohn)* עִתּוֹן
(vee-lohn) וִילוֹן	*(doh-ar) (tay-vaht)* תֵּיבַת דוֹאַר	*(shah-Hor)* שָׁחוֹר	*(sef-el)* סֵפֶל
(teh-leh-fohn) טֶלֶפוֹן	*(doh-ar)* דוֹאַר	*(kah-Hohl)* כָּחוֹל	*(mahz-leg)* מַזְלֵג
(Hah-lohn) חַלוֹן	*(ef-es)* אֶפֶס 0	*(yah-rohk)* יָרוֹק	*(sah-keen)* סַכִּין
(tmoo-nah) תְּמוּנָה	*(aH-aht)* אַחַת 1	*(tsiv-oh-nee)* צִבְעוֹנִי	*(mah-peet)* מַפִּית
(bite) בַּיִת	*(shtah-yeem)* שְׁתַּיִם 2	*(tohv) (boh-kair)* בֹּקֶר טוֹב	*(tsah-lah-Haht)* צַלַחַת
(ah-voh-dah) (Hah-dar) חֲדַר עֲבוֹדָה	*(shah-lohsh)* שָׁלוֹשׁ 3	*(tohv) (eh-rev)* עֶרֶב טוֹב	*(kah-peet)* כַּפִּית
(ahm-baht-yah) (Hah-dar) חֲדַר אַמְבַּטְיָה	*(ar-bah)* אַרְבַּע 4	*(tohv) (lie-lah)* לַיְלָה טוֹב	*(ah-rohn)* אָרוֹן
(meet-baH) מִטְבָּח	*(Hah-mesh)* חָמֵשׁ 5	*(shah-lohm)* שָׁלוֹם	*(tay)* תֵּה
(shay-nah) (Hah-dar) חֲדַר שֵׁינָה	*(shesh)* שֵׁשׁ 6	*(shlohm-Hah) (mah)* מַה שְׁלוֹמְךָ ?	*(kah-feh)* קָפֶה
(oh-Hel) (Hah-dar) חֲדַר אֹכֶל	*(sheh-vah)* שֶׁבַע 7	*(may-kah-reer)* מְקָרֵר	*(leh-Hem)* לֶחֶם
(sah-lohn) סָלוֹן	*(shmoh-neh)* שְׁמוֹנָה 8	*(tah-noor)* תַּנוּר	*(bay-vah-kah-shah)* בְּבַקָשָׁה
(moo-saH) מוּסָךְ	*(tay-shah)* תֵּשַׁע 9	*(yah-yeen)* יַיִן	*(toh-dah)* תּוֹדָה
(mar-tef) מַרְתֵּף	*(es-air)* עֶשֶׂר 10	*(meets)* מִיץ	*(slee-Hah)* סְלִיחָה

STICKY LABELS

This book has over 150 special sticky labels for you to use as you learn new words. When you are introduced to one of these words, remove the corresponding label from these pages. Be sure to use each of these unique self-adhesive labels by adhering them to a picture, window, lamp, or whatever object it refers to. And yes, they are removable! The sticky labels make learning to speak Hebrew much more fun and a lot easier than you ever expected. For example, when you look in the mirror and see the label, say

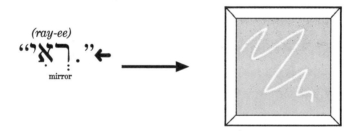

Don't just say it once, say it again and again. And once you label the refrigerator, you should never again open that door without saying

(may-kah-reer)
"מְקָרֵר."←
refrigerator

By using the sticky labels, you not only learn new words, but friends and family learn along with you! The sooner you start, the sooner you can use these labels at home or work.

7

(kes-ef)
כֶּסֶף
money

Before starting this Step, go back and review Step 5. It is important that you can count to

(es-reem)
עֶשְׂרִים ← without looking at this סֵפֶר ← *(sef-air)*. Let's learn the larger מִסְפָּרִים ← *(mis-pah-reem)* now. After
twenty   book   numbers

practicing aloud עִבְרִית ← *(eev-reet)* numbers 10 through 1,000 below, write these מִסְפָּרִים ← *(mis-pah-reem)* in the
          Hebrew   numbers

blanks provided. Again, notice the similarities between מִסְפָּרִים ← *(mis-pah-reem)* such as (4) אַרְבַּע ← *(ar-bah)* ,
                                                              numbers

(14) אַרְבַּע עֶשְׂרֵה ← *(ar-bah)* *(es-ray)* and (40) אַרְבָּעִים ← *(ar-bah-eem)*.

_____	10	*(es-air)* עֶשֶׂר _____	10
_____	20	*(es-reem)* עֶשְׂרִים _____	20
_____	30	*(shloh-sheem)* שְׁלוֹשִׁים _____	30
_____	40	*(ar-bah-eem)* אַרְבָּעִים _____	40
_____	50	*(Hah-mee-sheem)* חֲמִישִׁים _____	50
_____	60	*(shih-sheem)* שִׁשִּׁים _____	60
_____	70	*(sheev-eem)* שִׁבְעִים _____	70
_____	80	*(shmoh-neem)* שְׁמוֹנִים _____	80
_____	90	*(tee-sheem)* תִּשְׁעִים _____	90
_____	100	*(may-ah)* מֵאָה _____	100
_____	500	*(may-oht)* *(Hah-mesh)* חֲמֵשׁ מֵאוֹת _____	500
_____	1000	*(el-ef)* אֶלֶף _____	1000

Here are two important phrases to go with all these מִסְפָּרִים ← *(mis-pah-reem)*. Say them out loud over and

over and then write them out twice as many times.

_____ יֵשׁ לִי ← *(lee)(yesh)*
                                              I have

_____ יֵשׁ לָנוּ ← *(lah-noo)(yesh)*
                                              we have

_____	garden............ *(gahn)* .... גַּן ←☐
_____	zoo........... *(gahn-Hah-yoht)* ...... גַּן חַיּוֹת ☐
_____	Garden of Eden........... *(gahn-ay-den)* ...... גַּן עֵדֶן ☐
_____	Germany.......... *(gair-mahn-yah)* ...... גֶּרְמַנְיָה ☐
_____	German........... *(gair-mah-neet)* ...... גֶּרְמָנִית ☐

ג

The unit of currency *(buh-yiss-rah-el)* בְּיִשְׂרָאֵל ← *in Israel* is the *(shek-el)* שֶׁקֶל ← *shekel* abbreviated <u>NIS</u> which stands for "New Israeli Shekel." Let's learn the various kinds of *(shkah-leem)* שְׁקָלִים ←. *shekels* Always be sure to practice each *(mih-lah)* מִלָּה ← *word* out loud. You might want to exchange some money *(aH-shahv)* עַכְשָׁו ← *now* so that you can familiar-

ize yourself *(eem)* עִם ← *with* the various *(shkah-leem)* שְׁקָלִים ←. *shekels*

(shkah-leem)

שְׁקָלִים

shekels

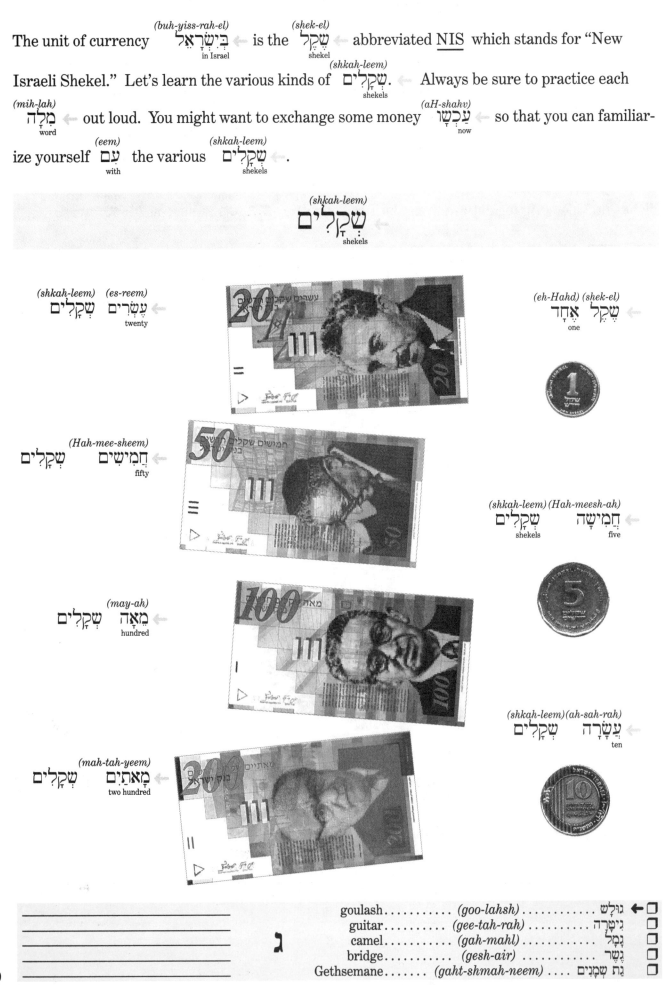

(shkah-leem) *(es-reem)*
שְׁקָלִים עֶשְׂרִים ←
twenty

(eh-Hahd) *(shek-el)*
שֶׁקֶל אֶחָד ←
one

(Hah-mee-sheem)
שְׁקָלִים חֲמִשִּׁים ←
fifty

(shkah-leem) *(Hah-meesh-ah)*
שְׁקָלִים חֲמִשָּׁה ←
shekels *five*

(may-ah)
שְׁקָלִים מֵאָה ←
hundred

(shkah-leem) *(ah-sah-rah)*
שְׁקָלִים עֲשָׂרָה ←
ten

(mah-tah-yeem)
שְׁקָלִים מָאתַיִם ←
two hundred

goulash	*(goo-lahsh)*	גּוּלָשׁ ←☐
guitar	*(gee-tah-rah)*	גִּיטָרָה ☐
camel	*(gah-mahl)*	גָּמָל ☐
bridge	*(gesh-air)*	גֶּשֶׁר ☐
Gethsemane	*(gaht-shmah-neem)*	גַּת שְׁמָנִים ☐

ג

Review *(hah-mis-pah-reem)* הַמִּסְפָּרִים ← *(es-air)* עֶשֶׂר – ten through *(el-ef)* אֶלֶף 1000 again. *(aH-shav)* עַכְשָׁו now how do you say "twenty-two"

(oh) אוֹ or "fifty-three" *(beev-reet)* בְּעִבְרִית in Hebrew ? Put the numbers together in a logical sequence just as you do in

English. See if you can say *(vuh)* וּ and write out *(hah-mis-pah-reem)* הַמִּסְפָּרִים the numbers on this *(ah-mood)* עַמּוּד page . *(hah-t'shoo-voht)* הַתְּשׁוּבוֹת the answers

are at the bottom of *(hah-ah-mood)* הָעַמּוּד the page .

	2.		1.
(25 = 20 + 5)		(47 = 40 + 7)	

	4.		3.
(84 = 80 + 4)		(51 = 50 + 1)	

Now, how would you say the following *(beev-reet)* בְּעִבְרִית ?

	5.
(I have 93 shekels.)	

	6.
(We have 68 shekels.)	

To ask how much something costs *(beev-reet)* בְּעִבְרִית , one asks — *(kah-mah)* כַּמָּה how much *(zeh)* זֶה it *(oh-leh)* עוֹלֶה? costs

Now you try it. _____
(How much does it cost?)

Answer the following questions based on the numbers in parentheses.

(shkah-leem) שְׁקָלִים shekels . _____ (10) _____ *(zeh)* זֶה it *(oh-leh)* עוֹלֶה costs *(kah-mah)* כַּמָּה how much *(zeh)* זֶה it *(oh-leh)* עוֹלֶה? costs ← 7.

(shkah-leem) שְׁקָלִים shekels . _____ (20) _____ *(zeh)* זֶה it *(oh-leh)* עוֹלֶה costs *(kah-mah)* כַּמָּה how much *(zeh)* זֶה it *(oh-leh)* עוֹלֶה? costs ← 8.

(shkah-leem) שְׁקָלִים shekels . _____ (8) _____ *(oh-leh)* עוֹלֶה *(hah-sef-air)* הַסֵּפֶר *(kah-mah)* כַּמָּה how much *(oh-leh)* עוֹלֶה *(hah-sef-air)* הַסֵּפֶר? the book ← 9.

(shkah-leem) שְׁקָלִים shekels . _____ (5) _____ *(oh-lah)* עוֹלָה *(hah-gloo-yah)* הַגְּלוּיָה *(oh-lah)* עוֹלָה *(kah-mah)* כַּמָּה how much *(hah-gloo-yah)* הַגְּלוּיָה? the postcard *(oh-lah)* עוֹלָה ← 10.

הַתְּשׁוּבוֹת

6. ← יֵשׁ לָנוּ שִׁשִּׁים וּשְׁמוֹנָה שְׁקָלִים.		1. ← אַרְבָּעִים וָשֶׁבַע	
7. עֲשָׂרָה		2. עֶשְׂרִים וְחָמֵשׁ	
8. עֶשְׂרִים		3. חֲמִשִּׁים וְאַחַת	
9. שְׁמוֹנָה		4. שְׁמוֹנִים וְאַרְבַּע	
10. חֲמִשָּׁה		5. יֵשׁ לִי תִּשְׁעִים וּשְׁלוֹשָׁה שְׁקָלִים.	

(et-mohl) אֶתְמוֹל
yesterday

 (vuh) וְ

(mah-Har) מָחָר
tomorrow

 (hah-yohm) הַיוֹם
today

(hah-shah-nah) (loo-aH) לוּחַ הַשָׁנָה
the calendar

_____

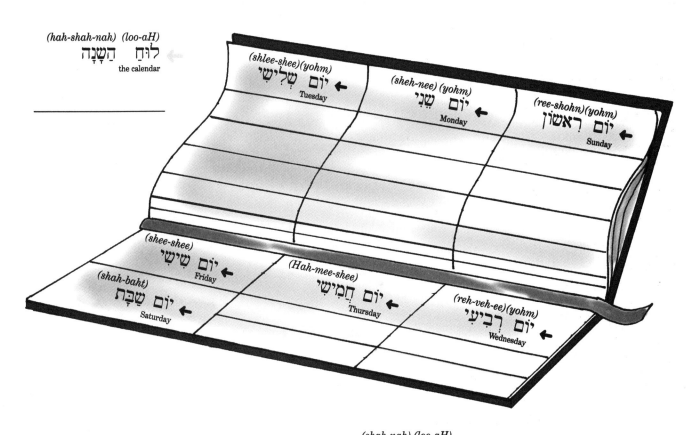

(shlee-shee) (yohm) יוֹם שְׁלִישִׁי
Tuesday

(sheh-nee) (yohm) יוֹם שֵׁנִי
Monday

(ree-shohn) (yohm) יוֹם רִאשׁוֹן
Sunday

(shee-shee) יוֹם שִׁישִׁי
Friday

(Hah-mee-shee) יוֹם חֲמִישִׁי
Thursday

(reh-veh-ee) (yohm) יוֹם רְבִיעִי
Wednesday

(shah-baht) יוֹם שַׁבָּת
Saturday

Learn the days of the week by writing them in the *(shah-nah) (loo-aH)* לוּחַ שָׁנָה calendar above and then move on to

the *(ar-bah)* אַרְבַּע four parts to each *(yohm)* יוֹם day.

(boh-kair) בֹּקֶר
morning

(hah-tsoh-hoh-rah-yeem) (aH-ah-ray) אַחֲרֵי הַצָהֳרַיִם
afternoon

(eh-rev) עֶרֶב
evening

(lie-lah) לַיְלָה
night

_____   _____

ד

_____
_____
_____
_____

flag	(deg-el)	דֶּגֶל ← ☐
mailman	(dah-var)	דּוָּר ☐
diet	(dee-eh-tah)	דִיאֵטָה ☐
dialogue	(dee-ah-lohg)	דִיאָלוֹג ☐
fisherman	(dah-yahg)	דַּיָּג ☐

It is very חָשׁוּב *(Hah-shoov)* **important** to know the days of the week וְ the various parts of the day as well as these three מִלִּים.

מָחָר *(mah-Har)* **tomorrow** → הַיּוֹם *(hah-yohm)* **today** → אֶתְמוֹל *(et-mohl)* **yesterday**

יוֹם → רְבִיעִי *(reh-veh-ee)*

יוֹם שַׁבָּת *(shah-baht)* **Saturday** →

יוֹם שִׁשִּׁי *(shee-shee)* →

חֲמִישִׁי *(Hah-mee-shee)* יוֹם → **Thursday**

יוֹם שְׁלִישִׁי *(shlee-shee) (yohm)* **Tuesday** →

יוֹם שֵׁנִי *(sheh-nee) (yohm)* →

יוֹם רִאשׁוֹן *(ree-shohn) (yohm)* **Sunday** →

_____ = מָחָר *(mah-Har)* **tomorrow**   _____ = הַיּוֹם *(hah-yohm)* **today**

_____ = יוֹם →   _____ = אֶתְמוֹל *(et-mohl)* **yesterday**

Notice that בְּ *(buh)* usually means "on" and בַּ *(bah)* means "in the." For example, בְּיוֹם שִׁשִּׁי *(shee-shee) (buh-yohm)* means "on Friday," and בַּבֹּקֶר *(bah-boh-kair)* means "in the morning." Fill in the following blanks וְ then check your answers at the bottom of הָעַמּוּד *(hah-ah-mood)* **the page**.

_____ = on Sunday (in the) morning a.

_____ = on Friday evening b.

_____ = on Saturday evening c.

_____ = on Tuesday afternoon d.

_____ = on Thursday afternoon e.

_____ = tomorrow morning f.

_____ = tomorrow afternoon g.

_____ = tomorrow evening h.

זֶה *(zeh)* ? _____ (when) _____ (when)   זֶה *(zeh)* ? _____ (who) _____ (who)

הַתְּשׁוּבוֹת

מָחָר אַחֲרֵי הַצָּהֳרַיִם g.   בְּיוֹם שְׁלִישִׁי אַחֲרֵי הַצָּהֳרַיִם d.   בְּיוֹם רִאשׁוֹן בַּבֹּקֶר → a.
מָחָר בָּעֶרֶב h.   בְּיוֹם חֲמִישִׁי אַחֲרֵי הַצָּהֳרַיִם e.   בְּיוֹם שִׁשִּׁי בָּעֶרֶב b.
מָחָר בַּבֹּקֶר f.   בְּיוֹם שַׁבָּת בָּעֶרֶב c.

Knowing the parts of the *(yohm)* יוֹם ← (day) will help you to learn the various *(eev-reet)* עִבְרִית ← (Hebrew) greetings below.

Practice these every day until your trip.

_____ *(tohv)* טוֹב *(boh-kair)* בֹּקֶר ←
(good) (morning)

_____ *(tohv)* טוֹב *(eh-rev)* עֶרֶב ←
(good) (evening)

_____ *(tohv)* טוֹב *(lie-lah)* לַיְלָה ←
(good) (night)

_____ *(shah-lohm)* שָׁלוֹם ←
good day/hello/peace

Take the next *(ar-bah)* אַרְבַּע ← (four) labels וְ stick them on the appropriate things in your *(bite)* בַּיִת ← (house) . Make

sure you attach them to the correct items, as they are only *(beev-reet)* בְּעִבְרִית ← . How about the bathroom

mirror for " *(tohv)* טוֹב *(boh-kair)* בֹּקֶר ← " ? *(oh)* אוֹ (or) your alarm clock for " *(tohv)* טוֹב *(lie-lah)* לַיְלָה ← " ? Let's not forget,

🧍 *(shlohm-Hah)* שְׁלוֹמְךָ ? *(mah)* מַה ← (how are you) _____

🧍 *(shloh-mayH)* שְׁלוֹמֵךְ ? *(mah)* מַה ← (how are you) _____

Now for some " *(ken)* כֵּן (yes) " or " *(loh)* לֹא (no) " questions –

Are your eyes *(kah-Hohl)* כָּחֹל ← (blue) ? _____   Are your shoes *(shah-Hor)* שָׁחֹר ← (black) ? _____

Is your favorite color *(tsah-hohv)* צָהֹב ← (yellow) ? _____   Is today *(sheh-nee)* שֵׁנִי *(yohm)* יוֹם ← ? _____

Do you own a *(kel-ev)* כֶּלֶב ← (dog) ? _____   Do you own a *(Hah-tool)* חָתוּל ← ? _____

You are about one-fourth of your way through this book and it is a good time to quickly review

the *(mih-lim)* מִלִּים ← you have learned before doing the crossword puzzle on the next *(ah-mood)* עַמּוּד ← (page) .

‏הַתְּשׁוּבוֹת TO THE CROSSWORD PUZZLE

DOWN					ACROSS	
אוֹפַנַּיִם	34.	שְׁקָלִים	13.	אָדֹם ←	1.	כֶּלֶב	31.	מְכוֹנִית	19.	אֵיפֹה ←	1.
עֶשֶׂר	35.	תְּמוּנָה	14.	לָבָן	2.	שָׁלוֹם	32.	כָּחֹל	20.	בַּיִת	3.
יוֹם שִׁשִּׁי	37.	מְנוֹרָה	15.	בֹּקֶר	3.	אַרְבַּע	34.	חָתוּל	21.	אוֹטוֹבּוּס	5.
		פְּרָחִים	17.	תְּשׁוּבוֹת	4.	דְּבָרִים	36.	חֶדֶר	22.	שְׁמוֹנָה	6.
		שָׁחֹר	18.	אָפֹר	5.	אֶתְמוֹל	38.	זֶה	23.	סֵפֶר	9.
		חָמֵשׁ	22.	הַיּוֹם	7.	יָרֹק	39.	מָלוֹן	24.	מִרְתֵּף	10.
		לָמָּה	25.	שְׁתַּיִם	8.	שְׁלוֹשִׁים	40.	יוֹם	26.	יִשְׂרָאֵל	11.
		עַכְשָׁו	27.	מָחָר	10.	עִבְרִית	41.	שָׁבוּעַ	28.	שַׁבָּת	13.
		צְבָעִים	29.	יֵשׁ	11.			צָהֹב	29.	מִסְפָּרִים	16.
		כַּמָּה	30.	לוּחַ הַשָּׁנָה	12.			כַּמָּה	30.	שֵׁשׁ	18.

CROSSWORD PUZZLE

ACROSS

1. where
3. house
5. bus
6. eight
9. book
10. basement
11. Israel
13. Saturday
16. numbers
18. six
19. car
20. blue
21. cat
22. room
23. it is
24. hotel
26. day
28. week
29. yellow
30. how much/many
31. dog
32. hello/goodbye/peace
34. four
36. things
38. yesterday
39. green
40. thirty
41. Hebrew

DOWN

1. red
2. white
3. morning
4. answers
5. gray
7. today
8. two
10. tomorrow
11. there is/are
12. the calendar
13. shekels
14. picture
15. lamp
17. flowers
18. black
22. five
25. why
27. now
29. colors
30. how much/many
34. bicycle
35. ten
37. Friday

stewardess	(dah-yel-et)	דַּיֶּלֶת ← ☐
gas	(del-ek)	דֶּלֶק ☐
fuel tanker	(may-Hah-leet-del-ek)	מְכָלִית דֶּלֶק ☐
gas pump	(mah-sheh-vaht-del-ek)	מַשְׁאֵבַת דֶּלֶק ☐
democracy	(deh-moh-krah-tee-yah)	דֶּמוֹקְרַטְיָה ☐

ד

25

9

(yahd) (ahl) (lif-nay) (meh-ah-Hoh-ray)
מֵאַחוֹרֵי, לִפְנֵי, עַל יַד ...
next to · in front of · behind

(eev-reet)
וְ עִבְרִית ← prepositions (words like "in," "on," "through" and "next to") are easy to learn

(eem) (shesh)
they allow you to be precise עִם ← a minimum of effort. Instead of having to point שֵׁשׁ ←
with · six

times at a piece of yummy pastry you would like, you can explain precisely which one you want

by saying it is behind, in front of, next to or under the piece of pastry that the salesperson is

(mih-lim)
starting to pick up. Let's learn some of these little מִלִים ←.
words

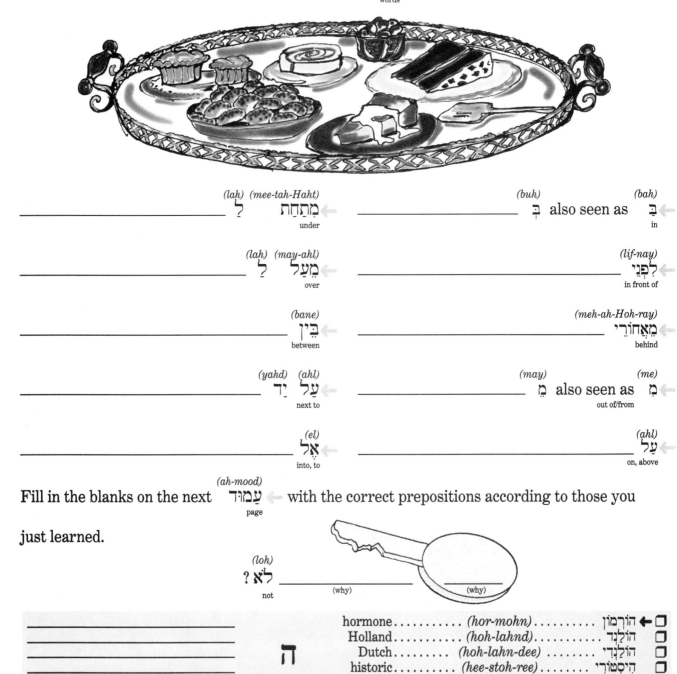

(lah) (mee-tah-Haht)	(buh) (bah)
_____ ל מִתַּחַת ←	_____ בְּ also seen as בַּ ←
under	in
(lah) (may-ahl)	(lif-nay)
_____ ל מֵעַל ←	_____ לִפְנֵי ←
over	in front of
(bane)	(meh-ah-Hoh-ray)
_____ בֵּין ←	_____ מֵאַחוֹרֵי ←
between	behind
(yahd) (ahl)	(may) (me)
_____ עַל יַד ←	_____ מֵ also seen as מֶ ←
next to	out of/from
(el)	(ahl)
_____ אֶל ←	_____ עַל ←
into, to	on, above

(ah-mood)
Fill in the blanks on the next עַמוּד ← with the correct prepositions according to those you
page

just learned.

(loh)
לֹא ? _____ _____
not   (why)   (why)

(hah-shool-Hahn) הַשׁוּלְחָן . _____ *(hah-mah-yeem) (kohs)* כּוֹס הַמַּיִם ⇐
table   (on)   the water glass

(shool-Hahn) שׁוּלְחָן . _____ *(hah-kel-ev)* הַכֶּלֶב ⇐
table   (under)   the dog

(mah-lohn) מָלוֹן . _____ *(hah-roh-fay)* הָרוֹפֵא ⇐
hotel   (in the)   the doctor

(hah-roh-fay) (ay-foh) אֵיפֹה הָרוֹפֵא ? _____ ⇐
doctor

(hah-mah-lohn) הַמָּלוֹן . _____ *(hah-eesh)* הָאִישׁ ⇐
the hotel   (in front of)   the man

(hah-eesh) (ay-foh) אֵיפֹה הָאִישׁ ? _____ ⇐
the man

(hah-tmoo-nah) הַתְּמוּנָה . _____ *(hah-teh-leh-fohn)* הַטֶּלֶפוֹן ⇐
picture   (next to)   the telephone

(hah-teh-leh-fohn) (ay-foh) אֵיפֹה הַטֶּלֶפוֹן ? _____ ⇐
the telephone

(aH-shahv) עַכְשָׁו ⇐ fill in each blank on the picture below with the best possible one of these little מִלִּים *(mih-lim)* .
now   words

Do you recognize the *(hah-mah-ah-rah-vee) (hah-koh-tel)* הַכֹּתֶל הַמַּעֲרָבִי ⇐ with the Dome of the Rock in the background?
Western Wall

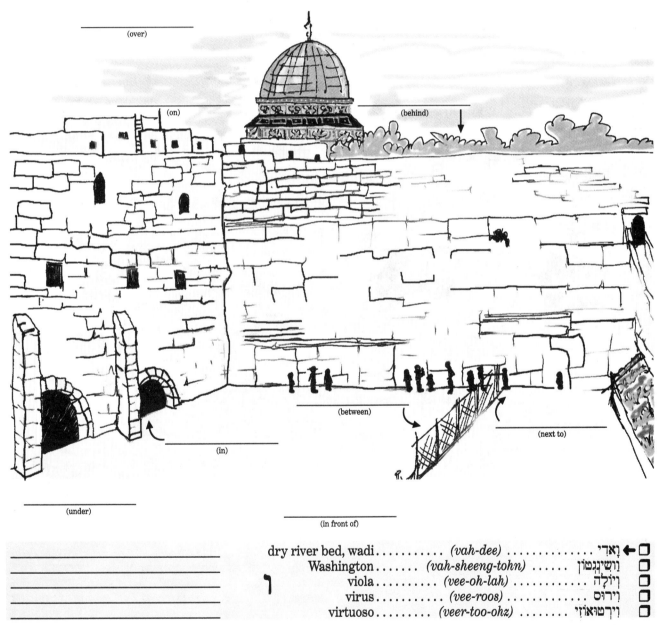

     _____ (over)

     _____ (on)   _____ (behind)

_____ (in)

_____ (between)   _____ (next to)

_____ (under)

_____ (in front of)

□ נָאדִי ⇐ .... *(vah-dee)* .... dry river bed, wadi
□ וָשִׁינְגְטוֹן ..... *(vah-sheeng-tohn)* .... Washington
□ וִיֹּלָה .... *(vee-oh-lah)* .... viola
□ וִירוּס .... *(vee-roos)* .... virus
□ וִירְטוּאוֹזִי .... *(veer-too-ohz)* .... virtuoso

ן

_____
_____
_____

You have learned days of the week, so now it is time to learn *(Hoh-dah-sheem)* חוֹדָשִׁים ← months of the *(shah-nah)* שָׁנָה ← year and

all the different kinds of *(hah-ah-veer) (meh-zeg)* מֶזֶג הָאֲוִיר ← weather. You can easily recognize the months of the year below.

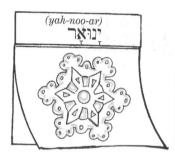

(yah-noo-ar)
יָנוּאָר

(feb-roo-ar)
פֶבְּרוּאָר

(mairts)
מֶרְץ

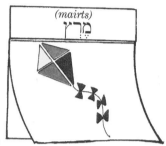

(ah-pril)
אַפְּרִיל

(my)
מַאי

(yoo-nee)
יוּנִי

(yoo-lee)
יוּלִי

(oh-goost)
אוֹגוּסְט

(sep-tem-bair)
סֶפְּטֶמְבֶּר

(ohk-toh-bair)
אוֹקְטוֹבֶּר

(noh-vem-bair)
נוֹבֶמְבֶּר

(deh-tsem-bair)
דֶצֶמְבֶּר

When someone asks, "*(hah-yohm) (hah-ah-veer) (meh-zeg) (mah)* מַה מֶזֶג הָאֲוִיר הַיּוֹם? today — weather what (is)" ← you have a variety of answers. Let's

learn them but first, does this sound familiar?

(yah-meem) (shloh-sheem) (yesh) (vuh-noh-vem-bair) (yoo-nee) (ah-pril) (sep-tem-bair) (bah-Hoh-dah-sheem)
יָמִים... שְׁלוֹשִׁים יֵשׁ וְנוֹבֶמְבֶּר יוּנִי, אַפְּרִיל, סֶפְּטֶמְבֶּר בַּחוֹדָשִׁים ←
days — thirty — there are — November and — June — April — September — in the months

---

זֶבְּרָה ←	zebra . . . . *(zeb-rah)* . . . . ☐
זוֹאוֹלוֹגְיָה	zoology . . . . *(zoh-oh-lohg-yah)* . . . . ☐
זִכָּרוֹן	memorial . . . . *(zih-kah-rohn)* . . . . ☐
זַמָּר	singer . . . . *(zah-mar)* . . . . ☐
זְמָן	time . . . . *(zeh-mahn)* . . . . ☐

ז

מַה מֶזֶג הָאֲוִיר הַיוֹם ?
(mah) (meh-zeg) (hah-ah-veer) (hah-yohm)
weather   today

_____

בְּיָנוּאָר יוֹרֵד שֶׁלֶג .
(byah-noo-ar) (yoh-red) (shel-eg)
in January   comes down   snow

_____

בִּפֶבְּרוּאָר יוֹרֵד גֶשֶׁם .
(buh-feb-roo-ar) (yoh-red) (gesh-em)
in February   comes down   rain

_____

בְּמֶרְץ יוֹרֵד גֶשֶׁם .
(buh-mairts) (yoh-red) (gesh-em)
rain comes down

_____

בְּאַפְּרִיל מֶזֶג הָאֲוִיר נָעִים .
(bah-pril) (meh-zeg) (hah-ah-veer) (nah-eem)
weather   pleasant

_____

בְּמַאי רוּחַ חֲזָקָה .
(buh-my) (roo-aH) (Hah-zah-kah)
wind   strong

_____

בְּיוּנִי נָעִים .
(buh-yoo-nee) (nah-eem)
pleasant

_____

בְּיוּלִי חַם מְאוֹד .
(buh-yoo-lee) (Hahm) (may-ohd)
hot   very

_____

בְּאוֹגוּסְט חַם מְאוֹד .
(buh-oh-goost) (Hahm) (may-ohd)
hot

_____

בְּסֶפְּטֶמְבֶּר נָעִים .
(buh-sep-tem-bair) (nah-eem)
pleasant

_____

בְּאוֹקְטוֹבֶּר עֲרָפֶל .
(buh-ohk-toh-bair) (ah-rah-fel)
fog

_____

בְּנוֹבֶמְבֶּר קַר .
(buh-noh-vem-bair) (kar)
cold

_____

בְּדֶצֶמְבֶּר מֶזֶג הָאֲוִיר רַע .
(buh-deh-tsem-bair) מֶזֶג הָאֲוִיר *(rah)*
bad

_____

מַה מֶזֶג הָאֲוִיר בִּפֶבְּרוּאָר ?
(mah) (meh-zeg) (hah-ah-veer) (buh-feb-roo-ar)
weather

_____

מַה מֶזֶג הָאֲוִיר בְּאַפְּרִיל ?
(mah) (meh-zeg) (hah-ah-veer) (bah-pril)
April

_____

מַה מֶזֶג הָאֲוִיר בְּמַאי ?
(buh-my)

_____

מַה מֶזֶג הָאֲוִיר בְּאוֹגוּסְט ?
(buh-oh-goost)

☐	← חַיִים	....	*(Hah-yeem)*	life
☐	חֲמוֹר	....	*(Hah-mor)*	donkey
☐	חֵמָר	....	*(Heh-mar)*	clay
☐	חֶרְמוֹן	....	*(Hair-mohn)*	Mt. Hermon
☐	חָשׁוּךְ	....	*(Hah-shooH)*	dark

ח

29

עַכְשָׁו ← for the seasons of the שָׁנָה ← *(shah-nah)* ...
year

חֹרֶף ← *(Hoh-ref)*
winter

קַיִץ ← *(kah-yits)*
summer

סְתָו ← *(stahv)*
autumn

אָבִיב ← *(ah-veev)*
spring

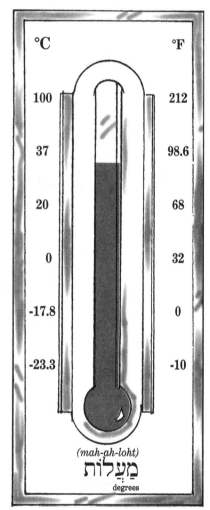

צֶלְסִיוּס ← *(tsel-see-oos)*
Celsius

פַרֶנְהַיְט ← *(far-en-hite)*
Fahrenheit

°C

°F

100   212
37   98.6
20   68
0   32
-17.8   0
-23.3   -10

מַעֲלוֹת *(mah-ah-loht)*
degrees

At this point, it is טוֹב ← *(tohv)* idea to familiarize
good
yourself with יִשְׂרְאֵלִי ← *(yiss-ruh-eh-lee)* temperatures.

Carefully study the thermometer because

טֶמְפֶּרָטוּרוֹת *(tem-peh-rah-too-roht)* in יִשְׂרָאֵל ← *(yiss-rah-el)* are calculated on
temperatures

the basis of Celsius (not Fahrenheit).

To convert °C to °F, multiply by 1.8 and add 32.

$$37\,°C \times 1.8 = 66.6 + 32 = 98.6\,°F$$

To convert °F to °C, subtract 32 and multiply by 0.55.

$$98.6\,°F - 32 = 66.6 \times 0.55 = 37\,°C$$

ט

11

(vuh-hah-bite) *(hah-mish-pah-Hah)*
הַמִּשְׁפָּחָה וְהַבַּיִת
and the house · the family

(buh-yiss-rah-el) *(vuh)*
There are many interesting family names → בְּיִשְׂרָאֵל which reflect the variety of national וְ

(hah-yiss-ruh-eh-leem) *(hah-mish-pah-Hah)* *(bah-eh-rev)*
cultural backgrounds of הַיִּשְׂרְאֵלִים ← הַמִּשְׁפָּחָה ← usually eats together בָּעֶרֶב ←
the Israelis · the family · in the evening

(shee-shee) *(buh-yohm)*
בְּיוֹם שִׁישִׁי ← and on holidays. Study the family tree below וְ then practice these new
on Friday

(ah-mood)
words on the next עַמּוּד.

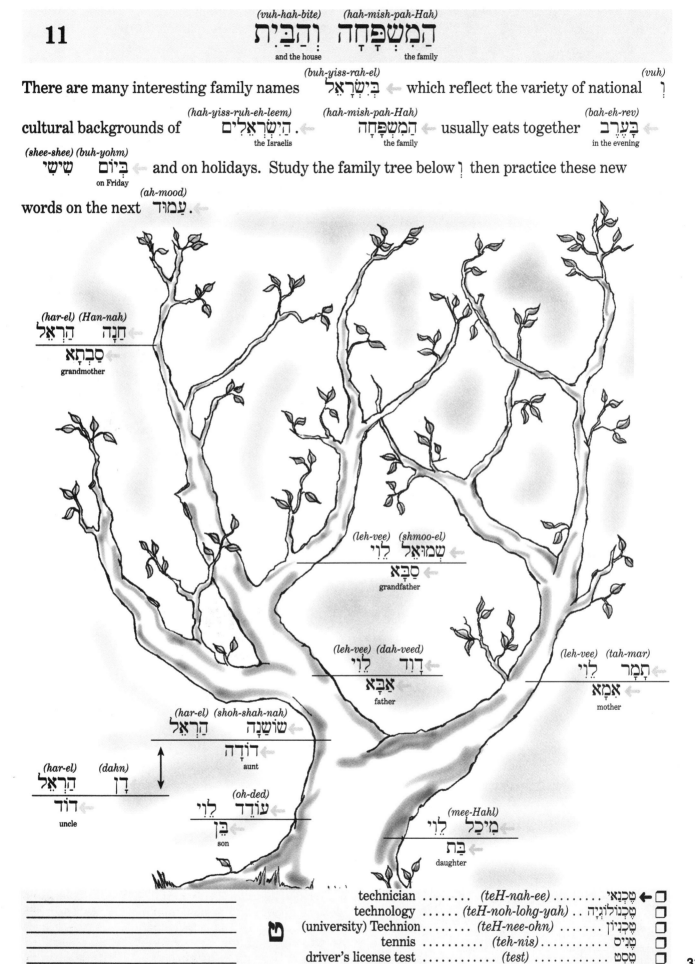

(har-el) *(Han-nah)*
חַנָּה הַרְאֵל
סַבְתָּא
grandmother

(leh-vee) *(shmoo-el)*
שְׁמוּאֵל לֵוִי ←
סַבָּא ←
grandfather

(leh-vee) *(dah-veed)*
דָּוִד לֵוִי ←
אַבָּא ←
father

(leh-vee) *(tah-mar)*
תָּמָר לֵוִי ←
אִמָּא ←
mother

(har-el) *(shoh-shah-nah)*
שׁוֹשַׁנָה הַרְאֵל
דּוֹדָה ←
aunt

(har-el) *(dahn)*
דָּן הַרְאֵל
דּוֹד ←
uncle

(oh-ded)
עוֹדֵד לֵוִי ←
בֵּן ←
son

(mee-Hahl)
מִיכַל לֵוִי ←
בַּת ←
daughter

☐ →	סְכְנַאי	*(teH-nah-ee)*	technician
☐	טֶכְנוֹלוֹגְיָה	*(teH-noh-lohg-yah)*	technology
☐	טֶכְנִיּוֹן	*(teH-nee-ohn)*	(university) Technion
☐	טֶנִיס	*(teh-nis)*	tennis
☐	טֶסְט	*(test)*	driver's license test

ט

Let's learn how to identify *(hah-mish-pah-Hah)* "הַמִּשְׁפָּחָה" ← by name. Study the following examples carefully.
the family

(sheem-Hah)
מַה שְׁמֵךְ ? ←
your name

_____ *(shmee)*
שְׁמִי ←
my name (is)

(hoh-reem)
הוֹרִים ←
parents

(ah-bah)
אַבָּא ←
father

(hah-ah-bah) *(shem)* *(mah)*
מַה שֵׁם הָאַבָּא ? ←
what name the father

(ee-mah)
אִמָּא ←
mother

(hah-ee-mah) *(shem)* *(mah)*
מַה שֵׁם הָאִמָּא ? ←
what name the mother

(yuh-lah-deem) *(baht)* *(ben)* *(ah-Hoht)* *(aH)*
יְלָדִים בַּת — בֵּן = אָחוֹת — אָח
children daughter son sister brother

(ben)
בֵּן ←
son

(hah-ben) *(shem)* *(mah)*
מַה שֵׁם הַבֵּן ? ←
what name the son

(baht)
בַּת ←
daughter

(hah-baht) *(shem)*
מַה שֵׁם הַבַּת ? ←
what name the daughter

(kroh-veem)
קְרוֹבִים ←
relatives

(hah-sah-bah)
מַה שֵׁם הַסַּבָּא ? ←
the grandfather

(hah-sahv-tah)
מַה שֵׁם הַסַּבְתָּא ? ←
the grandmother

Now you ask —

_____
(what's your name?)

And answer —

_____
(my name is . . .)

_____
_____
_____
_____

בּ

(meet-baH)

מִטְבָּח
kitchen

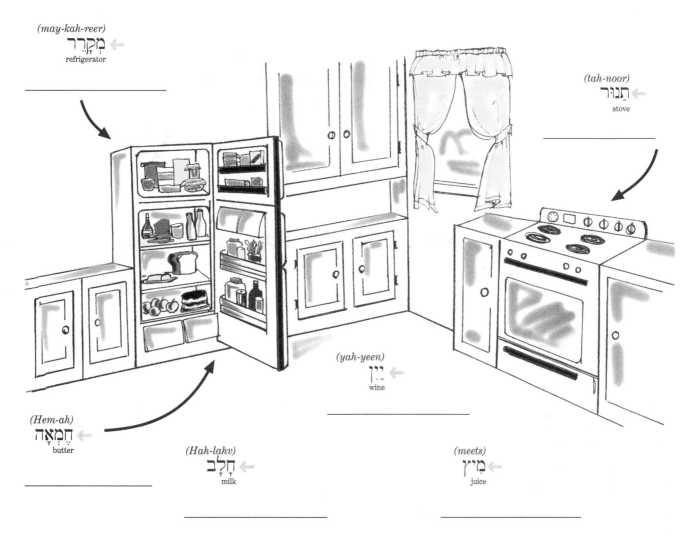

(may-kah-reer)
מְקָרֵר ←
refrigerator

_____

(tah-noor)
תָּנוּר ←
stove

_____

(yah-yeen)
יַיִן ←
wine

_____

(Hem-ah)
חֶמְאָה ←
butter

_____

(Hah-lahv)
חָלָב ←
milk

_____

(meets)
מִיץ ←
juice

_____

Answer these questions aloud.

(bah-may-kah-reer) *(hah-meets)*   *(hah-meets)*
בַּמְקָרֵר .   הַמִּיץ . . . . ? הַמִּיץ אֵיפֹה ←
in the refrigerator   the juice

(heh-Hah-lahv)   *(hah-yah-yeen)* *(ay-foh)*   *(hah-bah-nah-nah)*   *(hah-Hem-ah)*
הֶחָלָב ? אֵיפֹה ←   הַיַּיִן ? אֵיפֹה ←   הַבַּנָנָה ? אֵיפֹה ←   הַחֶמְאָה ? אֵיפֹה ←
the milk   the wine   banana   the butter

(ah-mood)   *(vuh)*
עַכְשָׁו ← open your book to the עַמוּד ← with the labels וְ remove the next group of labels וְ
and

proceed to label all these things in your *(meet-baH)* מִטְבָּח ← .
kitchen

Greece	*(yah-vahn)*	יָוָן ← ☐
jubilee	*(yoh-vel)*	יוֹבֵל ☐
birthday	*(yohm-hoo-led-et)* . . .	יוֹם הוּלֶדֶת ☐
yoga	*(yoh-gah)*	יוֹגָה ☐
yoghurt	*(yoh-goort)*	יוֹגוּרְט ☐

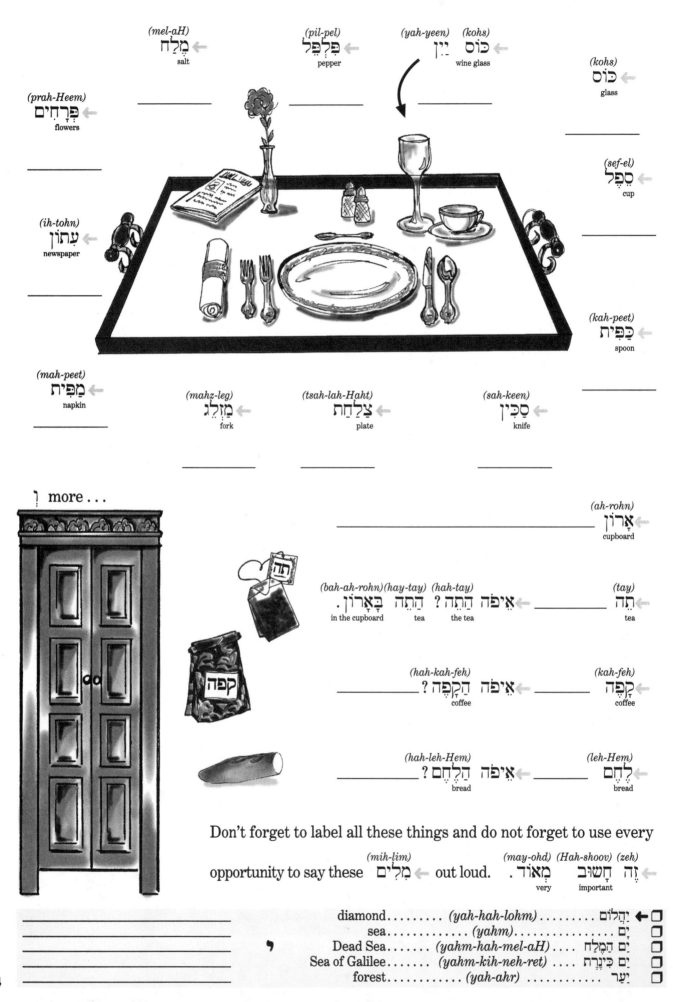

(mel-aH) **מֶלַח** ←
salt

(pil-pel) **פִּלְפֵּל** ←
pepper

(yah-yeen) **יַיִן** (kohs) **כּוֹס** ←
wine glass

(kohs) **כּוֹס** ←
glass

(prah-Heem) **פְּרָחִים** ←
flowers

(sef-el) **סֵפֶל** ←
cup

(ih-tohn) **עִתּוֹן** ←
newspaper

(kah-peet) **כַּפִּית** ←
spoon

(mah-peet) **מַפִּית** ←
napkin

(mahz-leg) **מַזְלֵג** ←
fork

(tsah-lah-Haht) **צַלַחַת** ←
plate

(sah-keen) **סַכִּין** ←
knife

וְ more . . .

(ah-rohn) **אָרוֹן** ←
cupboard

(bah-ah-rohn) (hay-tay) (hah-tay) **אֵיפֹה הַתֵּה? הַתֵּה בָּאָרוֹן.** ← (tay) **תֵּה** ←
in the cupboard / tea / the tea / tea

(hah-kah-feh) **אֵיפֹה הַקָּפֶה?** ← (kah-feh) **קָפֶה** ←
coffee / coffee

(hah-leh-Hem) **אֵיפֹה הַלֶּחֶם?** ← (leh-Hem) **לֶחֶם** ←
bread / bread

Don't forget to label all these things and do not forget to use every
opportunity to say these (mih-lim) **מִלִּים** ← out loud. (may-ohd) **מְאוֹד.** (Hah-shoov) **חָשׁוּב** (zeh) **זֶה** ←
very / important

diamond......... (yah-hah-lohm) .... יַהֲלוֹם ← ☐
sea............. (yahm)............. יָם ☐
Dead Sea...... (yahm-hah-mel-aH) .... יָם הַמֶּלַח ☐
Sea of Galilee...... (yahm-kih-neh-ret) .... יָם כִּנֶּרֶת ☐
forest.......... (yah-ahr) .... יַעַר ☐

34

(daht)
דָת
religion

(buh-yiss-rah-el)
בְּיִשְׂרָאֵל ← religion is very important in everyday life. A person's דָת ← *(daht)* is usually one
religion

of the following.

_____ יְהוּדִי *(yuh-hoo-dee)* ← 1.
Jewish man

_____ יְהוּדִיָּה *(yuh-hoo-dee-yah)* ←
Jewish woman

_____ נוֹצְרִי *(nohts-ree)* ← 2.
Christian man

_____ נוֹצְרִיָּה *(nohts-ree-yah)* ←
Christian woman

_____ מוּסְלְמִי *(moo-sluh-mee)* ← 3.
Muslim man

_____ מוּסְלְמִית *(moo-sluh-meet)* ←
Muslim woman

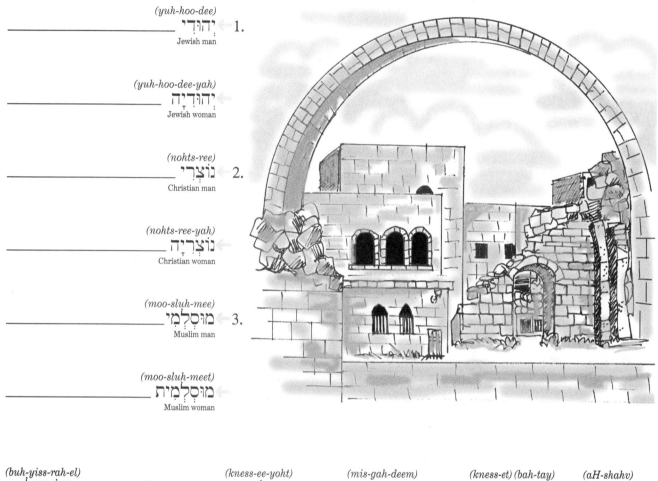

(buh-yiss-rah-el) *(kness-ee-yoht)* *(mis-gah-deem)* *(kness-et) (bah-tay)* *(aH-shahv)*
בְּיִשְׂרָאֵל ← you will see many כְּנֵסִיּוֹת ← plus מִסְגָּדִים ← and כְּנֶסֶת בָּתֵי ← עַכְשָׁו ←
churches mosques synagogues

(beev-reet)
let's learn how to say "I" בְּעִבְרִית ← : _____ אֲנִי ←
I

Test yourself - write each sentence on the next page for more practice. Add your own personal

variations as well.

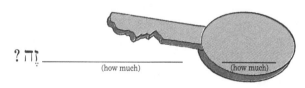

זֶה ? _____
(how much) (how much)

_____
_____ ׳
_____
_____

Japan............ *(yah-pahn)* .... יָפָן ← ☐
Japanese.......... *(yah-pah-nee)* .... יָפְנִי ☐
Jordan............ *(yar-dane)* .... יַרְדֵּן ☐
Jericho........... *(yuh-ree-Hoh)* .... יְרִיחוֹ ☐
Jesus............ *(yeh-shoo)* .... יֵשׁוּ ☐

37

אֲנִי נוֹצְרִי **.** (ah-nee) (nohts-ree) — I (am) / Christian man	אֲנִי נוֹצְרִיָה **.** (ah-nee) (nohts-ree-yah) — Christian woman
אֲנִי יְהוּדִיָה **.** (ah-nee) (yuh-hoo-dee-yah) — Jewish woman	אֲנִי אֲמֵרִיקָנִי **.** (ah-meh-ree-kahn-ee) — American man
אֲנִי בְּיִשְׂרָאֵל **.** (buh-yiss-rah-el)	אֲנִי אַנְגְלִיָה **.** (ahn-glee-yah) — English woman
אֲנִי אֲמֵרִיקָנִית **.** (ah-meh-ree-kahn-eet) — American woman	אֲנִי אַנְגְלִי **.** (ahn-glee) — I (am) / English man
אֲנִי מוּסְלְמִי **.** (moo-sluh-mee) — Muslim man	אֲנִי יְהוּדִי **.** (ah-nee) (yuh-hoo-dee) — Jewish man
אֲנִי בַּמָלוֹן **.** (bah-mah-lohn) — in the hotel	אֲנִי בַּמִסְעָדָה **.** (bah-mees-ah-dah) — in the restaurant
אֲנִי הָאִמָא **.** (hah-ee-mah) — the mother	אֲנִי דוֹד (dohd) — uncle

To negate any of these statements, simply add " לֹא " (loh) — not — after " אֲנִי " (ah-nee).

אֲנִי לֹא אֲמֵרִיקָנִית **.** (ah-meh-ree-kahn-eet) — not / American woman

אֲנִי לֹא מוּסְלְמִית **.** (moo-sluh-meet) — not / Muslim woman

Go through and drill these sentences above again but with " לֹא (loh) — not."

עַכְשָׁו (aH-shahv) take a piece of paper. Our מִשְׁפָּחָה (mish-pah-Hah) — family — from earlier had a reunion. Identify everyone below by writing the correct עברית (word) next to each person — אִמָא (ee-mah) — mother, אַבָּא (ah-bah) — father — and so on. Don't forget the כֶּלֶב (kel-ev) — dog!

☐← כַּבַּאי fireman............ (kah-by)
☐ כַּדוּר ball............ (kah-door)
☐ כַּדוּר בָּסִיס baseball........ (kah-door-bah-sees)
☐ כַּדוּר סַל basketball........... (kah-door-sahl)
☐ כַּדוּרֶגֶל soccer.......... (kah-doo-reg-el)

פ

(lil-mohd)
לִלְמֹד
to learn

You have already used two very important verbs: *(roht-seh)* רוֹצֶה *(ah-nee)* אֲנִי *want* *I* and *(lee)* לִי *(yesh)* יֵשׁ *I have* . Although

you might be able to get by with only these verbs, let's assume you want to do better. First a

quick review.

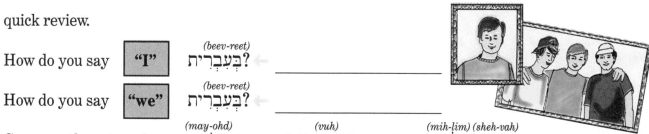

How do you say **"I"** *(beev-reet)* בְּעִבְרִית? _____

How do you say **"we"** *(beev-reet)* בְּעִבְרִית? _____

Compare these two charts *(may-ohd)* מְאֹד *very* carefully *(vuh)* וְ learn these *(mih-lim)* מִלִים *(sheh-vah)* שֶׁבַע now.

I = *(ah-nee)* אֲנִי _____   we = *(ah-naH-noo)* אֲנַחְנוּ _____

he = *(hoo)* הוּא _____   you = *(ah-tah)* אַתָּה ✦ _____

she = *(hee)* הִיא _____   you = *(aht)* אַתְּ ✦ _____

they = *(hem)* הֵם _____

Not too hard, is it? Draw lines between the matching *(ahn-gleet)* אַנְגְּלִית and *(eev-reet)* עִבְרִית words below to

see if you can keep these *(mih-lim)* מִלִים straight in your mind.

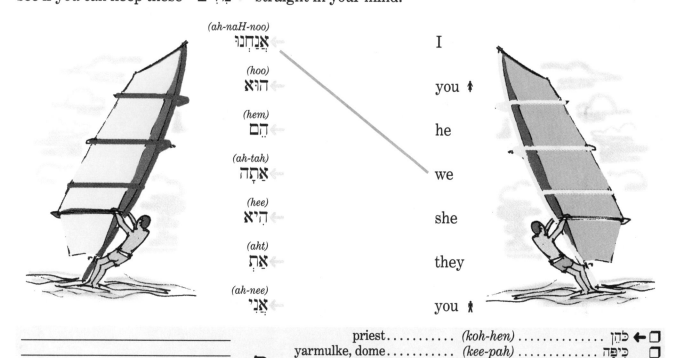

(ah-naH-noo) אֲנַחְנוּ

(hoo) הוּא

(hem) הֵם

(ah-tah) אַתָּה

(hee) הִיא

(aht) אַתְּ

(ah-nee) אֲנִי

I
you ✦
he
we
she
they
you ✦

_____

_____

_____

_____

ך

☐	priest.......... (koh-hen) .... כֹהֵן ←
☐	yarmulke, dome.......... (kee-pah) .... כִּיפָּה
☐	Dome of the Rock..... (kee-paht-hah-sel-ah) .. כִּיפַּת הַסֶּלַע
☐	village............ (kfar) .... כְּפָר
☐	Capernaum........ (kfar-nah-Hoom)...... כְּפַר נָחוּם

(aH-shahv) עַכְשָׁו ← close your *(sef-air)* סֵפֶר ← and write out both columns of this practice on *(nyar)* נְיָר ← . How did
paper

(ah-tah) אַתָּה ← do? *(rah)* רַע *(oh)* אוֹ *(tohv)* טוֹב ? *(tohv)* טוֹב *(loh)* לֹא *(oh)* אוֹ *(tohv)* טוֹב *(aH-shahv)* עַכְשָׁו *(ah-tah)* אַתָּה ← know these *(mih-lim)* מִלִּים ,
you   bad   or   good   good not or good   you

(ah-tah) אַתָּה ← can say almost anything *(beev-reet)* בְּעִבְרִית ← with one basic formula: the "plug-in" formula.
you

To demonstrate, let's take *(shee-shah)* שִׁשָּׁה ← basic וְ practical verbs וְ see how the "plug-in" formula works.
six

Write the verbs in the blanks after *(ah-tah)* אַתָּה ← have practiced saying them out loud many times.

_____ *(leer-tsoht)* לִרְצוֹת   _____ *(lah-voh)* לָבוֹא
to want   to come

_____ *(lik-noht)* לִקְנוֹת   _____ *(lin-soh-ah)* לִנְסוֹעַ
to buy   to travel

_____ *(lil-mohd)* לִלְמוֹד   _____ *(luh-dah-bair)* לְדַבֵּר
to learn   to speak

Besides the familiar words already circled, can *(ah-tah)* אַתָּה ← find *(ar-bah)* אַרְבַּע ← of the above verbs in the
four

puzzle below? When *(ah-tah)* אַתָּה ← find them, write them in the blanks to the right.

ל	ר	צ	ו	ת	פ	ת	ו	ד	שׁ	ל	ק
שׁ	ג	כ	ל	ד	ר	ב	ר	נ	ס	פ	ת
ט	א	ת	ה	צ	ח	ל	ל	ק	נ	ו	ת
ו	ב	ר	ע	ח	שׁ	ק	ד	מ	י	ז	
שׁ	כ	ג	ו	ר	ל	א	פ	ל	ס	ה	
ז	ר	ב	נ	ק	ג	כ	ב	כ	ק	שׁ	
ח	צ	ר	כ	ל	א	נ	ר	ו	ח	פ	
מ	ס	ע	ד	ה	ג	פ	צ	א	י	ת	

1. _____

2. _____

3. _____

4. _____

	cotton	*(koot-nah)*	כֻּתְנָה ←	☐ ☐ ☐
	ticket	*(kar-tees)*	כַּרְטִיס	☐ ☐
	ticket collector	*(kar-tee-sahn)*	כַּרְטִיסָן	☐ ☐
	Carmel	*(kar-mel)*	כַּרְמֶל	☐ ☐
	kosher	*(kah-shair)*	כָּשֵׁר	☐ ☐

כ

_____
_____
_____
_____

Study the following patterns carefully then practice your new verbs in the space provided.

_____ *(muh-dah-bair)* מְדַבֵּר speak(s)

_____ *(loh-med)* לוֹמֵד learn(s)

_____ *(noh-seh-ah)* נוֹסֵעַ travel(s)

_____ *(bah)* בָּא come(s)

_____ *(koh-neh)* קוֹנֶה buy(s)

_____ *(roht-seh)* רוֹצֶה want(s)

{ *(ah-nee)* אֲנִי I

(ah-tah) אַתָה you

(hoo) הוּא he

Note: • With all these verbs, the first thing you do is drop the initial "לְ" from the basic

verb form or stem.

• The verb form used with ✦ *(ah-nee)* אֲנִי I is the same form used with ✦ *(ah-tah)* אַתָה you and *(hoo)* הוּא he.

• The verb form used with ✦ *(ah-nee)* אֲנִי I is the same form used with ✦ *(aht)* אַתְ you and *(hee)* הִיא she.

_____ *(muh-dah-bair-et)* מְדַבֶּרֶת speak(s)

_____ *(loh-med-et)* לוֹמֶדֶת learn(s)

_____ *(noh-sah-aht)* נוֹסַעַת travel(s)

_____ *(bah-ah)* בָּאָה come(s)

_____ *(koh-nah)* קוֹנָה buy(s)

_____ *(roht-sah)* רוֹצָה want(s)

{ *(ah-nee)* אֲנִי I

(aht) אַתְ you

(hee) הִיא she

_____
_____
_____
_____

ל

Here's your pattern for *(ah-naH-noo)* אֲנַחְנוּ ← and הֶם ← *(hem)*. This verb form always ends in ־ים. Easy, isn't it?

_____	בָּאִים *(bah-im)* ← come
_____	קוֹנִים *(koh-nim)* ← buy
_____	רוֹצִים *(roht-sim)* ← want
_____	מְדַבְּרִים *(muh-dah-brim)* ← speak
_____	לוֹמְדִים *(lohm-dim)* ← learn
_____	נוֹסְעִים *(noh-sim)* ← travel

(ah-naH-noo)
אֲנַחְנוּ
we

(hem)
הֶם
they

Some verbs just will not conform to the rules! But don't worry. Speak slowly וְ clearly, וְ you

will be perfectly understood whether you say קוֹנֶה *(koh-neh)* or קוֹנָה *(koh-nah)*. יִשְׂרְאֵלִים *(yiss-ruh-eh-leem)* ← Israelis will be

delighted that you have taken the time to learn their language. Here are six more verbs.

_____	לוֹמַר *(loh-mar)* to say	_____	לְבַקֵשׁ *(luh-vah-kesh)* to order
_____	לִרְאוֹת *(luh-roht)* to see	_____	לְהַגִיעַ *(luh-hah-gee-ah)* to arrive
_____	לְהִישָׁאֵר *(luh-hish-ah-air)* to stay	_____	לְחַפֵּשׂ *(luh-Hah-pes)* to look for

At the back of this *(sef-air)* סֵפֶר, אַתָה ← *(ah-tah)* will find

twelve pages of flash cards to help you learn

these מִלִים חֲדָשׁוֹת *(mih-lim) (Hah-dah-shoht)* new. Cut them out;

carry them in your briefcase, purse, pocket אוֹ

knapsack; וְ review them whenever אַתָה *(ah-tah)*

have a free moment.

_____	ל	liberal......... *(lee-beh-rah-lee)* ...... לִיבְּרָלִי ← ☐
_____		league.......... *(lee-gah)* .... לִיגָה ☐
_____		liter............ *(lee-tair)* .... לִיטֶר ☐
		lemon.......... *(lee-mohn)* .... לִימוֹן ☐
		lemonade........ *(lee-moh-nah-dah)* .... לִימוֹנָדָה ☐

42

Practice what *(ah-tah)* אַתָּה ← have learned by filling in the following blanks with the correct form of the verb.

(luh-dah-bair)
לְדַבֵּר
to speak

מַה זֶה?

(ah-nee) אֲנִי _____ עִבְרִית. *(eev-reet)*
I — Hebrew

הוּא / אַתָּה ♂ _____ עִבְרִית. *(eev-reet)*
he you *(hoo)* *(ah-tah)*

הִיא / אַתְּ ♀ _____ עִבְרִית. *(eev-reet)*
she you *(hee)* *(aht)*

אֲנַחְנוּ / הֵם _____ עִבְרִית. *(eev-reet)*
we they *(ah-naH-noo)* *(hem)*

(lil-mohd)
לִלְמוֹד
to learn

(ah-nee) אֲנִי _____ עִבְרִית. *(eev-reet)*
I — Hebrew

♂ הוּא / אַתָּה _____ עִבְרִית. *(eev-reet)*
he you *(hoo)* *(ah-tah)*

♀ הִיא / אַתְּ _____ עִבְרִית. *(eev-reet)*
she you *(hee)* *(aht)*

הֵם / אֲנַחְנוּ _____ עִבְרִית. *(eev-reet)*
they we *(hem)* *(ah-naH-noo)*

(lin-soh-ah)
לִנְסוֹעַ
to travel

(ah-nee) אֲנִי _____ לְיִשְׂרָאֵל. *(luh-yiss-rah-el)*
I to Israel

♂ הוּא / אַתָּה _____ לְיִשְׂרָאֵל. *(ah-tah)*
he you

♀ הִיא / אַתְּ _____ לַמָּלוֹן. *(lah-mah-lohn)*
she you *(aht)* to the hotel

אֲנַחְנוּ / הֵם _____ לַמָּלוֹן. *(hem)*
we they

(lah-voh)
לָבוֹא
to come

(ah-nee) אֲנִי _____ מֵאָמֵרִיקָה. *(may-ah-meh-ree-kah)*
I from America

♂ הוּא / אַתָּה _____ מֵאָמֵרִיקָה. *(hoo)*
he you

♀ הִיא / אַתְּ _____ מֵאַנְגְלִיָה. *(hee)* *(may-ahn-glee-yah)*
she you from England

הֵם / אֲנַחְנוּ _____ מֵאַנְגְלִיָה. *(ah-naH-noo)*
they we

(lik-noht)
לִקְנוֹת
to buy

(ah-nee) אֲנִי _____ סֵפֶר. *(sef-air)*
book

♂ הוּא / אַתָּה _____ סֵפֶר.
he you

♀ הִיא / אַתְּ _____ כַּרְטִיס. *(hee)* *(kar-tees)*
she you ticket

אֲנַחְנוּ / הֵם _____ כַּרְטִיס.

(leer-tsoht)
לִרְצוֹת
to want

(ah-nee) אֲנִי _____ כּוֹס יַיִן. *(kohs)* *(yah-yeen)*
glass wine

♂ הוּא / אַתָּה _____ כּוֹס יַיִן. *(hoo)* *(ah-tah)*
he you

♀ הִיא / אַתְּ _____ כּוֹס מִיץ. *(kohs)* *(meets)*
she you juice

הֵם / אֲנַחְנוּ _____ כּוֹס מִיץ. *(ah-naH-noo)* *(hem)*
they we

☐ ← מִגְדָּל	tower.......... *(mig-dahl)*	
☐ מִגְדָּל דָוִד	Tower of David....... *(mig-dahl-dah-veed)*	
מ ☐ מִגְדָּל פִּיקוּחַ	control tower...... *(mig-dahl-pih-koo-aH)*	
☐ מְגִילָה	scroll.......... *(muh-gee-lah)*	
☐ מְגִילוֹת יַם הַמֶּלַח	Dead Sea Scrolls *(muh-gee-loht-yahm-hah-mel-aH)*	

Now take a break, walk around the room, take a deep breath and do the next six verbs.

(loh-mar)
לוֹמַר
to say

(luh-vah-kesh)
לְבַקֵּשׁ
to order

(shah-lohm)
שָׁלוֹם . _____ אוֹמֵר / אֲנִי
hello/goodbye

(mah-yeem) (kohs)
כּוֹס מַיִם . _____ מְבַקֵּשׁ / אֲנִי
water — I

_____ אוֹמֵר / אַתָּה / הוּא . שָׁלוֹם
(ah-tah) you — *(hoo)* he

(meets)
כּוֹס מִיץ . _____ מְבַקֵּשׁ / אַתָּה / הוּא
meets — *(ah-tah)* you — *(hoo)* he

(tohv) (boh-kair)
בֹּקֶר טוֹב . _____ אוֹמֶרֶת / אַתְּ / הִיא
good morning — *(aht)* — *(hee)*

(Hah-lahv)
כּוֹס חָלָב . _____ מְבַקֶּשֶׁת / אַתְּ / הִיא
milk — *(aht)* you — *(hee)* she

(hem) (ah-naH-noo)
בֹּקֶר טוֹב . _____ אוֹמְרִים / הֵם / אֲנַחְנוּ

(yah-yeen)
כּוֹס יַיִן . _____ מְבַקְשִׁים / הֵם / אֲנַחְנוּ
(hem) they — *(ah-naH-noo)* we

(luh-roht)
לִרְאוֹת
to see

(luh-Hah-pes)
לְחַפֵּשׂ
to look for

(sef-air)
סֵפֶר . _____ רוֹאֶה / אֲנִי

(sef-air)
סֵפֶר . _____ מְחַפֵּשׂ / אֲנִי
book

(mah-lohn)
מָלוֹן . _____ רוֹאֶה / אַתָּה / הוּא
(hoo)

(mah-lohn)
מָלוֹן . _____ מְחַפֵּשׂ / אַתָּה / הוּא
hotel — *(hoo)*

(may-Hoh-neet)
מְכוֹנִית . _____ רוֹאָה / אַתְּ / הִיא
(aht) you — *(hee)*

(oh-toh-boos)
אוֹטוֹבּוּס . _____ מְחַפֶּשֶׂת / אַתְּ / הִיא
(aht) you — *(hee)* she

(bahnk)
בַּנְק . _____ רוֹאִים / הֵם / אֲנַחְנוּ
(hem)

(bahnk)
בַּנְק . _____ מְחַפְּשִׂים / הֵם / אֲנַחְנוּ
(hem) (ah-naH-noo)

(luh-hah-gee-ah)
לְהַגִּיעַ
to arrive

(luh-hish-ah-air)
לְהִישָׁאֵר
to stay

(buh-yiss-rah-el)
בְּיִשְׂרָאֵל . _____ מַגִּיעַ / אֲנִי
in Israel

(buh-yiss-rah-el)
בְּיִשְׂרָאֵל . _____ נִשְׁאָר / אֲנִי
in Israel

(ah-veev) (buh-tel)
בְּתֵל אָבִיב . _____ מַגִּיעַ / אַתָּה / הוּא
in Tel Aviv — *(hoo)*

(ah-veev) (buh-tel)
בְּתֵל אָבִיב . _____ נִשְׁאָר / אַתָּה / הוּא
in Tel Aviv — *(hoo)*

(bee-roo-shah-lah-yeem)
בִּירוּשָׁלַיִם . _____ מַגִּיעָה / אַתְּ / הִיא
in Jerusalem — *(aht)* — *(hee)*

(bee-roo-shah-lah-yeem)
בִּירוּשָׁלַיִם . _____ נִשְׁאֶרֶת / אַתְּ / הִיא
in Jerusalem — *(aht)* — *(hee)*

(buh-Hay-fah)
בְּחֵיפָה . _____ מַגִּיעִים / הֵם / אֲנַחְנוּ
in Haifa

(buy-ay-roh-pah)
בְּאֵירוֹפָּה . _____ נִשְׁאָרִים / הֵם / אֲנַחְנוּ
in Europe — *(hem)* they — *(ah-naH-noo)* we

☐	מִדְבָּר ←	desert........... *(mid-bar)*
☐	מִדְרָכָה	sidewalk.......... *(mid-rah-Hah)*
☐	מוּזֵיאוֹן	museum.......... *(moo-zay-ohn)*
☐	מוּזֵיאוֹן הָאִסְלָאם	Islam Museum.... *(moo-zay-ohn-hah-iss-lahm)*
☐	מוּזֵיאוֹן יִשְׂרָאֵל	Israel Museum..... *(moo-zay-ohn-yiss-rah-el)*

מ

_____
_____
_____
_____

(ken)
כֵּן , it is hard to get used to all those מִלִים חֲדָשׁוֹת *(Hah-dah-shoht) (mih-lim)* . ← But just keep practicing וְ , before
yes   new

you know it, אַתָּה *(ah-tah)* ← will be using them naturally. עַכְשָׁו *(aH-shahv)* ← is a perfect time to turn to the back

(sef-air)
of this סֵפֶר , ← clip out your verb flash cards וְ start flashing. Don't skip over your free מִלִים *(mih-lim)*

either. Check them off in the box provided as אַתָּה לוֹמֵד *(loh-med) (ah-tah)* ← each one. See if אַתָּה *(ah-tah)* ← can fill
learn

in the blanks below. The correct תְּשׁוּבוֹת *(t'shoo-voht)* ← are at the bottom of this עַמוּד *(ah-mood)* . ←
answers

_____ 1.
(I (↑) speak Hebrew.)

_____ 2.
(We learn Hebrew.)

_____ 3.
(He orders a glass of juice.)

_____ 4.
(He comes from America.)

_____ 5.
(I stay in Tel Aviv.)

_____ 6.
(You (↑) buy a book.)

(ah-tah)
In the following Steps, אַתָּה ← will be introduced

to more verbs and אַתָּה ← should drill them in

(ah-tah)
exactly the same way as אַתָּה ← did in this section.

Look up new מִלִים *(mih-lim)* ← in your מִלּוֹן *(mih-lohn)* ← and make
dictionary

up your own sentences. Try out your new מִלִים *(mih-lim)* ←

for that's how you make them yours to use on your

holiday. Remember, the more אַתָּה ← practice

עַכְשָׁו ← the more enjoyable your trip will be.

(buh-hahts-lah-Hah)
בְּהַצְלָחָה ! ←
good luck

הַתְּשׁוּבוֹת

4. הוּא בָּא מֵאֲמֶרִיקָה .   1. ← אֲנִי מְדַבֶּרֶת עִבְרִית .
5. אֲנִי נִשְׁאָר בְּתֵל אָבִיב .   2. אֲנַחְנוּ לוֹמְדִים עִבְרִית .
6. אַתְּ קוֹנָה סֵפֶר .   3. הוּא מְבַקֵשׁ כּוֹס מִיץ .

45

(hah-shah-ah) *(mah)* **מָה הַשָׁעָה** ?
time is it   what

(ayH) אֵיךְ know אַתָּה to tell *(hah-yah-mim)* הַיָּמִים of *(hah-shah-voo-ah)* הַשָׁבוּעַ and *(hah-Hoh-dah-shim)* הַחֳדָשִׁים of *(hah-shah-nah)* הַשָׁנָה.
how   the days   the week   the months   the year

As a traveler *(buh-yiss-rah-el)* בְּיִשְׂרָאֵל , you need to be able to tell time in order to make reservations and to

catch *(oh-toh-boo-seem)* אוֹטוֹבּוּסִים . Here are the "basics."
buses

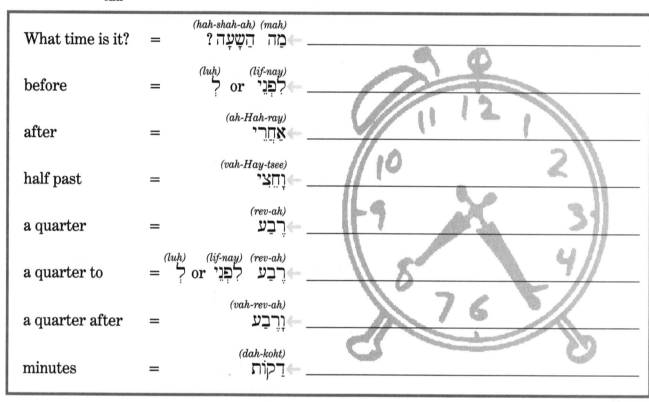

What time is it?	=	*(hah-shah-ah)* *(mah)* מָה הַשָׁעָה ? _____
before	=	*(luh)* *(lif-nay)* לִפְנֵי or לְ _____
after	=	*(ah-Hah-ray)* אַחֲרֵי _____
half past	=	*(vah-Hay-tsee)* וָחֵצִי _____
a quarter	=	*(rev-ah)* רֶבַע _____
a quarter to	=	*(luh)* *(lif-nay)* *(rev-ah)* רֶבַע לִפְנֵי or לְ _____
a quarter after	=	*(vah-rev-ah)* וָרֶבַע _____
minutes	=	*(dah-koht)* דַקוֹת _____

עַכְשָׁו quiz yourself. Fill in the missing letters below.

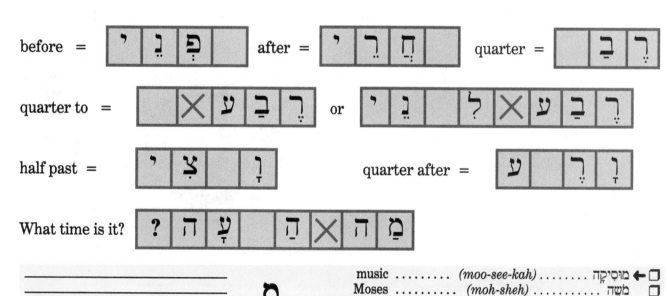

before = פְּ נֵ י   after = חֲ רֵ י   quarter = רֶ ב

quarter to = רֶ ב עַ ✕ or רֶ ב עַ ✕ ל נֵ י

half past = רָ צִ י   quarter after = רֶ עַ וָ

What time is it? מַ ה ✕ ה עָ ה ?

☐ ←	מוּסִיקָה	music .... *(moo-see-kah)*	
☐	מֹשֶׁה	Moses .... *(moh-sheh)*	
☐	מֻחֲמָד	Muhammed .... *(moo-Hah-mahd)*	
☐	מוֹשָׁב	cooperative farm/moshav .... *(moh-shahv)*	
☐	מַטָע	orchard .... *(mah-tah)*	

מ

(ayH) אֵיךְ *how* ← עַכְשָׁו are these (mih-lim) מִלִים ← used? Study the examples (luh-mah-tah) לְמַטָה *below* . When אַתָה

think it through, it really is not too difficult.

(Hah-mesh) חָמֵשׁ *five* — (hah-shah-ah) הַשָׁעָה *the hour*	5:00	_____
(dah-koht) דַקוֹת *minutes* — (vuh-es-air) וְעֶשֶׂר *and ten* — (Hah-mesh) חָמֵשׁ *five* — (hah-shah-ah) הַשָׁעָה *the time*	5:10	_____
(vah-rev-ah) וָרֶבַע *and a quarter* — (Hah-mesh) חָמֵשׁ — (hah-shah-ah) הַשָׁעָה	5:15	_____
(vuh-es-reem) וְעֶשְׂרִים דַקוֹת *and twenty* — (Hah-mesh) חָמֵשׁ *five* — (hah-shah-ah) הַשָׁעָה	5:20	_____
(vah-Hay-tsee) וָחֵצִי *half past* — (Hah-mesh) חָמֵשׁ — (hah-shah-ah) הַשָׁעָה	5:30	_____
(luh-shesh) לְשֵׁשׁ *before six* — (es-reem) עֶשְׂרִים דַקוֹת *twenty* — (hah-shah-ah) הַשָׁעָה	5:40	_____
(shesh) שֵׁשׁ *six* — (lif-nay) לִפְנֵי *before* — (rev-ah) רֶבַע *quarter* — (hah-shah-ah) הַשָׁעָה	5:45	_____
(luh-shesh) לְשֵׁשׁ *before six* — (dah-koht) דַקוֹת *minutes* — (es-air) עֶשֶׂר *ten* — (hah-shah-ah) הַשָׁעָה	5:50	_____
(shesh) שֵׁשׁ *six* — (hah-shah-ah) הַשָׁעָה *the hour*	6:00	_____

See how (Hah-shoov) חָשׁוּב *important* learning (mis-pah-reem) מִסְפָּרִים *numbers* עַכְשָׁו is? answer the following (shuh-eh-laht) שְׁאֵלוֹת *questions* based

on (luh-mah-tah) לְמַטָה *the clocks* (hah-shoh-neem) הַשָׁעוֹנִים . (hah-t'shoo-voht) הַתְשׁוּבוֹת are at the bottom of (hah-ah-mood) הָעַמוּד . (hah-shah-ah) הַשָׁעָה ? (mah) מַה

1. 8:00 _____

2. 12:15 _____

3. 7:30 _____

4. 9:20 _____

הַתְשׁוּבוֹת

3. הַשָׁעָה שֶׁבַע וְחֵצִי .   1. → הַשָׁעָה שְׁמוֹנֶה .

4. הַשָׁעָה תֵּשַׁע וְעֶשְׂרִים דַקוֹת .   2. הַשָׁעָה שְׁתֵּים עֶשְׂרֵה וָרֶבַע .

47

When אַתָּה ← answer a "מָתַי" ← question, say "בְּ" before אַתָּה ← give the time.

(mah-tie) above מָתַי — "when"
(buh) above בְּ — "at"

1. מָתַי *(mah-tie)* מַגִּיעַ *(mah-gee-ah)* arrives הָאוֹטוֹבּוּס *(hah-oh-toh-boos)* the bus ? _____ (at 7:30)

2. מָתַי *(mah-tie)* מַגִּיעַ *(mah-gee-ah)* arrives הָאוֹטוֹבּוּס *(hah-oh-toh-boos)* מִבְּאֵר *(mee-bair)* from Beersheba שֶׁבַע *(sheh-vah)* ? _____ (at 6:00)

3. מָתַי *(mah-tie)* when (is) הַקוֹנְצֶרְט *(hah-kohn-tsairt)* the concert ? _____ (at 8:00)

4. מָתַי *(mah-tie)* הַסֶּרֶט *(hah-sair-et)* the movie ? _____ (at 9:00)

5. מָתַי *(mah-tie)* when (is) הַמִּסְעָדָה *(hah-mees-ah-dah)* the restaurant פְּתוּחָה *(ptoo-Hah)* open ? _____ (at 11:30)

6. מָתַי *(mah-tie)* הַמּוּזֵיאוֹן *(hah-moo-zay-ohn)* the museum פָּתוּחַ *(pah-too-aH)* open ? _____ (at 8:30)

7. מָתַי *(mah-tie)* הַמּוּזֵיאוֹן *(hah-moo-zay-ohn)* the museum סָגוּר *(sah-goor)* closed ? _____ (at 5:30)

8. מָתַי *(mah-tie)* הַמִּסְעָדָה *(hah-mees-ah-dah)* the restaurant סְגוּרָה *(sgoo-rah)* closed ? _____ (at 10:30)

הִנֵּה *(hin-ay)* ← a quick quiz. Fill in the blanks with the correct מִסְפָּרִים *(mis-pah-reem)* numbers.

9. בְּדַקָּה *(buh-dah-kah)* in (a) minute יֵשׁ *(yesh)* there (are) _____ *(?)* שְׁנִיּוֹת *(shnee-yoht)* seconds .

12. בְּשָׁנָה *(buh-shah-nah)* in year יֵשׁ *(yesh)* _____ *(?)* חוֹדָשִׁים *(Hoh-dah-shim)* months .

10. בְּשָׁעָה *(buh-shah-ah)* in (an) hour יֵשׁ *(yesh)* there (are) _____ *(?)* דַּקּוֹת *(dah-koht)* minutes .

13. בְּשָׁנָה *(buh-shah-nah)* יֵשׁ *(yesh)* _____ *(?)* שָׁבוּעוֹת *(shah-voo-oht)* weeks .

11. בְּשָׁבוּעַ *(buh-shah-voo-ah)* in (a) week יֵשׁ *(yesh)* _____ *(?)* יָמִים *(yah-mim)* days .

14. בְּשָׁנָה *(buh-shah-nah)* יֵשׁ *(yesh)* _____ *(?)* יָמִים *(yah-mim)* days .

הַתְּשׁוּבוֹת

1. ← בְּשָׁעָה שֶׁבַע וָחֵצִי
2. בְּשָׁעָה שֵׁשׁ
3. בְּשָׁעָה שְׁמוֹנֶה
4. בְּשָׁעָה תֵּשַׁע
5. בְּשָׁעָה אַחַת עֶשְׂרֵה וָחֵצִי
6. בְּשָׁעָה שְׁמוֹנֶה וָחֵצִי
7. בְּשָׁעָה חָמֵשׁ וָחֵצִי

8. בְּשָׁעָה עֶשֶׂר וָחֵצִי
9. שִׁישִׁים
10. שִׁישִׁים
11. שִׁבְעָה
12. שְׁנֵים עָשָׂר
13. חֲמִישִׁים וּשְׁנַיִם
14. שְׁלוֹשׁ מֵאוֹת שִׁישִׁים וַחֲמִישָׁה

Do אַתָּה *(ah-tah)* ← remember your greetings from earlier? It is a good time to review them as they will

always be very important.

בְּשָׁעָה שְׁמוֹנֶה בַּבֹּקֶר אוֹמְרִים: "בֹּקֶר טוֹב, גְּבֶרֶת לֵוִי!"
(buh-shah-ah) (shmoh-neh) (bah-boh-kair) (ohm-rim) (boh-kair) (tohv) (gveh-ret) (leh-vee)
at hour — eight — in the morning — (we say) — — Mrs. — Levy

_____ מָה אֲנַחְנוּ אוֹמְרִים ?
(mah) (ah-naH-noo)
what

בְּיוֹם שַׁבָּת אוֹמְרִים: "שַׁבָּת שָׁלוֹם!"
(buh-yohm) (shah-baht) (ohm-rim) (shah-baht) (shah-lohm)
on Saturday

_____ מָה אֲנַחְנוּ אוֹמְרִים ?
(mah) (ah-naH-noo)

בְּשָׁעָה שְׁמוֹנֶה בָּעֶרֶב אוֹמְרִים: "עֶרֶב טוֹב, מַר הָרְאֵל!"
(buh-shah-ah) (shmoh-neh) (bah-eh-rev) (ohm-rim) (eh-rev) (tohv) (mar) (har-el)
at hour — eight — in the evening — (we say) — — Mr. — Harel

_____ מָה אֲנַחְנוּ אוֹמְרִים ?
(mah) (ah-naH-noo)

בְּשָׁעָה עֶשֶׂר בַּלַּיְלָה אוֹמְרִים: "לַיְלָה טוֹב!"
(buh-shah-ah) (es-air) (bah-lie-lah) (ohm-rim) (lie-lah) (tohv)

_____ מָה אֲנַחְנוּ אוֹמְרִים ?
(mah) (ah-naH-noo)

לֶאֱכֹל *(leh-eh-Hohl)* ← and לִשְׁתּוֹת *(lish-toht)* ← will be very important for you during your stay בְּיִשְׂרָאֵל *(buh-yiss-rah-el)*.
to eat — to drink

Learn them well! If אַתָּה *(ah-tah)* ← are visiting יִשְׂרָאֵל *(yiss-rah-el)* ← on a special occasion, אַתָּה *(ah-tah)* ← may want to

use one of the following greetings.

Congratulations! = מַזָּל טוֹב! ← *(mah-zahl) (tohv)*	Happy Holiday! = חַג שָׂמֵחַ! ← *(Hahg) (sah-may-aH)*
Good Sabbath! = שַׁבָּת שָׁלוֹם! ← *(shah-baht) (shah-lohm)*	Happy New Year! = שָׁנָה טוֹבָה! ← *(shah-nah) (toh-vah)*

_____	meter............ *(meh-tair)*	מֶטֶר ← ☐
_____	milkshake....... *(milk-shake)*	מִילְק שֵׁיק ☐
מ	water............ *(mah-yim)*	מַיִם ☐
_____	waterfall........ *(mah-pahl-mah-yim)*	מַפַּל מַיִם ☐
_____	minimum......... *(mee-nee-moom)*	מִינִימוּם ☐

49

(hin-ay)
הִנֵּה
here
are the new verbs for Step 13.

(leh-eh-Hohl)
לֶאֱכֹל ←
to eat

(lish-toht)
לִשְׁתּוֹת ←
to drink

(leh-eh-Hohl)
לֶאֱכֹל ←
to eat

(lish-toht)
לִשְׁתּוֹת ←
to drink

(mah-rahk)
מָרָק .
soup
אֲנִי אוֹכֵל/ _____

(Hah-lahv)
חָלָב .
milk
אֲנִי שׁוֹתֶה/ _____

(steak)
סְטֵייק .
steak
הוּא / אַתָּה אוֹכֵל/ _____ ♙

(yah-yin)
יַיִן .
wine
(hoo)
הוּא / אַתָּה שׁוֹתֶה/ _____ ♙

(har-bay)
הַרְבֵּה .
a lot
הִיא / אַתְּ אוֹכֶלֶת/ _____ ♀

(meets)
מִיץ .
juice
(aht) *(hee)*
הִיא / אַתְּ שׁוֹתָה/ _____ ♀
you she

הַרְבֵּה . אֲנַחְנוּ / הֵם אוֹכְלִים/ _____

(har-bay)
הַרְבֵּה .
a lot
(hem)
אֲנַחְנוּ / הֵם שׁוֹתִים/ _____

> **Note:** All those dots and dashes known as vowels are only used to help you when you first begin to learn Hebrew. When you arrive in Israel you will see these same familiar words but without most of the dots and dashes. As soon as you feel comfortable with your new language and its pronunciation, you may stop including them.

_____	mechanic.......... *(muh-Hoh-nee)* .... מְכוֹנַאי ←	☐
_____	dirty........ *(muh-looH-laH)* .... מְלֻכְלָךְ	☐
מ _____	million.......... *(meel-yohn)* .... מִילְיוֹן	☐
_____	millionaire........ *(meel-yoh-nair)* .... מִילְיוֹנֶר	☐
_____	missionary.......... *(mees-yoh-nair)* .... מִיסְיוֹנֶר	☐

(aht)
אַתְּ ← have learned a lot of material in the last few steps וְ that means it is time to quiz yourself.

Don't panic, this is just for you וְ no one else needs to know how אַתְּ ← (aht) did. Remember, this is a

chance to review, find out מָה אַתְּ ← (aht) (mah) remember וְ מָה אַתְּ ← need to spend more time on. After

אַתְּ ← have finished, check your תְּשׁוּבוֹת ← (t'shoo-voht) in the glossary at the back of this book. Circle the

correct answers.

קָפֶה	tea	coffee
לֹא	yes	no
דּוֹד	aunt	uncle
אוֹ	and	or
(lil-mohd) לִלְמוֹד	to drink	to learn
(lie-lah) לַיְלָה	morning	night
(shee-shee) יוֹם שִׁישִׁי	Friday	Tuesday
(luh-roht) לִרְאוֹת	to see	to look for
חַם	cold	hot
כֶּסֶף	money	page
תֵּשַׁע	nine	ten
(leh-Hem) לֶחֶם	many	bread

מִשְׁפָּחָה	seven	family
(yuh-lah-deem) יְלָדִים	children	grandfather
חָלָב	butter	(milk)
פִּלְפֵּל	pepper	salt
(may-ahl) מֵעַל לְ	under	over
(roh-fay) רוֹפֵא	man	doctor
בְּיוּלִי	in June	in July
דָּת	kitchen	religion
יֵשׁ לִי	I want	I have
(luh-Hah-pes) לְחַפֵּשׂ	to look for	to stay
(mah-Har) מָחָר	yesterday	tomorrow
טוֹב	good	yellow

(shlohm-Hah) (mah)
מַה שְׁלוֹמְךָ ? ← __What time is it?__   __How are you?__   Well, how are you after this quiz?

_____	maximum......... (mahk-see-moom) .... מַקְסִימוּם ← ☐
_____	margarine........ (mar-gah-ree-nah) .... מַרְגָּרִינָה ☐
_____ מ	marzipan.......... (mar-tsee-pahn) .... מַרְצִיפָּן ☐
_____	Messiah......... (mah-shee-aH) .... מָשִׁיחַ ☐
_____	mathematics...... (mah-tay-mah-tee-kah) .... מָתֶמָטִיקָה ☐

51

(ah-tah)

If אַתָּה ← are looking at a (mah-pah) מַפָּה ← and you see the following (mih-lim) מִלִּים ←, it should not be too
map

difficult to figure out (mah) מַה ← they mean. Take an educated guess. (hah-t'shoo-voht) (luh-mah-tah) הַתְּשׁוּבוֹת לְמַטָּה.
what   below

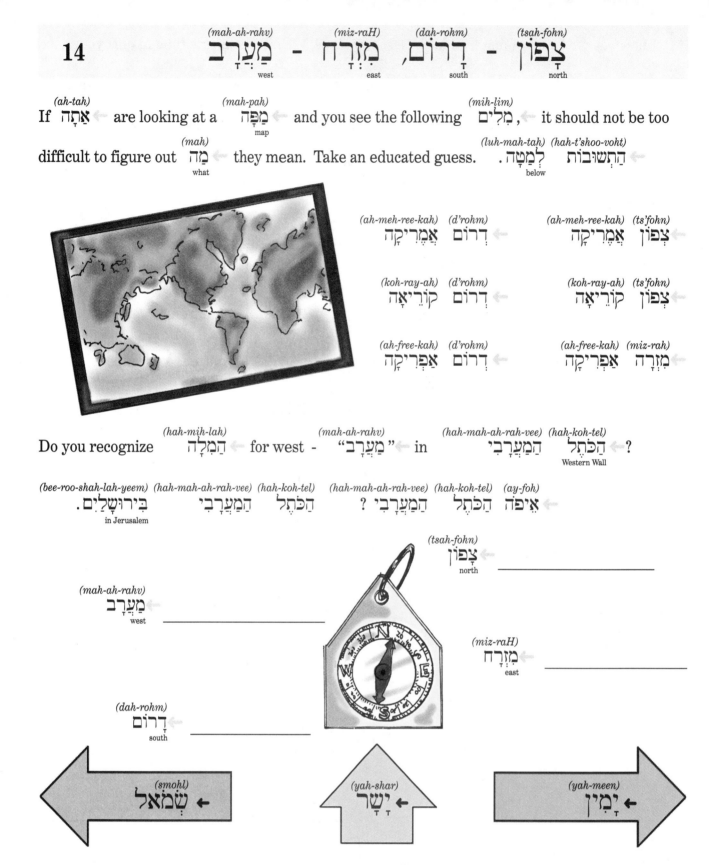

(ts'fohn) (ah-meh-ree-kah)   (d'rohm) (ah-meh-ree-kah)

צָפוֹן אֲמֶרִיקָה   דָּרוֹם אֲמֶרִיקָה

(ts'fohn) (koh-ray-ah)   (d'rohm) (koh-ray-ah)

צָפוֹן קוֹרֵיאָה   דָּרוֹם קוֹרֵיאָה

(miz-rah) (ah-free-kah)   (d'rohm) (ah-free-kah)

מִזְרָח אַפְרִיקָה   דָּרוֹם אַפְרִיקָה

Do you recognize (hah-mih-lah) הַמִּלָּה ← for west - "(mah-ah-rahv) מַעֲרָב" in (hah-mah-ah-rah-vee) (hah-koh-tel) הַכֹּתֶל הַמַּעֲרָבִי ←?
Western Wall

(ay-foh) (hah-koh-tel) (hah-mah-ah-rah-vee) ← אֵיפֹה הַכֹּתֶל הַמַּעֲרָבִי? (hah-koh-tel) (hah-mah-ah-rah-vee) (bee-roo-shah-lah-yeem) הַכֹּתֶל הַמַּעֲרָבִי בִּירוּשָׁלַיִם.
in Jerusalem

(tsah-fohn) צָפוֹן ← _____
north

(mah-ah-rahv) מַעֲרָב ← _____
west

(miz-raH) מִזְרָח ← _____
east

(dah-rohm) דָּרוֹם ← _____
south

(smohl) שְׂמֹאל ←   (yah-shar) יָשָׁר ←   (yah-meen) יָמִין ←

_____   _____   _____
(left)   (straight ahead)   (right)

הַתְּשׁוּבוֹת

South America	North America
South Korea	North Korea
South Africa	East Africa

These (mih-lim) (ar-bah) אַרְבַּע מִלִּים can go a long way. Say them aloud each time you write them in the

blanks below.

_____ (bay-vah-kah-shah) בְּבַקָשָׁה
please

_____ (toh-dah) תּוֹדָה
thank you

_____ (slee-Hah) סְלִיחָה
excuse me

_____ (bay-vah-kah-shah) בְּבַקָשָׁה
you're welcome

(hin-ay) הִנֵּה are (shtay) שְׁתֵּי typical (see-Hoht) שִׂיחוֹת for someone who is trying to find something. Write them out.
two   conversations

(yuh-roo-shah-lah-yeem) (mah-lohn) (slee-Hah) (dah-veed)
דָוִד : ← סְלִיחָה, אֵיפֹה מָלוֹן יְרוּשָׁלַיִם ?

_____

(hah-sheh-nee) (bah-ruh-Hohv) (smoh-lah) (pneh) (reh-Hoh-voht) (shnay) (leH) (gahd)
גַד : ← לֵךְ שְׁנֵי רְחוֹבוֹת . פְּנֵה שְׂמֹאלָה בָּרְחוֹב הַשֵּׁנִי .
second   in the street   to the left   turn   streets   two   go

_____

(mee-yah-meen) (yuh-roo-shah-lah-yeem) (mah-lohn)
מָלוֹן יְרוּשָׁלַיִם מִיָמִין .
on right

_____

(hah-iss-lahm) (moo-zay-ohn) (oh-ded)
עוֹדֵד : ← סְלִיחָה, אֵיפֹה מוּזֵיאוֹן הָאִיסְלַאם ?
Islam   museum

_____

(met-reem) (es-reem) (leH) (yuh-mee-nah) (pneh) (root)
רוּת : ← פְּנֵה יָמִינָה . לֵךְ עֶשְׂרִים מֶטְרִים .
meters   go   to the right   turn

_____

(bah-pee-nah) (vuh-hah-moo-zay-ohn) (smoh-lah) (pneh)
פְּנֵה שְׂמֹאלָה וְהַמּוּזֵיאוֹן בַּפִּנָה .
on the corner   to the left

_____

	(orchestra) conductor ... (muh-nah-tsay-aH) .... מְנַצֵּחַ ← ☐
_____	מ key ...... (mahf-tay-aH) .... מַפְתֵּחַ ☐
_____	king .... (mel-eH) .... מֶלֶךְ ☐
_____	King David Hotel (mah-lohn-hah-mel-eH-dah-veed) מָלוֹן הַמֶּלֶךְ דָוִד ☐
_____	truck .... (mah-sah-eet) .... מַשָׂאִית ☐

53

Are אַתָה *(ah-tah)* lost? There is no need to be lost if אַתָה ← have learned the basic direction words.

Do not try to memorize these שִׂיחוֹת *(see-Hoht)* conversations because אַתָה ← will never be looking for precisely these

places. One day, אַתָה ← might need to ask for directions to הַכְּנֶסֶת *(hah-kness-et)* the Knesset or הַשׁוּק *(hah-shook)* the market. Learn

the key direction words and be sure אַתָה ← can find your destination. אַתָה ← may want to

לִקְנוֹת *(lik-noht)* buy a guidebook to start planning what places אַתָה ← would like to visit. מַה *(mah)* what if the

person responding to your שְׁאֵלָה *(shuh-eh-lah)* question answers too quickly for אַתָה ← to understand the entire

reply? Just ask עוֹד פַּעַם *(ohd)* *(pahm)* once more saying,

---

← סְלִיחָה, אֲנִי מְדַבֵּר רַק קְצָת עִבְרִית. בְּבַקָשָׁה. לַחֲזוֹר. תוֹדָה.
(toh-dah) *(lah-Hah-zor)* repeat *(bay-vah-kah-shah)* *(eev-reet)* *(k'tsaht)* little *(rahk)* only *(muh-dah-bair)* speak

---

עַכְשָׁו *(aH-shahv)* ← say it again וְ then write it out below.

_____

(Excuse me. I speak only a little Hebrew. Please repeat. Thank you.)

כֵּן, *(ken)* ← it is difficult at first but don't give up! עַכְשָׁו ← when the directions are repeated, אַתָה ←

will be able to understand if אַתָה ← have learned the key מִלִּים ← for directions.

right

left

(north)

(west)

(east)

(south)

← מִשְׁטָרָה	police .... (mish-tah-rah)	
מְכוֹנִית מִשְׁטָרָה	police car (may-Hoh-neet-mish-tah-rah)	
מַתָּנָה	gift .... (mah-tah-nah)	
מוֹרָה	teacher (↑) .... (moh-rah)	
מִצְרַיִם	Egypt ...... (mits-rah-yim)	

מ

Here are (ar-bah) אַרְבַּע ← new verbs. Quick — (mah) מַה ← is the (eev-reet) עִבְרִית ← word for "they"? For "we"?

For "she"?

_____

(luh) (luh-Hah-koht) לִחְכּוֹת לְ
to wait for

(luh-hah-veen) לְהָבִין
to understand

_____

(ahl) (lah-Hah-zor) לַחֲזוֹר עַל ←
to repeat

(tsah-reeH) צָרִיךְ ←
to need

As always, say each sentence out loud. Say each ן every (mih-lah) מִלָה ← carefully, pronouncing each

(eev-reet) עִבְרִית ← sound as well as אַתָה ← can.

(luh) (luh-Hah-koht) לִחְכּוֹת לְ
to wait for

(oh-toh-boos) אוֹטוֹבּוּס. _____ מְחַכָּה לְ אֲנִי ←

(ah-tah) (hoo) אוֹטוֹבּוּס. _____ מְחַכָּה לְ הוּא / אַתָה ♦
you he

(tahk-see) טַקְסִי. _____ מְחַכָּה לְ הִיא / אַת ♦
the taxi (aht) (hee)
you she

(hem) (ah-naH-noo) טַקְסִי. _____ מְחַכִּים לְ אֲנַחְנוּ / הֵם

(luh-hah-veen) לְהָבִין
to understand

(eev-reet) עִבְרִית. _____ מֵבִין אֲנִי ← (ah-nee)
I

(ah-tah) (hoo) עִבְרִית. _____ מֵבִין הוּא / אַתָה ♦
you he

(ah-rah-veet) עֲרָבִית. _____ מְבִינָה הִיא / אַת ♦
Arabic (aht) (hee)
you she

(ee-tahl-keet) אִיטַלְקִית. _____ מְבִינִים אֲנַחְנוּ / הֵם
Italian (hem) (ah-naH-noo)
they we

(tsah-reeH) צָרִיךְ
to need

(tahk-see) טַקְסִי. _____ צָרִיךְ אֲנִי ←
taxi (ah-nee)
I

(bahnk) בַּנְק. _____ צָרִיךְ הוּא / אַתָה ♦
bank (ah-tah) (hoo)
you he

(mah-lohn) מָלוֹן. _____ צְרִיכָה הִיא / אַת ♦
hotel (aht) (hee)
you she

(kah-feh) (sef-el) סֵפֶל קָפֶה. _____ צְרִיכִים אֲנַחְנוּ / הֵם
coffee cup (hem) (ah-naH-noo)
they we

מַה ? מַה ?

(ahl) (lah-Hah-zor) לַחֲזוֹר עַל ←
to repeat

(hah-mih-lah) הַמִלָה. _____ חוֹזֵר עַל / אֲנִי ←
(ah-nee)
I

(hah-t'shoo-vah) הַתְשׁוּבָה. _____ חוֹזֵר עַל / הוּא / אַתָה ♦
the answer (ah-tah) (hoo)
you he

(hah-shem) הַשֵׁם. _____ חוֹזֶרֶת עַל / הִיא / אַת ♦
the name (aht) (hee)
you she

(hah-mis-pah-rim) הַמִסְפָּרִים. _____ חוֹזְרִים עַל / אֲנַחְנוּ / הֵם
(hem) (ah-naH-noo)
they we

_____
_____
_____   נ
_____

prophet	(nah-vee)	נָבִיא ← ☐
carpenter	(nah-gar)	נַגָּר ☐
river	(nah-har)	נָהָר ☐
Nahariya	(nah-hah-ree-yah)	נַהֲרִיָה ☐
stream	(nah-Hahl)	נַחַל ☐

55

15

(luh-mah-tah) *(luh-mah-uh-lah)*

לְמַעְלָה - לְמַטָּה ←

downstairs, below   upstairs, above

(mih-lim) *(buh-yiss-rah-el)* *(bite)* *(hin-ay)* *(shay-nah)* *(Hah-dar)*

עַכְשָׁו ← let's learn more מִלִּים . הִנֵּה בַּיִת בְּיִשְׂרָאֵל . Go to your חֲדַר שֵׁינָה and
bedroom

(Hed-air) *(hah-shay-nah)* *(bah-Hah-dar)*

look around the חֶדֶר . Let's learn the names of the things בַּחֲדַר הַשֵּׁינָה , just like
in the bedroom

(ah-naH-noo) *(hah-bite)*

אֲנַחְנוּ ← learned the various parts of הַבַּיִת .
we

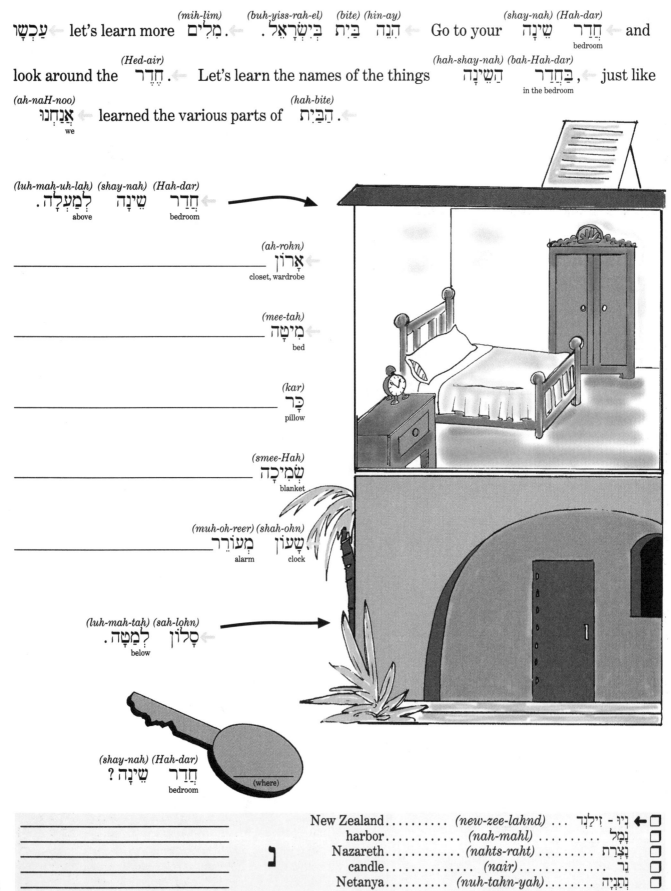

(luh-mah-uh-lah) *(shay-nah)* *(Hah-dar)*

חֲדַר שֵׁינָה לְמַעְלָה . ←
bedroom   above

(ah-rohn)

אָרוֹן ←
closet, wardrobe

(mee-tah)

מִיטָה ←
bed

(kar)

כַּר ←
pillow

(smee-Hah)

שְׂמִיכָה ←
blanket

(muh-oh-reer) *(shah-ohn)*

שָׁעוֹן מְעוֹרֵר ←
alarm   clock

(luh-mah-tah) *(sah-lohn)*

סָלוֹן לְמַטָּה . ←
below

(shay-nah) *(Hah-dar)*

חֲדַר שֵׁינָה ?
bedroom   _____ (where)

New Zealand	*(new-zee-lahnd)*	נְיוּ - זִילָנְד ←
harbor	*(nah-mahl)*	נָמֵל
Nazareth	*(nahts-raht)*	נָצְרַת
candle	*(nair)*	נֵר
Netanya	*(nuh-tahn-yah)*	נְתַנְיָה

נ

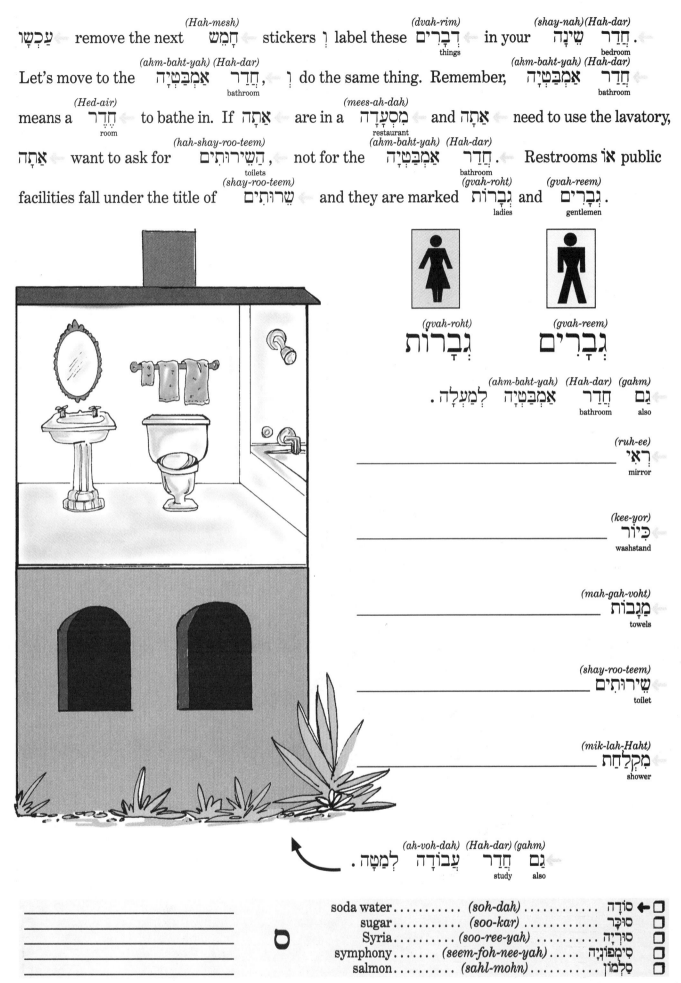

עַכְשָׁו remove the next חָמֵשׁ *(Hah-mesh)* ← stickers וְ label these דְּבָרִים *(dvah-rim)* ← **things** in your שֵׁנָה *(shay-nah)* חֲדַר *(Hah-dar)* **bedroom** .

Let's move to the אַמְבַּטְיָה *(ahm-baht-yah)* חֲדַר *(Hah-dar)*, **bathroom** וְ do the same thing. Remember, אַמְבַּטְיָה *(ahm-baht-yah)* חֲדַר *(Hah-dar)* **bathroom**

means a חֶדֶר *(Hed-air)* ← **room** to bathe in. If אַתָּה are in a מִסְעָדָה *(mees-ah-dah)* **restaurant** and אַתָּה ← need to use the lavatory,

אַתָּה want to ask for הַשֵּׁרוּתִים *(hah-shay-roo-teem)* ← **toilets**, not for the אַמְבַּטְיָה *(ahm-baht-yah)* חֲדַר *(Hah-dar)* **bathroom** . Restrooms אוֹ public

facilities fall under the title of שֵׁרוּתִים *(shay-roo-teem)* ← and they are marked גְּבָרוֹת *(gvah-roht)* **ladies** and גְּבָרִים *(gvah-reem)* **gentlemen** .

(gvah-roht) *(gvah-reem)*
גְּבָרוֹת גְּבָרִים
ladies **gentlemen**

גַּם *(gahm)* חֲדַר *(Hah-dar)* אַמְבַּטְיָה *(ahm-baht-yah)* לְמַעְלָה .
also **bathroom**

רְאִי *(ruh-ee)*
mirror

כִּיוֹר *(kee-yor)*
washstand

מַגָּבוֹת *(mah-gah-voht)*
towels

שֵׁרוּתִים *(shay-roo-teem)*
toilet

מִקְלַחַת *(mik-lah-Haht)*
shower

גַּם *(gahm)* חֲדַר *(Hah-dar)* עֲבוֹדָה *(ah-voh-dah)* לְמַטָּה .
also **study**

soda water	*(soh-dah)*	סוֹדָה ←
sugar	*(soo-kar)*	סוּכָּר
Syria	*(soo-ree-yah)*	סוּרְיָה
symphony	*(seem-foh-nee-yah)*	סִימְפוֹנְיָה
salmon	*(sahl-mohn)*	סַלְמוֹן

ס

Do not forget to remove the next group of stickers וְ **label these things in your**

(ahm-baht-yah) *(Hah-dar)*

חֲדַר אַמְבַּטְיָה
bathroom

← Okay, it is time to review. Here's a quick quiz to see what you **remember.**

men's (restroom)   *(luh-mah-tah)*
                                                      לְמַטָּה ←

I need   *(gvah-rim)*
                                                      גְּבָרִים

downstairs   *(bay-vah-kah-shah)*
                                                      בְּבַקָשָׁה

please   *(yah-shar)*
                                                      יָשָׁר

towels   *(shay-roo-teem)*
                                                      שֵׁירוּתִים

upstairs   *(gvah-roht)*
                                                      גְּבָרוֹת

bathroom   *(mah-gah-voht)*
                                                      מַגְּבוֹת

lavatory/restroom   *(luh-mah-uh-lah)*
                                                      לְמַעְלָה

straight ahead   *(tsah-reeH)*
                                                      אֲנִי צָרִיךְ

women's (restroom)   *(ahm-baht-yah)* *(Hah-dar)*
                                                      חֲדַר אַמְבַּטְיָה

	China............. *(seen)* .... סִין ←
	Chinese........... *(see-nee)*........... סִינִי
	boat............. *(see-rah)* .... סִירָה
ס	fishing boat......... *(see-raht-dah-yig)* ... סִירַת דַיְג
	celery............ *(seh-leh-ree)* .... סֶלֶרִי

Next stop — *(hah-ah-voh-dah)* *(Hah-dar)* חֲדַר הָעֲבוֹדָה, specifically *(hah-ktee-vah)* *(shool-Hahn)* הַכְּתִיבָה שׁוּלְחָן in this room.
the study   the desk

(hah-ktee-vah) *(shool-Hahn)* *(ahl)* *(mah)* מַה יֵשׁ עַל שׁוּלְחָן הַכְּתִיבָה ? Let's identify *(hah-dvah-rim)* הַדְּבָרִים that one normally finds on
on   what   the things

(hah-ktee-vah) *(shool-Hahn)* שׁוּלְחָן הַכְּתִיבָה or strewn about *(hah-bite)* הַבַּיִת .
the desk

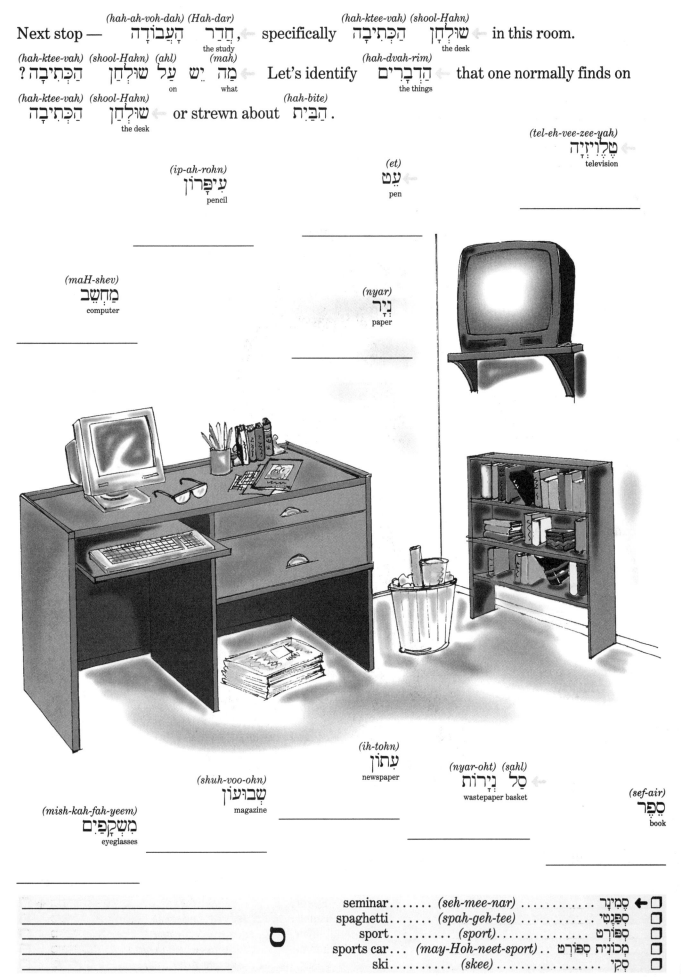

(tel-eh-vee-zee-yah)
טֶלֶוִיזְיָה
television

(ip-ah-rohn)
עִיפָּרוֹן
pencil

(et)
עֵט
pen

(maH-shev)
מַחְשֵׁב
computer

(nyar)
נְיָר
paper

(ih-tohn)
עִתּוֹן
newspaper

(nyar-oht) *(sahl)*
סַל נְיָרוֹת
wastepaper basket

(sef-air)
סֵפֶר
book

(shuh-voo-ohn)
שָׁבוּעוֹן
magazine

(mish-kah-fah-yeem)
מִשְׁקָפַיִם
eyeglasses

ס

seminar	*(seh-mee-nar)*	סֶמִינָר ← ☐
spaghetti	*(spah-geh-tee)*	סְפָּגֶטִי ☐
sport	*(sport)*	סְפּוֹרְט ☐
sports car	*(may-Hoh-neet-sport)*	מְכוֹנִית סְפּוֹרְט ☐
ski	*(skee)*	סְקִי ☐

Don't forget these essentials!

(miH-tahv)
מִכְתָּב
letter

(bool)
בּוּל
stamp

(gloo-yah)
גלוּיָה
postcard

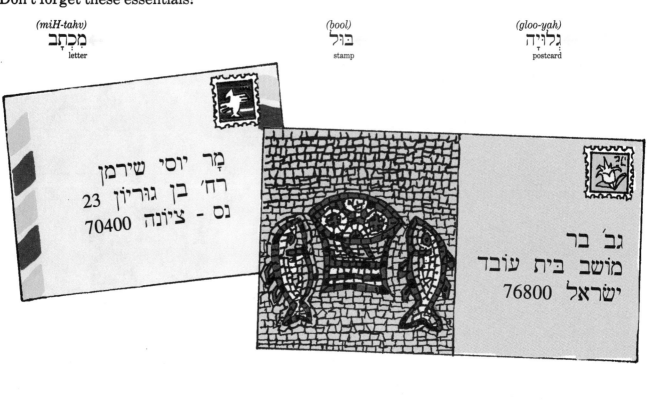

מָר יוֹסִי שירמן
רח׳ בֶּן גוּריוֹן 23
נס - ציוֹנה 70400

גב׳ בר
מוֹשב בית עוֹבד
ישראל 76800

_____ (letter)   _____ (stamp)   _____ (postcard)

(ah-veer) (ee-gair-et)   *(ah-veer)*   *(ah-veer) (buh-doh-ar)*
You can also purchase אֲוִיר אִיגֶרֶת . The word " אֲוִיר " is also found in " בְּדוֹאַר אֲוִיר ."
                      aerograms   air   by airmail

(mar)   *(beev-reet)*
Note that " מָר " and " גב׳ " are used when addressing letters בְּעִבְרִית .
        Mr.   Mrs.

(hah-ah-voh-dah) (Hah-dar)
(ah-Hshav)
עַכְשָׁו label these things in הַעֲבוֹדָה חֶדֶר with your stickers. Do not forget to say these
                              the study

(mih-lim)   *(ah-tah)*   *(ah-tah)*   *(ah-tah)*
מִלים out loud whenever אַתָה write them, אַתָה see them וְ אַתָה apply the stickers.

(loh)
The word לֹא is extremely useful בְּעִברִית . Add לֹא before a verb וְ you negate the sentence.
         not

(miH-tahv) (shoh-lay-aH) (loh)   *(miH-tahv) (shoh-lay-aH)*
← אֲנִי לֹא שוֹלֵחַ מִכְתָּב .   ← אֲנִי שוֹלֵחַ מִכְתָּב .
  a letter send do not I   a letter send   I

(ah-Hshav)
Simple, isn't it? עַכְשָׁו , after you fill in the blanks on the next page, go back a second time

_____
_____   ס
_____
_____

Spain........ *(sfah-rahd)* .... סְפָרַד ←
Spanish....... *(sfah-rah-dee)* .... סְפָרַדִי
Scandinavia... *(skahn-dee-nahv-yah)* ..... סְקַנְדִינַבְיָה
Scandinavian.... *(skahn-dee-nah-vee)* .... סְקַנְדִינַבִי
sardines....... *(sar-dee-neem)* .... סַרְדִינִים

and negate all these sentences by adding לֹא ← before each verb. Practice saying these

sentences out loud many times. Don't get discouraged! Just look at *(kah-mah)* כַּמָה ← *how much* אַתָה have

already learned וְ think ahead to *(hah-yahm)* הַיָם *the sea* at *(ay-laht)* אֵילַת *Eilat* or sightseeing in *(yuh-roo-shah-lah-yeem)* יְרוּשָׁלַיִם .

_____ *(luh) (luh-tahl-pane)* ← ל לְטַלְפֵּן *to phone*

_____ *(lee-shohn)* לִישׁוֹן *to sleep*

_____ *(lish-loh-aH)* ← לִשְׁלוֹחַ *to send*

_____ *(lim-kor)* ← לִמְכֹּר *to sell*

(luh) (luh-tahl-pane)
לְטַלְפֵּן ל
to phone

(mah-lohn) מָלוֹן *hotel* . _____ אֲנִי

(mees-ah-dah) מִסְעָדָה *restaurant* . _____ *(ah-tah)* הוּא / אַתָה *he you*

(ah-meh-ree-kah) אֲמֶרִיקָה . _____ *(aht)* הִיא / אַת *she you*

(ah-veev) *(tel)* תֵּל אָבִיב . _____ *(hem) (ah-naH-noo)* אֲנַחְנוּ / הֵם *we they*

(lish-loh-aH)
לִשְׁלוֹחַ
to send

(miH-tahv) מִכְתָּב *letter* . _____ *(ah-nee)* אֲנִי *I*

(gloo-yah) גְלוּיָה *postcard* . _____ *(ah-tah)* הוּא / אַתָה *he you*

(sef-air) סֵפֶר . _____ *(aht)* הִיא / אַת *she you*

(gloo-yoht) *(ar-bah)* אַרְבַּע גְלוּיוֹת *postcards* . _____ *(hem) (ah-naH-noo)* אֲנַחְנוּ / הֵם *we they*

(lee-shohn)
לִישׁוֹן
to sleep

(shay-nah) (bah-Hah-dar) בַּחֶדֶר שֵׁינָה *in bedroom* . _____ אֲנִי

(bah-mee-tah) בַּמִיטָה *in the bed* . _____ *(ah-tah)* הוּא / אַתָה *he you*

(bah-mah-lohn) בַּמָלוֹן . _____ *(aht)* הִיא / אַת *she you*

(bah-bite) בַּבַּיִת . _____ *(hem) (ah-naH-noo)* אֲנַחְנוּ / הֵם *we they*

(lim-kor)
לִמְכֹּר
to sell

(boo-leem) בּוּלִים *stamps* . _____ *(ah-nee)* אֲנִי *I*

(ih-toh-neem) עִתּוֹנִים *newspapers* . _____ *(ah-tah)* הוּא / אַתָה *he you*

(mish-kah-fah-yeem) מִשְׁקָפַיִם *eyeglasses* . _____ *(aht)* הִיא / אַת *she you*

(prah-Heem) פְּרָחִים *flowers* . _____ *(hem) (ah-naH-noo)* אֲנַחְנוּ / הֵם *we they*

_____

_____

_____

_____

ע

cloud	*(ah-nahn)*	עָנָן ← ☐
tree	*(ehts)*	עֵץ ☐
Arab	*(ah-rah-vee)*	עֲרָבִי ☐
Arabic	*(ah-rah-veet)*	עֲרָבִית ☐
antique	*(ah-teek)*	עַתִּיק ☐

Before אַתָּה proceed with the next step, 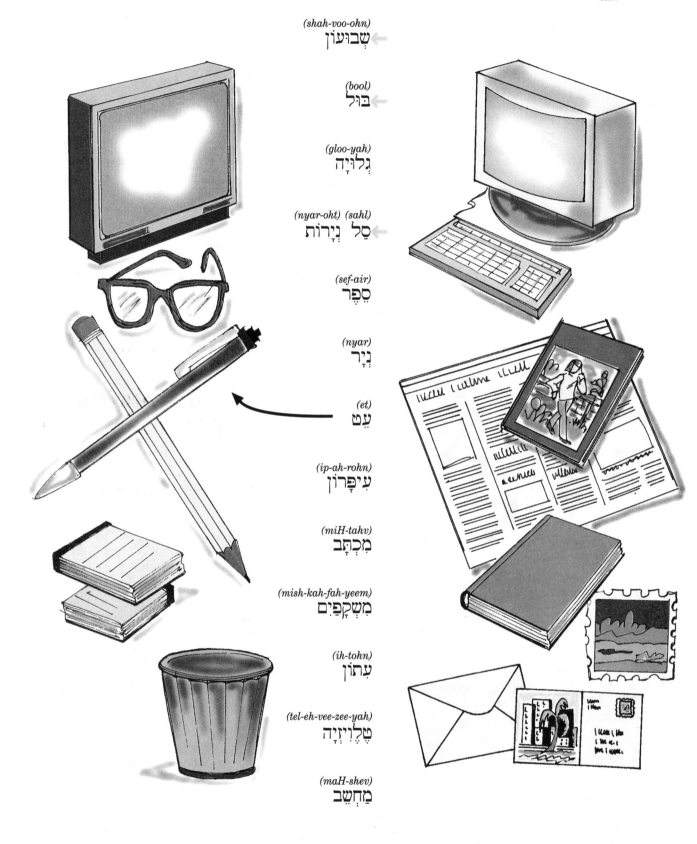 בְּבַקָּשָׁה (bay-vah-kah-shah) ← identify all the items לְמַטָּה (luh-mah-tah)
below.

שְׁבוּעוֹן (shah-voo-ohn) ←

בּוּל (bool) ←

גְּלוּיָה (gloo-yah) ←

סַל נֵירוֹת (sahl) (nyar-oht) ←

סֵפֶר (sef-air) ←

נְיָר (nyar) ←

עֵט (et) ←

עִפָּרוֹן (ip-ah-rohn) ←

מִכְתָּב (miH-tahv) ←

מִשְׁקָפַיִם (mish-kah-fah-yeem) ←

עִתּוֹן (ih-tohn) ←

טֶלֶוִיזְיָה (tel-eh-vee-zee-yah) ←

מַחְשֵׁב (maH-shev) ←

puzzle	(pah-zel)	פָּאזֶל	← ☐
pie	(pie)	פָּאי	☐
political	(poh-lee-tee)	פּוֹלִיטִי	☐
politics	(poh-lee-tee-kah)	פּוֹלִיטִיקָה	☐
policy	(poh-lee-sah)	פּוֹלִיסָה	☐

פ

אַתָּה know עַכְשָׁו how to count, אֵיךְ ← to ask שְׁאֵלוֹת, ← how to use verbs with the "plug-in"
(ayH) *(shuh-eh-loht)*
how questions

formula, אֵיךְ ← to make statements וְ how to describe something, be it the location of a מָלוֹן or

the color of a בַּיִת. ← Let's now take the basics that אַתָּה ← have learned וְ expand them in
(bite)
house

special areas that will be most helpful in your travels. מַה ← does everyone do on a holiday?

Send גְּלוּיוֹת, ← of course! Let's learn exactly אֵיךְ the הַדּוֹאַר מִשְׂרַד ← works בְּיִשְׂרָאֵל.
(gloo-yoht) *(ayH)* *(hah-doh-ar)* *(mis-rahd)* *(buh-yiss-rah-el)*
the post office

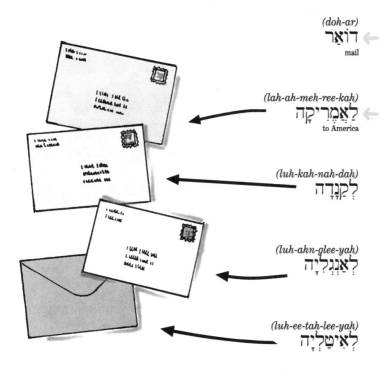

(doh-ar)
דּוֹאַר ←
mail

(lah-ah-meh-ree-kah)
לַאֲמֵרִיקָה ←
to America

(luh-kah-nah-dah)
לְקַנָדָה ←

(luh-ahn-glee-yah)
לְאַנְגְּלִיָּה ←

(luh-ee-tah-lee-yah)
לְאִיטַלְיָה ←

(hah-doh-ar) *(mis-rahd)* *(buh-yiss-rah-el)* *(hah-doh-ar)* *(mis-rahd)*
הַדּוֹאַר מִשְׂרַד בְּיִשְׂרָאֵל ← has everything. הַדּוֹאַר מִשְׂרַד ← is where אַתָּה need to go
the post office

to buy a בּוּל, mail a package, and send וּגְלוּיוֹת מִכְתָבִים. הַדּוֹאַר מִשְׂרַד ← is generally
(bool) *(oo-gloo-yoht)* *(miH-tah-veem)*
and postcards letters

open from בַּבֹּקֶר שְׁמוֹנֶה ← until בָּעֶרֶב שֵׁשׁ ← Sunday through Thursday and until
(bah-boh-kair) *(shmoh-neh)* *(bah-eh-rev)* *(shesh)*

שְׁתַּיִם ← on יוֹם שִׁישִׁי.
(shtah-yeem) *(shee-shee)* *(yohm)*

		פ

popcorn....... *(pohp-korn)* .... פּוֹפְּ קוֹרֶן ← ☐
poker....... *(poh-kair)* .... פּוֹקֶר ☐
picnic....... *(peek-neek)* .... פִּיקְנִיק ☐
lantern....... *(pah-nahs)* .... פָּנָס ☐
lamppost... *(pah-nahs-ruh-Hohv)* ...... פָּנָס רְחוֹב ☐

Here are the necessary *(mih-lim)* מִלִים ← for *(hah-doh-ar) (mis-rahd)* מִשְׂרַד הַדוֹאַר. Practice them aloud וְ write the מִלִים

in the blanks.

(miH-tahv)
מִכְתָב ←
letter

(gloo-yah)
גְלוּיָה
postcard

(Hah-vee-lah)
חֲבִילָה
package

(miv-rahk)
מִבְרָק
telegram

(ah-veer) (buh-doh-ar)
בְּדוֹאַר אֲוִיר ←
by airmail

(fahks)
פַקְס
fax

(bool)
בּוּל
stamp

(tsih-boo-ree) (teh-leh-fohn)
טֶלֶפוֹן צִיבּוּרִי ←
public telephone

(doh-ar) (tay-vaht)
תֵיבַת דוֹאַר ←
mailbox

(teh-leh-fohn)
טֶלֶפוֹן
telephone

 פ

← Passover	*(pes-aH)*	פֶּסַח
statue	*(pes-el)*	פֶּסֶל
project	*(proh-yekt)*	פְּרוֹיֶקְט
permanent (hair)	*(pair-mah-nent)*	פֶּרְמָנֶנְט
park	*(park)*	פַּרְק

Next step — אַתָּה ask שְׁאֵלוֹת *(shuh-eh-loht)* like those לְמַטָּה *(luh-mah-tah)*, depending on what אַתָּה רוֹצֶה.

Repeat these sentences aloud many times.

_____ אֵיפֹה אֶפְשָׁר לִקְנוֹת בּוּלִים ?
(ay-foh) *(ef-shar)* *(lik-noht)* *(boo-leem)*
(is it) possible to buy stamps

_____ אֵיפֹה אֶפְשָׁר לִקְנוֹת גְּלוּיוֹת ?
(ef-shar) *(lik-noht)* *(gloo-yoht)*
(is it) possible to buy postcards

_____ אֵיפֹה יֵשׁ טֶלֶפוֹן ?
(teh-leh-fohn)

_____ אֵיפֹה יֵשׁ תֵּיבַת דּוֹאַר ?
(tay-vaht) *(doh-ar)*
mailbox

_____ אֵיפֹה יֵשׁ טֶלֶפוֹן צִיבּוּרִי ?
(tsih-boo-ree)
public

_____ אֵיפֹה אֶפְשָׁר לִשְׁלֹחַ גְּלוּיוֹת ?
(ef-shar) *(lish-loh-aH)* *(gloo-yoht)*
to send postcards

_____ אֵיפֹה אֶפְשָׁר לִשְׁלֹחַ פַקְס ?
(lish-loh-aH) *(fahks)*
fax

_____ כַּמָּה זֶה עוֹלֶה ?
(kah-mah) *(zeh)* *(oh-leh)*
it costs

עַכְשָׁו, quiz yourself. See if אַתָּה can translate the following thoughts בְּעִבְרִית.

1. Where is a public telephone? _____

2. Where is it possible to buy stamps? _____

3. Where is it possible to send a fax? _____

4. Where is it possible to send postcards? _____

5. Where is the post office? _____

6. Where is it possible to buy aerograms? _____

7. By airmail? _____

8. Where is it possible to send a package? _____

הֵנֵה are more verbs.

_____ (lee) (ten)
תֵּן לִי
give me

_____ (liH-tohv)
לִכְתּוֹב
to write

_____ (luh-shah-lem)
לְשַׁלֵם
to pay

_____ (shmee)
שְׁמִי
my name is

Practice these verbs by not only filling in the blanks, but by saying them aloud many, many

times until you are comfortable with the sounds and the words.

(lee) (ten)
תֵּן לִי
give me

(liH-tohv)
לִכְתּוֹב
to write

(bay-vah-kah-shah) (sef-air)
סֵפֶר, בְּבַקָשָׁה. _____ תֵּן לִי ←

(miH-tahv)
מִכְתָּב. _____ כּוֹתֵב/ אֲנִי ←
letter   I
(ah-nee)

(kar-tees)
כַּרְטִיס, בְּבַקָשָׁה. _____
ticket

(sef-air)
סֵפֶר. _____ כּוֹתֵב/ הוּא / אַתָּה ♂
you   he
(ah-tah) (hoo)

(gloo-yah)
גְלוּיָה, בְּבַקָשָׁה. _____

(gloo-yah)
גְלוּיָה. _____ כּוֹתֶבֶת/ הִיא / אַתְּ ♀
you   she
(aht) (hee)

(boo-leem)
בּוּלִים, בְּבַקָשָׁה. _____

(miv-rahk)
מִבְרָק. _____ כּוֹתְבִים/ אֲנַחְנוּ / הֵם
they   we
(hem) (ah-naH-noo)

(luh-shah-lem)
לְשַׁלֵם
to pay

(shmee)
שְׁמִי ...
my name is

שְׁמִי אֶפְרִי

(bah-mah-lohn)
בְּמָלוֹן. _____ מְשַׁלֵם/ אֲנִי
in the hotel

(shmee)
שְׁמִי _____

(bah-tahk-see)
בְּטַקְסִי. _____ מְשַׁלֵם/ הוּא / אַתָּה ♂
in the taxi   you   he
(ah-tah) (hoo)

(shmoh)
שְׁמוֹ _____
his name is

(bah-oh-toh-boos)
בְּאוֹטוֹבּוּס. _____ מְשַׁלֶמֶת/ הִיא / אַתְּ ♀
in the bus   you   she
(aht) (hee)

(shmah)
שְׁמָה _____
her name is

(bah-mees-ah-dah)
בְּמִסְעָדָה. _____ מְשַׁלְמִים/ אֲנַחְנוּ / הֵם
in the restaurant   we   they
(hem) (ah-naH-noo)

(shim-Hah)
שְׁמֵךְ _____
your name is (♀)

(sh'meyH)
שְׁמֵךְ _____
your name is (♂)

_____
_____
_____   פ
_____

66

Some of these signs you probably recognize, but take a couple of minutes to review them anyway.

road closed to vehicles

customs

no entrance

main road, you have
the right of way

yield

speed limit

no parking

no passing

stop

(mah-kahf)
detour

What follows are approximate conversions, so when you order something by liters, kilograms or grams you will have an idea of what to expect and not find yourself being handed one piece of candy when you thought you ordered an entire bag.

To Convert		Do the Math		
liters (l) to gallons,	multiply by 0.26	4 liters x 0.26	=	1.04 gallons
gallons to liters,	multiply by 3.79	10 gal. x 3.79	=	37.9 liters
kilograms (kg) to pounds,	multiply by 2.2	2 kilograms x 2.2	=	4.4 pounds
pounds to kilos,	multiply by 0.46	10 pounds x 0.46	=	4.6 kg
grams (g) to ounces,	multiply by 0.035	100 grams x 0.035	=	3.5 oz.
ounces to grams,	multiply by 28.35	10 oz. x 28.35	=	283.5 g.
meters (m) to feet,	multiply by 3.28	2 meters x 3.28	=	6.56 feet
feet to meters,	multiply by 0.3	6 feet x 0.3	=	1.8 meters

For fun, take your weight in pounds and convert it into kilograms. It sounds better that way, doesn't it? How many kilometers is it from your home to school, to work, to the post office?

The Simple Versions		
one liter	=	approximately one US quart
four liters	=	approximately one US gallon
one kilo	=	approximately 2.2 pounds
100 grams	=	approximately 3.5 ounces
500 grams	=	slightly more than one pound
one meter	=	slightly more than three feet

The distance between יְרוּשָׁלַיִם וְ תֵל אָבִיב ← is approximately 40 miles. How many kilometers would that be? יִשְׂרָאֵל is only 420 kilometers from north to south. How many miles is that?

kilometers (km.) to miles,	multiply by 0.62	1000 km. x 0.62	=	620 miles
miles to kilometers,	multiply by 1.6	1000 miles x 1.6	=	1,600 km.

Inches	1		2		3		4		5		6		7

To convert centimeters into inches, multiply by 0.39   Example: 9 cm. x 0.39   = 3.51 in.

To convert inches into centimeters, multiply by 2.54   Example: 4 in. x 2.54   = 10.16 cm.

cm 1	2	3	4	5	6	7	8	9	10	11	12	13	14	15	16	17	18

18

(luh-shah-lem) *(ayH)*
אֵיךְ לְשַׁלֵּם
to pay · how

(ken)
כֵּן, there are also חֶשְׁבּוֹנוֹת *(Hesh-boh-noht)* to pay בְּיִשְׂרָאֵל. You have just finished your delicious dinner וְ

bills

you would like הַחֶשְׁבּוֹן *(hah-Hesh-bohn)*. אֵיךְ *(ayH)* ← do you do this? אַתָּה call for the מֶלְצָר *(mel-tsar)*, or the מֶלְצָרִית *(mel-tsah-reet)*:

the bill · waiter · waitress

(mel-tsah-reet) *(bay-vah-kah-shah)* *(Hesh-bohn)* *(mel-tsar)*
← מֶלְצָר, חֶשְׁבּוֹן בְּבַקָּשָׁה. מֶלְצָרִית, חֶשְׁבּוֹן בְּבַקָּשָׁה.

(hah-mel-tsar)
הַמֶּלְצָר will normally reel off what אַתָּה have eaten, while writing rapidly. הוּא *(hoo)* will then

place a piece of paper on הַשֻּׁלְחָן *(hah-shool-Hahn)*. ← "זֶה עוֹלֶה חֲמִישִׁים שְׁקָלִים." אַתָּה

(zeh) *(oh-leh)* *(Hah-mee-sheem)* *(shkah-leem)*

אַתָּה will pay הַמֶּלְצָר *(hah-mel-tsar)* or perhaps אַתָּה will pay the קוּפַּאי *(koo-pah-ee)*.

cashier

Remember, the service may be included in הַחֶשְׁבּוֹן *(hah-Hesh-bohn)*. When אַתָּה *(ah-tah)* dine out בְּיִשְׂרָאֵל, always

make a reservation. It can be very difficult to get into a popular מִסְעָדָה *(mees-ah-dah)*. Nevertheless the

experience is well worth the trouble אַתָּה will go to to obtain a reservation. וְ remember, אַתָּה

know enough עִבְרִית ← to make a reservation! Just speak slowly and clearly.

---

painter	*(tsah-bah)*	צַבָּע ←☐
paint	*(tseh-vah)*	צֶבַע ☐
diver	*(tsoh-luh-lahn)*	צוֹלְלָן ☐
civilization	*(tsee-vee-lee-zah-tsee-yah)*	צִיבִילִיזַצְיָה ☐
painting	*(tsee-yoor)*	צִיּוּר ☐

צ

Remember these key *(mih-lim)* מִלִּים when dining out בְּיִשְׂרָאֵל.

(mel-tsar) מֶלְצַר ← waiter	*(mel-tsah-reet)* מֶלְצָרִית ← waitress
(Hesh-bohn) חֶשְׁבּוֹן bill	*(bay-vah-kah-shah)* בְּבַקָשָׁה you're welcome
(tahf-reet) תַּפְרִיט menu	*(shay-root) (d'may)* דְמֵי שֵׁירוּת service charge
(slee-Hah) סְלִיחָה excuse me	*(rah-bah) (toh-dah)* תּוֹדָה רַבָּה very much thank you
(bay-vah-kah-shah) בְּבַקָשָׁה please	*(kah-bah-lah)* קַבָּלָה receipt

(hin-ay) הִנֵּה is a sample conversation involving paying *(hah-Hesh-bohn)* הַחֶשְׁבּוֹן. Practice by writing it in the blanks.

the bill

דָּן ← *(dahn)* סְלִיחָה. אֲנִי רוֹצָה לְשַׁלֵּם אֶת הַחֶשְׁבּוֹן בְּבַקָשָׁה.
(bay-vah-kuh-shah) (hah-Hesh-bohn) (luh-shah-lem) (slee-Hah)
the bill to pay

_____

פָּקִיד: *(pah-keed)* מַה מִסְפַּר הַחֶדֶר בְּבַקָשָׁה?
(hah-Hed-air) (mis-par) (mah)
clerk the room number what

_____

דָּן: חֶדֶר שָׁלֹשׁ מֵאוֹת וְעֶשֶׂר.
(vah-es-air) (may-oht) (shlohsh)
and ten hundred three

_____

פָּקִיד: *(pah-keed)* רַק רֶגַע. הִנֵּה הַקַבָּלָה. תּוֹדָה רַבָּה וְשָׁלוֹם.
(vuh-shah-lohm) (rah-bah) (toh-dah) (hah-kah-bah-lah) (reh-gah) (rahk)
the receipt just a minute

_____

If אַתָּה have any problems with *(hah-mis-pah-reem)* הַמִּסְפָּרִים, just ask someone to write out הַמִּסְפָּרִים, so that

אַתָּה can be sure you understand everything correctly,

בְּבַקָשָׁה לִכְתוֹב אֶת הַמִּסְפָּרִים. תּוֹדָה.
(hah-mis-pah-reem) (liH-tohv)
write

Practice: _____

(Please write out the numbers. Thank you.)

_____	cynical	*(tsee-nee)*	צִינִי ← ☐
_____	plant	*(tseh-maH)*	צֶמַח ☐
_____	**צ** bird	*(tsih-por)*	צִיפּוֹר ☐
_____	France	*(tsar-faht)*	צָרְפַת ☐
	French	*(tsar-fah-tee)*	צָרְפָתִי ☐

Let's take a break from כֶּסֶף *(kes-ef)* / money and learn some fun new מִלִּים *(mih-lim)* ← אַתָּה ← can always practice these מִלִּים by using your flash cards at the back of this book. Carry these flash cards in your purse, pocket, briefcase אוֹ knapsack וְ *use them!*

(pah-too-aH)
← פָּתוּחַ
open
_____

(sah-goor)
← סָגוּר
closed
_____

(gah-dohl)
← גָּדוֹל
big
_____

(kah-tahn)
← קָטָן
small
_____

(bah-ree)
← בָּרִיא
healthy
_____

(Hoh-leh)
← חוֹלֶה
sick
_____

(tohv)
← טוֹב
good
_____

(rah)
← רָע
bad
_____

(Hahm)
← חַם
hot
_____

(kar)
← קַר
cold
_____

_____

ק

71

(kah-tsar)
קָצָר
short

(ah-roH)
אָרוֹך
long

(luh-aht)
לְאַט
slow

(mah-hair)
מַהֵר
fast

(gah-voh-hah)
גָּבוֹהַ
tall

(nah-mooH)
נָמוּך
short

(zah-ken)
זָקֵן
old

(tsah-eer)
צָעִיר
young

(yah-kar)
יָקָר
expensive

(zohl)
זוֹל
cheap

(ah-sheer)
עָשִׁיר
rich

(ah-nee)
עָנִי
poor

(har-bay)
הַרְבֵּה
a lot

(muh-aht)
מְעַט
a little

ק

kiosk	(kee-yohsk)	קִיוֹסְק	← ☐
easy	(kahl)	קַל	☐
client	(klee-ent)	קְלִיֶּנט	☐
campus	(kahm-poos)	קַמְפּוּס	☐
Canada	(kah-nah-dah)	קָנָדָה	☐

(hin-ay)
הִנֵּה are some new verbs.

(lik-roh) לִקְרוֹא ← to read	*(tsah-reeH)* צָרִיךְ ← I must, have to
(lah-dah-aht) לָדַעַת ← to know	*(yah-Hohl)* יָכוֹל ← I can

Study the patterns closely as אַתָּה will use these verbs a lot.

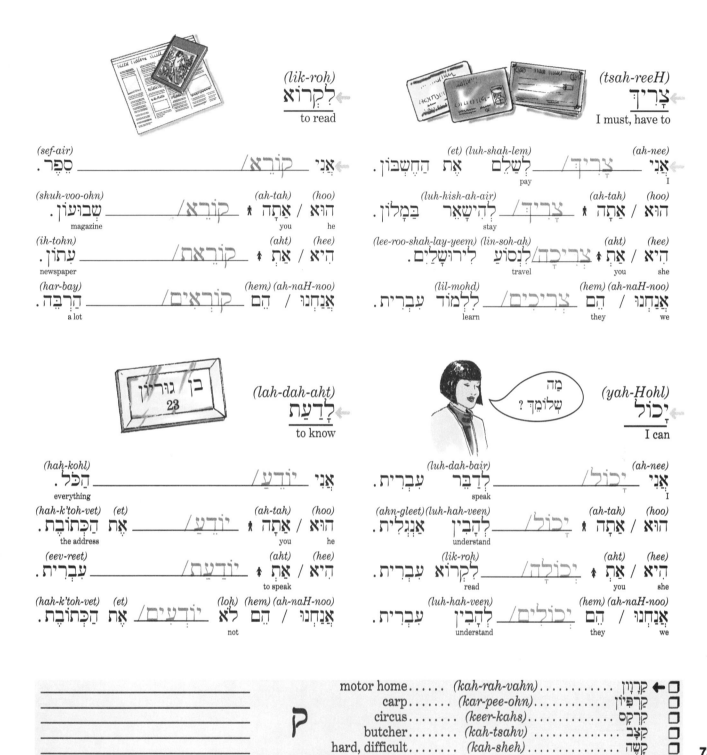

(lik-roh)
לִקְרוֹא ← to read

(sef-air) סֵפֶר . _____ קוֹרֵא / אֲנִי

(shuh-voo-ohn) שָׁבוּעוֹן . הוּא / אַתָּה ♂ קוֹרֵא _____ *(ah-tah)* you *(hoo)* he
magazine

(ih-tohn) עִתּוֹן הִיא / אַתְּ ♀ קוֹרֵאת _____ *(aht)* you *(hee)* she
newspaper

(har-bay) הַרְבֵּה . אֲנַחְנוּ / הֵם קוֹרְאִים _____ *(hem)* they *(ah-naH-noo)* we
a lot

(tsah-reeH)
צָרִיךְ ← I must, have to

(et) (luh-shah-lem) אֲנִי _____ צָרִיךְ / לְשַׁלֵּם אֶת הַחֶשְׁבּוֹן . *(ah-nee)* I
pay

(luh-hish-ah-air) הוּא / אַתָּה ♂ צָרִיךְ _____ לְהִשָּׁאֵר בַּמָּלוֹן . *(ah-tah)* you *(hoo)* he
stay

(lee-roo-shah-lay-yeem) (lin-soh-ah) הִיא / אַתְּ ♀ צְרִיכָה _____ לִנְסוֹעַ לִירוּשָׁלַיִם . *(aht)* you *(hee)* she
travel

(lil-mohd) אֲנַחְנוּ / הֵם צְרִיכִים _____ לִלְמֹד עִבְרִית . *(hem)* they *(ah-naH-noo)* we
learn

(lah-dah-aht)
לָדַעַת ← to know

(hah-kohl) הַכֹּל . _____ יוֹדֵעַ / אֲנִי
everything

(hah-k'toh-vet) (et) אֶת הַכְּתֹבֶת . הוּא / אַתָּה ♂ יוֹדֵעַ _____ *(ah-tah)* you *(hoo)* he
the address

(eev-reet) עִבְרִית . הִיא / אַתְּ ♀ יוֹדַעַת _____ *(aht)* you *(hee)* she
to speak

(hah-k'toh-vet) (et) אֶת הַכְּתֹבֶת . אֲנַחְנוּ / הֵם לֹא יוֹדְעִים _____ *(loh) (hem)* they *(ah-naH-noo)* we
not

(yah-Hohl)
יָכוֹל ← I can

מַה שְׁלוֹמֵךְ ?

(luh-dah-bair) אֲנִי _____ יָכוֹל / לְדַבֵּר עִבְרִית . *(ah-nee)* I
speak

(ahn-gleet) (luh-hah-veen) הוּא / אַתָּה ♂ יָכוֹל _____ לְהָבִין אַנְגְּלִית . *(ah-tah)* you *(hoo)* he
understand

(lik-roh) הִיא / אַתְּ ♀ יְכוֹלָה _____ לִקְרוֹא עִבְרִית . *(aht)* you *(hee)* she
read

(luh-hah-veen) אֲנַחְנוּ / הֵם יְכוֹלִים _____ לְהָבִין עִבְרִית . *(hem)* they *(ah-naH-noo)* we
understand

motor home......	*(kah-rah-vahn)*	קָרָוָן ←	☐
carp......	*(kar-pee-ohn)*	קַרְפִּיוֹן	☐
circus......	*(keer-kahs)*	קִרְקָס	☐
butcher......	*(kah-tsahv)*	קַצָּב	☐
hard, difficult.......	*(kah-sheh)*	קָשֶׁה	☐

ק

Use the flash cards at the back of הַסֵּפֶר to drill these וְ other verbs. You will see the (�) and (♀)

"I" form of each verb, so choose the appropriate one for you and drill yourself. The verbs

(yah-Hohl)
יָכוֹל ← and   *(tsah-reeH)*
צָרִיךְ can be joined with another verb:
can   must

(eev-reet) *(lil-mohd)* *(tsah-reeH)*
← אֲנִי צָרִיךְ לִלְמוֹד עִבְרִית .
learn
(gloo-yah) *(lik-noht)* *(tsah-reeH)*
← אֲנִי צָרִיךְ לִקְנוֹת גְּלוּיָה .
buy
(luh-yiss-rah-el) *(lin-soh-ah)*
← אֲנִי צָרִיךְ לִנְסוֹעַ לְיִשְׂרָאֵל .
travel

(eev-reet) *(lik-roh)* *(yah-Hohl)*
← אֲנִי יָכוֹל לִקְרוֹא עִבְרִית .
(luh-hah-veen) *(yah-Hohl)*
← אֲנִי יָכוֹל לְהָבִין עִבְרִית .
understand
(luh-dah-bair)
← אֲנִי יָכוֹל לְדַבֵּר עִבְרִית .

Can אַתָּה translate the sentences below into עִבְרִית ?   ← *(luh-mah-tah)* *(hah-t'shoo-voht)*
הַתְּשׁוּבוֹת לְמַטָּה .

1. I (♂) can speak Hebrew. _____

2. He must pay now. _____

3. We don't know the address. _____

4. They can pay. _____

5. She knows a lot. _____

6. You (♀) can speak Hebrew. _____

7. I can pay. _____

8. We are not able to (cannot) understand Hebrew. _____

9. I (♂) want to travel to Israel. _____

10. She reads a newspaper. _____

הַתְּשׁוּבוֹת

6. אַתְּ יְכוֹלָה לְדַבֵּר עִבְרִית .   1. ← אֲנִי יָכוֹל לְדַבֵּר עִבְרִית .
7. אֲנִי יָכוֹל לְשַׁלֵּם .   2. הוּא צָרִיךְ לְשַׁלֵּם עַכְשָׁו .
8. אֲנַחְנוּ לֹא יְכוֹלִים לְהָבִין עִבְרִית .   3. אֲנַחְנוּ לֹא יוֹדְעִים אֶת הַכְּתוֹבֶת .
9. אֲנִי רוֹצֶה לִנְסוֹעַ לְיִשְׂרָאֵל .   4. הֵם יְכוֹלִים לְשַׁלֵּם .
10. הִיא קוֹרֵאת עִתּוֹן .   5. הִיא יוֹדַעַת הַרְבֵּה .

(aH-shahv) עַכְשָׁו draw lines *(bane)* בֵּין between the opposites *(luh-mah-tah)* לְמַטָּה . Don't forget to say them out loud. Use these

מִלִּים every day to describe *(hah-dvah-rim)* הַדְּבָרִים ← in your *(bite)* בֵּית , ← in your *(hah-sef-air)* הַסֵּפֶר *(bait)* בֵּית school ← and at work.

(gah-voh-hah) גָּבוֹהַּ ←

(smohl) שְׂמֹאל

(kah-tahn) קָטָן

(ah-nee) עָנִי

(bah-ree) בָּרִיא

(ah-roH) אָרוֹךְ

(har-bay) הַרְבֵּה

(tohv) טוֹב

(Hahm) חַם

(lah) לְ *(mee-tah-Haht)* מִתַּחַת

(luh-aht) לְאַט

(yah-kar) יָקָר

(pah-too-aH) פָּתוּחַ

(lah) לְ *(may-ahl)* מֵעַל ←

(nah-mooH) נָמוּךְ

(kah-tsar) קָצָר

(zohl) זוֹל

(Hoh-leh) חוֹלֶה

(zah-ken) זָקֵן

(mah-hair) מַהֵר

(yah-meen) יָמִין

(kar) קַר

(ah-sheer) עָשִׁיר

(rah) רַע

(muh-aht) מְעַט

(sah-goor) סָגוּר

אַתָּה will probably want to try swimming in *(hah-mel-aH)* הַמֶּלַח *(yahm)* יָם ← Dead Sea — it is very *(nah-mooH)* נָמוּךְ low . In fact it is

the lowest place on earth! Not far away is the fortress of *(muh-tsah-dah)* מְצָדָה Masada — it is *(gah-voh-hah)* גָּבוֹהַּ high ←. In your

travels, you should also include *(kin-eh-ret)* כִּינֶרֶת *(yahm)* יָם ← Sea of Galilee and of course *(hah-ah-tee-kah)* הָעַתִּיקָה Old *(hah-eer)* הָעִיר the City ← on your list

of places to visit בְּיִשְׂרָאֵל .

ר

_____

rabbi	*(rahv)*	רַב ←	☐
radio	*(rahd-yoh)*	רַדְיוֹ	☐
radical	*(rah-dee-kahl-ee)*	רָדִיקָלִי	☐
zipper	*(roH-sahn)*	רוֹכְסָן	☐
romantic	*(roh-mahn-tee)*	רוֹמַנְטִי	☐

75

(lin-soh-ah)
לִנְסוֹעַ
to travel

(et-mohl) *(buh-ay-laht)*
← אֶתְמוֹל בְּאֵילַת
yesterday   in Eilat

(hah-yohm) *(buh-Hay-fah)*
← הַיוֹם בְּחֵיפָה
today   in Haifa

(mah-Har) *(bee-ree-Hoh)*
← מָחָר בִּירִיחוֹ
tomorrow   in Jericho

(shee-shee) *(buh-vait)* *(leH-em)*
← בְּיוֹם שִׁישִׁי בְּבֵית לֶחֶם
in Bethlehem

(buh-yohm) *(buh-tel)* *(ah-veev)*
← בְּיוֹם שֵׁנִי בְּתֵל אָבִיב
Monday

(bair) *(shev-ah)*
← בְּיוֹם רְבִיעִי בִּבְאֵר שֶׁבַע
Wednesday   in Beersheba

אַתָּה will find it easy to travel around בְּיִשְׂרָאֵל , as it is a very small country. אַתָּה will also be

surprised at the variety of scenery בְּיִשְׂרָאֵל .

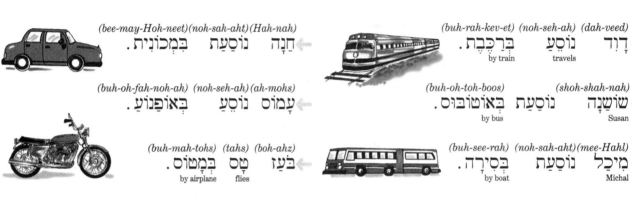

(Hah-nah) *(noh-sah-aht)* *(bee-may-Hoh-neet)*
← חַנָה נוֹסַעַת בִּמְכוֹנִית .

(dah-veed) *(noh-seh-ah)* *(buh-rah-kev-et)*
← דָוִד נוֹסֵעַ בְּרַכֶּבֶת .
travels   by train

(ah-mohs) *(noh-seh-ah)* *(buh-oh-fah-noh-ah)*
← עָמוֹס נוֹסֵעַ בְּאוֹפַנוֹעַ .

(shoh-shah-nah) *(buh-oh-toh-boos)*
← שׁוֹשַׁנָה נוֹסַעַת בְּאוֹטוֹבּוּס .
Susan   by bus

(boh-ahz) *(tahs)* *(buh-mah-tohs)*
← בּוֹעַז טָס בְּמָטוֹס .
flies   by airplane

(mee-Hahl) *(noh-sah-aht)* *(buh-see-rah)*
← מִיכָל נוֹסַעַת בְּסִירָה .
Michal   by boat

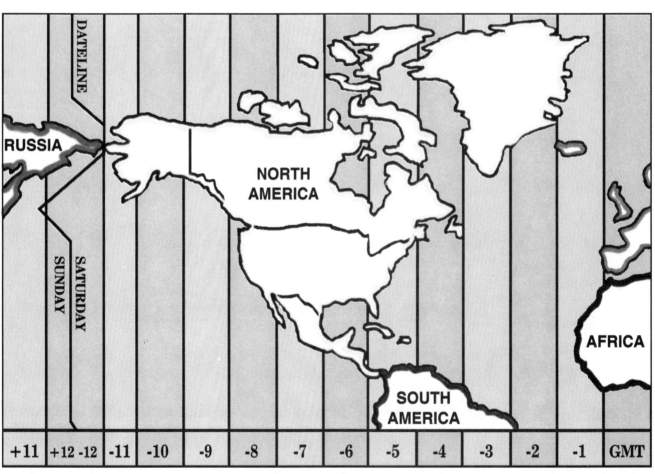

DATELINE

RUSSIA

NORTH AMERICA

SATURDAY SUNDAY

SOUTH AMERICA

AFRICA

| +11 | +12 -12 | -11 | -10 | -9 | -8 | -7 | -6 | -5 | -4 | -3 | -2 | -1 | GMT |

When אַתָּה are traveling, אַתָּה will want to tell others your nationality and אַתָּה will meet people from all corners of the world. Can you guess where someone is from if they say one of the following? הַתְּשׁוּבוֹת are in your glossary beginning on page 108.

(mee-mitz-rah-eem) (bah) (ah-nee) אֲנִי בָּא מִמִּצְרַיִם.	*(may-ah-meh-ree-kah) (bah) (ah-nee)* אֲנִי בָּא מֵאָמֶרִיקָה.
(mee-yar-den) (bah) (ah-nee) אֲנִי בָּא מִיַרְדֵן.	*(may-ahn-glee-yah) (bah) (ah-nee)* אֲנִי בָּא מֵאַנְגְלִיָה.
(mee-leh-vah-nohn) (bah) אֲנִי בָּא מִלְבָנוֹן.	*(mee-gair-mahn-yah) (bah)* אֲנִי בָּא מִגֶרְמַנְיָה.
(mee-soo-ree-yah) אֲנִי בָּא מִסוּרְיָה.	*(mee-kah-nah-dah)* אֲנִי בָּא מִקַנָדָה.
(mee-toor-kee-yah) אֲנִי בָּא מִטוּרְקְיָה.	*(may-ee-tah-lee-yah)* אֲנִי בָּא מֵאִיטַלְיָה.
(mee-shvit-zah-ree-yah) אֲנִי בָּא מִשְׁוֵיצַרְיָה.	*(mee-tsar-faht)* אֲנִי בָּא מִצָרְפַת.
(mee-nor-veg-ee-yah) אֲנִי בָּא מִנוֹרְבֶגְיָה.	*(may-hoh-lahnd)* אֲנִי בָּא מֵהוֹלַנְד.
(mee-shved-ee-yah) אֲנִי בָּא מִשְׁבֶדְיָה.	*(may-roo-see-yah)* אֲנִי בָּא מֵרוּסְיָה.

EUROPE

ASIA

AFRICA

DATELINE

SUNDAY | SATURDAY

-1	GMT	+1	+2	+3	+4	+5	+6	+7	+8	+9	+10	+11	+12 -12

(hah-yiss-ruh-eh-leem) הַיִשְׂרְאֵלִים the Israelis love *(lin-soh-ah)* לִנְסוֹעַ to travel so *(loh)* לֹא no *(zeh)* זֶה it (is) ← wonder to find many מְלִים revolving around the concept of travel which is exactly what אַתָּה want to do. Practice saying the following מְלִים many times. אַתָּה will see them often.

_____ *(lin-soh-ah)* לִנְסוֹעַ — to travel

_____ *(nuh-see-oht) (soH-noot)* סוֹכְנוּת נְסִיעוֹת — travel agency

_____ *(noh-say-ah)* נוֹסֵעַ — traveler

_____ *(nuh-see-ah)* נְסִיעָה — trip, journey

If אַתָּה choose to go *(bee-may-Hoh-neet)* בִּמְכוֹנִית by car, here are a few key מְלִים.

_____ *(deh-reH)* דֶּרֶךְ — road

_____ *(del-ek) (tah-Hah-naht)* תַחֲנַת דֶּלֶק ← gas station

_____ *(ruh-Hohv)* רְחוֹב — street

_____ *(mah-heer) (k'veesh)* כְּבִישׁ מָהִיר ← freeway

(luh-mah-tah) לְמַטָּה some basic signs which אַתָּה should learn to recognize quickly without vowel points.

_____ *(luh-hih-kah-ness)* לְהִכָּנֵס — to enter

_____ *(lah-tset)* לָצֵאת — to exit

כְּנִיסָה

יְצִיאָה

_____ *(kuh-nee-sah)* כְּנִיסָה — entrance

_____ *(yuh-tsee-ah)* יְצִיאָה — exit

_____ *(kuh-nee-sah) (ayn)* אֵין כְּנִיסָה — no

_____ *(yuh-tsee-ah) (ayn)* אֵין יְצִיאָה — no

דְּחוֹף

מְשׁוֹךְ

_____ *(duh-Hohf)* דְּחוֹף ← push

_____ *(muh-shoH)* מְשׁוֹךְ ← pull

_____
_____
_____ ך

doctor......... *(roh-fay)*............. רוֹפֵא ←	☐
dentist... *(roh-fay-shih-nah-yim)* ... רוֹפֵא שִׁנַיִם	☐
Russian......... *(roo-see)*............. רוּסִי	☐
Russia......... *(roos-yah)*............. רוּסְיָה	☐
wet......... *(rah-tohv)*............. רָטוֹב	☐

Let's learn the basic travel verbs. Take out a piece of paper ו make up your own sentences

with these new מִלִּים. Follow the same pattern you have in previous Steps.

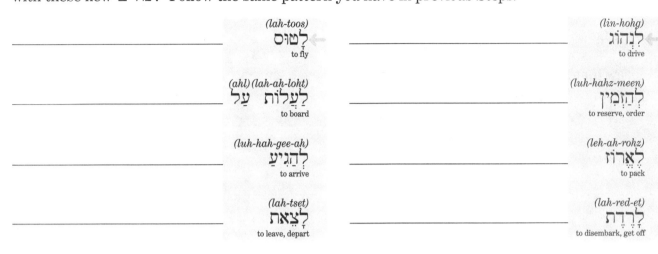

(lah-toos) לָטוּס — to fly	*(lin-hohg)* לִנְהֹג — to drive
(ahl) (lah-ah-loht) לַעֲלוֹת עַל — to board	*(luh-hahz-meen)* לְהַזְמִין — to reserve, order
(luh-hah-gee-ah) לְהַגִּיעַ — to arrive	*(leh-ah-rohz)* לֶאֱרֹז — to pack
(lah-tset) לָצֵאת — to leave, depart	*(lah-red-et)* לָרֶדֶת — to disembark, get off

(hin-ay) הִנֵּה are some new מִלִּים for your *(nuh-see-ah)* נְסִיעָה.

(too-fah) (sday) שְׂדֵה תְּעוּפָה
airport

(oh-toh-boos) (tah-Hah-naht) תַּחֲנַת אוֹטוֹבּוּס
bus station

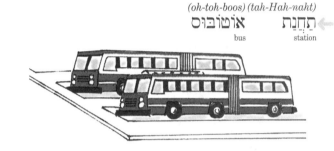

(zmah-neem) (loo-aH) לוּחַ זְמַנִּים
timetable

(rah-kev-et) (tah-Hah-naht) תַּחֲנַת רַכֶּבֶת
train station

(yuh-roo-shah-lah-yeem) תֵּל אָבִיב - יְרוּשָׁלַיִם *(ah-veev) (tel)*		
(mah-gee-ah) מַגִּיעַ arrives	אוֹטוֹבּוּס	*(yoh-tseh)* יוֹצֵא departs
10:15	50	8:00
10:45	19	8:15
11:00	10	8:30
11:15	4	8:45
11:30	22	9:00

ר

empty	*(rake)*	רֵיק ←	☐
Ramadan	*(rah-mah-dahn)*	רַמַדָּן	☐
traffic lights	*(rahm-zoh-reem)*	רַמְזוֹרִים	☐
dancer	*(rahk-dahn)*	רַקְדָּן	☐
rational	*(rah-tsee-oh-nah-lee)*	רַצְיוֹנָלִי	☐

(eem)
עִם these words אַתָּה are ready for any *(nuh-see-ah)* נְסִיעָה anywhere. אַתָּה should have no problem
with

(eem)
עִם these verbs, just remember the basic "plug-in" formula *(ah-naH-noo)* אֲנַחְנוּ learned already. Use that

knowledge to translate the following thoughts into *(eev-reet)* עִבְרִית . By now you have learned enough

Hebrew that the vowel points can be omitted for some of your words. Congratulations!

1.   I (🚶) reserve a car. _____

2.   He boards the bus to Bethlehem. _____

3.   The bus leaves at 9:30. _____

4.   We arrive tomorrow in Israel. _____

5.   You (🚶) get off in Haifa. _____

6.   They travel to Tel Aviv. _____

7.   Where is the bus to Jerusalem? _____

8.   How do we fly to Israel? With KLM or EL AL? _____

(hin-ay)
הִנֵּה some very important words for the traveler.

_____ *(tah-foos)* תָּפוּס ⬅ occupied	_____ *(yuh-tsee-ah)* יְצִיאָה ⬅ (bus/train) departure
_____ *(pah-noo-ee)* פָּנוּי ⬅ free	_____ *(hahm-rah-ah)* הַמְרָאָה ⬅ (plane) departure
_____ *(mah-kohm)* מָקוֹם ⬅ seat	_____ *(luh-oo-meet)* *(bane)* *(tee-sah)* טִיסָה בֵּין לְאוּמִית international flight
_____ *(nuh-Hee-tah)* נְחִיתָה ⬅ arrival	_____ *(ar-tseet)* *(pnim)* *(tee-sah)* טִיסָה פְּנִים אַרְצִית domestic flight

הַתְּשׁוּבוֹת

1. ← אֲנִי מַזְמִין מְכוֹנִית.
2. הוּא עוֹלֶה עַל הָאוֹטוֹבּוּס לְבֵית לֶחֶם.
3. הָאוֹטוֹבּוּס יוֹצֵא בְּתֵשַׁע וָחֵצִי.
4. אֲנַחְנוּ מַגִּיעִים מָחָר לְיִשְׂרָאֵל.
5. אַתְּ יוֹרֶדֶת בְּחֵיפָה.
6. הֵם נוֹסְעִים לְתֵל אָבִיב.
7. אֵיפֹה הָאוֹטוֹבּוּס לִירוּשָׁלַיִם?
8. אֵיךְ טָסִים לְיִשְׂרָאֵל?
בְּקָ. לָ. מָ. אוֹ בְּאֵל עַל?

Increase your travel מִלִּים by writing out *(hah-mih-lim)* הַמִּלִּים ← *(luh-mah-tah)* לְמַטָּה and practicing the sample

sentences out loud. Practice asking " אֵיפֹה " questions. It will help you later.

(luh)
לְ
to

אֵיפֹה הָאוֹטוֹבּוּס לְחֵיפָה ?

(kar-tees)
כַּרְטִיס
ticket

כַּמָּה עוֹלֶה כַּרְטִיס לְתֵל אָבִיב ?

(mis-rahd) *(hah-ah-veh-doht)*
מִשְׂרַד הָאֲבֵידוֹת
office   lost-and-found

סְלִיחָה, אֵיפֹה מִשְׂרַד הָאֲבֵידוֹת ?

(may)
מֵ
from

אֵיפֹה הָאוֹטוֹבּוּס מֵאֵילַת ?

(hah-moh-dee-een)
הַמּוֹדִיעִין
information

אֵיפֹה הַמּוֹדִיעִין ?

(shmee-raht) *(Hah-fah-tseem)*
שְׁמִירַת חֲפָצִים
left-luggage office

אֵיפֹה שְׁמִירַת חֲפָצִים ?

(ah-gah-lah)
עֲגָלָה
cart

אֵיפֹה יֵשׁ עֲגָלָה ?

(mah-kohm)
מָקוֹם
seat

הַאִם הַמָּקוֹם הַזֶּה תָּפוּס ? (is this seat occupied)

הַאִם הַמָּקוֹם הַזֶּה פָּנוּי ? (is this seat free)

(bahnk)
בַּנְק
bank

סְלִיחָה, אֵיפֹה יֵשׁ בַּנְק ?

(esh-nahv)
אֶשְׁנָב
counter

סְלִיחָה, אֵיפֹה אֶשְׁנָב שְׁמוֹנֶה ?

(yoh-tseh)
יוֹצֵא הָאוֹטוֹבּוּס ? ___ (when)   ___ (when)

אַתָּה שׁוֹתֶה ? ___ (what)   ___ (what)

שׁ

	path.........	*(shveel)*	שְׁבִיל ← ☐
	Swedish......	*(shveh-dee)*	שְׁבֵדִי ☐
	Sweden......	*(shved-ee-yah)*	שְׁבֵדְיָה ☐
	Switzerland....	*(shvit-zah-ree-yah)*	שְׁוֵיצָרְיָה ☐
	policeman.......	*(shoh-tair)*	שׁוֹטֵר ☐

81

Can אַתָּה read the following paragraph?

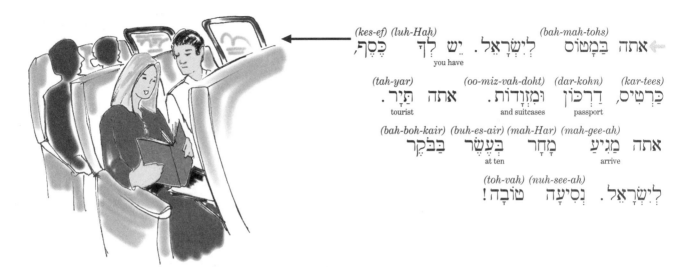

(bah-mah-tohs)   *(kes-ef) (luh-Hah)*
אַתָּה בַּמָּטוֹס לְיִשְׂרָאֵל. יֵשׁ לְךָ כֶּסֶף,
you have

(kar-tees) (dar-kohn) (oo-miz-vah-doht) (tah-yar)
כַּרְטִיס, דַּרְכּוֹן וּמִזְוָדוֹת. אַתָּה תַּיָּר.
tourist   and suitcases   passport

(mah-gee-ah) (mah-Har) (buh-es-air) (bah-boh-kair)
אַתָּה מַגִּיעַ מָחָר בְּעֶשֶׂר בַּבֹּקֶר
arrive   at ten

(nuh-see-ah) (toh-vah)
לְיִשְׂרָאֵל. נְסִיעָה טוֹבָה!

(rah-kev-et)
בְּיִשְׂרָאֵל the bus is the most common form of transport. A רַכֶּבֶת runs along the coast from
train

(nah-hah-ree-yah)   *(ah-veev) (tel)*   *(ah-veev) (tel)*   *(yah-roo-shah-lah-yeem)*
נַהֲרִיָּה to תֵּל אָבִיב ←, and from תֵּל אָבִיב ← to יְרוּשָׁלַיִם.
Nahariya

(oh-toh-boo-seem)   *(rah-kah-voht)*   *(ayn)*   *(shah-baht)*   *(oo-vuh-yohm)*   *(bah-eh-rev)*
Note that אוֹטוֹבּוּסִים אוֹ רַכָּבוֹת אֵין שַׁבָּת וּבְיוֹם בָּעֶרֶב שִׁישִׁי בְּיוֹם. ←
trains   no

(sheh-root)
But don't worry, you will not be stranded. You can always take a שֵׁירוּת which runs in and
shared taxi

between towns וְ cities. It is an interesting way to meet יִשְׂרָאֵלִים.

☐ ←	table....... *(shool-Hahn)*.............	שֻׁלְחָן
☐	tablecloth.. *(mah-paht-shool-Hahn)* ...	מַפַּת שֻׁלְחָן
☐	table tennis.... *(teh-nis-shool-Hahn)*	טֶנִיס שֻׁלְחָן
☐	judge........ *(shoh-fet)*	שׁוֹפֵט
☐	market........... *(shook)*	שׁוּק

שׁ

Knowing these travel מִלִּים will make your holiday twice as enjoyable וּ at least three times as easy. Review these new מִלִּים by doing the crossword puzzle below. Drill yourself on this Step by selecting other destinations וּ ask your own שְׁאֵלוֹת about רַכָּבוֹת *(rah-kah-voht)* ← אוֹטוֹבּוּסִים ← and *trains* מְטוֹסִים *(mah-toh-seem)* ← that go there. Select new מִלִּים from your מָלוֹן *(mih-lohn)* and ask your own questions *planes* that begin with מָתַי ,כַּמָּה and כַּמָּה עוֹלֶה . ← הַתְּשׁוּבוֹת to the crossword puzzle are at the bottom of the next page.

ACROSS
1. to eat
3. tower
5. to send
8. bread
10. I, you (♀) arrive
11. men
15. toilets
16. pleasant
18. ladies
19. stamp
20. we
22. west
24. September
26. street
27. north
28. closed
29. right
31. you (♂)

DOWN
2. I, you (♂) learn
3. salt
4. eyeglasses
6. hot
7. June
9. towels
12. tomorrow
13. autumn
14. winter
17. kitchen
18. postcard
19. in Bethlehem
21. I, you (♂) travel
22. refrigerator
23. a quarter
24. knife
25. shower
27. I, you (♂) need
28. grandmother
30. fork

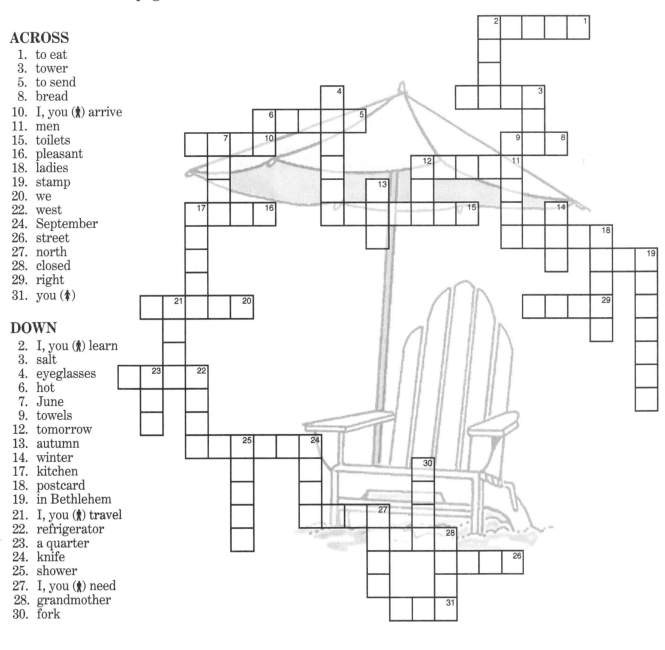

_____	wristwatch...... *(shuh-ohn-yahd)* .... שְׁעוֹן יָד ← ☐
_____	gate......... *(shah-ar)* .... שַׁעַר ☐
_____ שׁ	Jaffa Gate..... *(shah-ar-yah-foh)* .... שַׁעַר יָפוֹ ☐
_____	Damascus Gate.... *(shah-ar-shuh-Hem)* ..... שַׁעַר שְׁכֶם ☐
_____	sun....... *(sheh-mesh)* .... שֶׁמֶשׁ ☐

What about inquiring about the price of כַּרְטִיסִים? Remember, אַתָּה מְדַבֵּר *(muh-dah-bair)* עִבְרִית
speak
and

and אַתָּה can ask שְׁאֵלוֹת *(shuh-eh-loht)*.

_____ כַּמָּה עוֹלֶה כַּרְטִיס לְחֵיפָה ? *(kah-mah) (oh-leh) (kar-tees) (luh-Hay-fah)*
costs   ticket

_____ כַּמָּה עוֹלֶה כַּרְטִיס לִירוּשָׁלַיִם ? *(kah-mah) (oh-leh) (kar-tees)*

_____ כַּמָּה עוֹלֶה כַּרְטִיס לִבְאֵר שֶׁבַע ? *(lee-bair) (sheh-vah)*
to Beersheba

_____ הָלוֹךְ וָשׁוֹב ? *(hah-loH) (vah-shohv)*
round trip

מַה *(mah)* about times of הַמִּגְרָאוֹת *(hahm-rah-oht)* and נְחִיתוֹת *(nuh-Hee-toht)* ? אַתָּה can also ask these שְׁאֵלוֹת *(shuh-eh-loht)*.
what   departures   arrivals

_____ מָתַי יוֹצֵאת הָרַכֶּבֶת לְתֵל אָבִיב ? *(mah-tie) (yoh-tset) (hah-rah-kev-et) (luh-tel) (ah-veev)*
when   leaves   the train

_____ מָתַי יוֹצֵא הָאוֹטוֹבּוּס לִנְתַנְיָה ? *(mah-tie) (yoh-tseh) (lee-nuh-tahn-yah)*
to Netanya

_____ מָתַי מַגִּיעַ הָאוֹטוֹבּוּס מִבְּאֵר שֶׁבַע ? *(mah-tie) (mah-gee-ah) (mee-bair) (sheh-vah)*
arrives   from Beersheba

_____ מָתַי מַגִּיעַ הַמָּטוֹס מִנְיוּ יוֹרְק ? *(mah-tie) (mah-gee-ah) (hah-mah-tohs) (mee-new) (york)*
arrives   the plane   from New   York

_____ מָתַי יוֹצֵא הָאוֹטוֹבּוּס לִטְבֶרְיָה ? *(mah-tie) (yoh-tseh) (lee-t'veh-ree-yah)*
leaves   to Tiberias

אַתָּה רוֹצֶה לִנְסוֹעַ לְחֵיפָה ? תַּחֲנַת הָאוֹטוֹבּוּס at עַכְשָׁו are אַתָּה
(roh-tseh) (lin-soh-a) (luh-Hay-fah) Well, tell that to
to travel   to Haifa   station *(tah-Hah-naht)*

the person at הָאֶשְׁנָב *(hah-esh-nahv)* selling כַּרְטִיסִים *(kar-tih-seem)*.
the counter

נְסִיעָה טוֹבָה *(nuh-see-ah)*
Have a good trip

DOWN						ACROSS	
רֶבַע	23.	סְתָו	13.	לוֹמֵד	2.	צָפוֹן	27.	נָעִים	16.	→ לֶאֱכוֹל	1.
סַכִּין	24.	חֹרֶף	14.	מֶלַח	3.	סָגוּר	28.	גְבָרוֹת	18.	מִגְדָל	3.
מִקְלַחַת	25.	מִטְבָּח	17.	מִשְׁקָפַיִם	4.	יָמִין	29.	בּוּל	19.	לְשַׁלֵם	5.
צָרִיךְ	27.	גְלוּיָה	18.	חַם	6.	אַתָּה	31.	אֲנַחְנוּ	20.	לֶחֶם	8.
סַבְתָא	28.	בֵּית לֶחֶם	19.	יוֹנִי	7.			מַעֲרָב	22.	מַגִּיעַ	10.
מַזְלֵג	30.	נוֹסֵעַ	21.	מַגָבוֹת	9.			סֶפְּטֶמְבֶּר	24.	גְבָרִים	11.
		מְקָרֵר	22.	מָחָר	12.			רְחוֹב	26.	שֵׁרוּתִים	15.

עַכְשָׁו that אתה know the words essential for traveling – to Eilat, Beer Sheva, the Hula Valley, Nahariya אוֹ Caesarea – what are some speciality items אתה might go in search of?

(taH-shee-teem)
תַּכְשִׁיטִים
jewelry

(bed-wee-yeem) (buh-gah-deem)
בְּדְוִיִים בְּגָדִים
Bedouin clothing

(feen-zhahn)
פִינְגַ׳ן
Arab coffee set

(neh-Hoh-shet) (klay)
כְּלֵי נְחוֹשֶׁת
copper and brass goods

(zay-yit) (muh-etz) (mah-tah-noht)
מַתָּנוֹת מֵעֵץ זַיִת
olivewood

(keh-rah-mee-kah)
קֶרָמִיקָה
ceramics

Consider using HEBREW *a language map*® as well. HEBREW *a language map*® is the perfect companion for your travels when אתה may not wish to take along this book. Each section focuses on essentials for your trip. Your *Language Map*® is not meant to replace learning Hebrew, but will help you in the event אתה forget something and need a little bit of help. For more information about the *Language Map*® Series, please turn to page 132.

field	(sah-deh)	שָׂדֶה ◄ ▢
strawberries, field berries	(toot-sah-deh)	תּוּת שָׂדֶה ▢
bush	(see-aH)	שִׂיחַ ▢
language	(sah-fah)	שָׂפָה ▢
seaside	(s'faht-hah-yahm)	שְׂפַת הַיָּם ▢

שׂ

(toh-vah) *(mees-ah-dah)* *(rah-ev)* *(buh-mah-lohn)* *(buh-Hed-air)*

עַכְשָׁו אַתָה בְּיִשְׂרָאֵל. אַתָה בְּחֶדֶר בְּמָלוֹן. אַתָה רָעֵב. אֵיפֹה יֵשׁ מִסְעָדָה טוֹבָה ?
restaurant   hungry   in a room

First of all, there are different types of places to eat. Let's learn them.

(mees-ah-dah)
← מִסְעָדָה
restaurant

Many different national cuisines are represented,
so אַתָה have plenty of interesting choices.

(miz-rah-Heet) *(mees-ah-dah)*
← מִסְעָדָה מִזְרָחִית

serves Middle Eastern food

(steak-ee-yah)
← סְטֵיקִיָה

serves a variety of beef dishes: steaks, kebabs, shashlik

(fah-lah-fel)
← פָלָפֶל

Israeli "fast-food." Here you can try פָלָפֶל (fried chick pea balls with lettuce
in pita bread) which you can garnish with a variety of pickles and sauces.

(kah-feh) *(bait)*
← בֵּית קָפֶה

coffee shop, serves beverages and light snacks.

(Hoo-moos) *(tuh-Hee-nah)*
You may want to begin your meal with a plate of חוּמוּס ← or → טְחִינָה (sauce of ground
humus   tehina

(pee-tah) *(Hoo-moos)* *(tuh-Hee-nah)*
sesame seeds). Use your פִּיתָה to scoop up your חוּמוּס or טְחִינָה. Before beginning your
pita

(ah-roo-Hah) *(buh-tay-ah-vohn)*
אֲרוּחָה, be sure to wish those sharing your table בְּתֵיאָבוֹן.
meal   enjoy your meal

_____
(enjoy your meal)

And at least one more time for practice!

_____
(enjoy your meal)

Do not pass up the opportunity to enjoy פִּלְפֶּל *(fah-lah-fel)* or fresh פִּיתָה *(pee-tah)* at a דּוּכָן *(doo-Hahn)*.

falafel stand

מִסְעָדוֹת בְּיִשְׂרָאֵל *(buh-yiss-rah-el) (mees-ah-doht)* are generally כְּשֵׁרוֹת *(k'shair-oht)*. They follow the dietary law of כַּשְׁרוּת *(kahsh-root)*,

restaurants   kosher   purity

which forbids eating certain foods such as pork and shellfish. Milk ו meat dishes are not served

together. Most מִסְעָדוֹת *(mees-ah-doht)* – except עֲרָבִיּוֹת *(ah-rah-vee-yoht)* מִסְעָדוֹת *(mees-ah-doht)* – close for שַׁבָּת *(shah-baht)* (from Friday

Arab

evening to Saturday evening). Once you have found a מִסְעָדָה טוֹבָה *(toh-vah) (mees-ah-dah)* enter הַמִּסְעָדָה *(hah-mees-ah-dah)* and

good

find a שׁוּלְחָן *(shool-Hahn)*. אתה call הַמֶּלְצַר *(hah-mel-tsar)* and say "מֶלְצַר, הַתַפְרִיט בְּבַקָשָׁה." *(hah-tah-freet)* →

_____
(Waiter, the menu please.)

If your מֶלְצַר asks if אתה enjoyed your

"כֵּן, תּוֹדָה רַבָּה *(ken) (toh-dah) (rah-bah)* ו a", a smile אֲרוּחָה *(ah-roo-Hah)*

will tell him that אתה did.

עַכְשָׁו, it may be breakfast time at home, but אתה are בְּיִשְׂרָאֵל and it is 20:00. Some מִסְעָדוֹת *(mees-ah-doht)*

post הַתַפְרִיט *(hah-tah-freet)* outside. Always read it before entering so אתה know what type of meals ו prices

the menu

אתה will encounter inside. Did you notice that the words פִּלְפֶּל and פִּלְפֵּל are very similar

falafel   pepper

once the vowels are removed? Keep an eye out for those slight differences.

_____		picture........ *(tmoo-nah)*........... תְּמוּנָה ☐ ←
_____		photo album... *(ahl-bohm-tmoo-noht)*.. אַלְבּוֹם תְּמוּנוֹת ☐
_____	ח	signpost........ *(tahm-roor)*......... תַּמְרוּר ☐
_____		photograph........ *(tahts-loom)*......... תַּצְלוּם ☐
_____		medicine........ *(troo-fah)*......... תְּרוּפָה ☐

בְּיִשְׂרָאֵל there are *(shah-lohsh)* שָׁלוֹשׁ main meals to enjoy every *(yohm)* יוֹם , plus *(kah-feh)* קָפֶה and perhaps *(oo-gah)* עוּגָה
three   cake

for the tourist *(hah-tsoh-hoh-rah-yeem)* *(aH-ah-ray)* אַחֲרֵי הַצָּהֳרַיִם .
in the afternoon

(boh-kair) *(ah-roo-Haht)* אֲרוּחַת בֹּקֶר _____
breakfast

an Israeli breakfast may include yoghurt, cheese, herring, as well as תֵה or קָפֶה and לֶחֶם .

(tsoh-hoh-rah-yeem) *(ah-roo-Haht)* אֲרוּחַת צָהֳרַיִם _____
lunch

the main meal of the day. Usually served between 12:00 and 14:00, but you will find felafel stands open all day.

(eh-rev) אֲרוּחַת עֶרֶב _____
dinner

Israelis eat a light meal in the evening. Dinner is usually served from 18:00 until the late evening.

Perhaps אתה would like to try *(yah-yeen)* *(kohs)* כּוֹס יַיִן with your *(ah-roo-Hah)* אֲרוּחָה . Ask about the local wine.
wine glass (of)

עַכְשׁוּ a preview of delights to come . . . . At the back of this סֵפֶר you will find a sample

(yiss-ruh-eh-lee) *(tah-freet)* תַּפְרִיט יִשְׂרְאֵלִי . Read *(hah-tah-freet)* הַתַּפְרִיט today וּ learn the new מִלִים ! When אתה are ready to
menu

leave for יִשְׂרָאֵל , cut out *(hah-tah-freet)* הַתַּפְרִיט , fold it וּ carry it in your pocket, wallet אוֹ purse. Before you

go, how do אתה say these שָׁלוֹשׁ phrases which are so very important for the hungry traveler?

I am hungry. _____

Waiter! Menu, please. _____

Enjoy your meal! _____

(mah-rahk) אוֹכֵל מָרָק ? _____ _____
soup   eats   (who)

(yah-yeen) שׁוֹתֶה יַיִן ? _____
drinks   (who)

(who)

(lee-roo-shah-lah-yeem) *(noh-seh-ah)* נוֹסֵעַ לִירוּשָׁלַיִם ? _____
(who)

The following should help you identify what kind of meat אוֹ poultry אתה have ordered and אֵיךְ it will be prepared.

_____	beef . . . . *(buh-sar-bah-kar)*	◄ בְּשַׂר בָּקָר ☐
_____	veal . . . . *(buh-sar-ay-gel)*	בְּשַׂר עֵגֶל ☐
_____	mutton . . . . *(buh-sar-keh-ves)*	בְּשַׂר כֶּבֶשׂ ☐
_____	poultry . . . . *(buh-sar-ohf)*	בְּשַׂר עוֹף ☐

(hah-tah-freet) הַתַּפְרִיט *(luh-mah-tah)* לְמַטָּה has the main categories אתה will find in most restaurants. Learn them

(hah-yohm) הַיוֹם
today
so that אתה will easily recognize them when you dine בְּיִשְׂרָאֵל. Be sure to write the

words in the blanks below.

(hah-tah-freet)
הַתַּפְרִיט
the menu

(ree-shoh-noht) (mah-noht)
מָנוֹת רִאשוֹנוֹת
appetizers
_____

(meh-rah-keem)
מְרָקִים
soups
_____

(bay-tseem)
בֵּיצִים
eggs
_____

(dah-geem)
דָגִים
fish
_____

(bah-sar)
בָּשָׂר
meat
_____

(ohf)
עוֹף
poultry
_____

(yuh-rah-koht)
יְרָקוֹת
vegetables
_____

(sah-lah-teem)
סָלָטִים
salads
_____

(kee-noo-aH)
קִנוּחַ
dessert
_____

(glee-doht)
גְלִידוֹת
ice cream
_____

(peh-roht)
פֵּרוֹת
fruit
_____

(oo-goht)
עוּגוֹת
pastries, small cakes
_____

(mahsh-kah-oht)
מַשְׁקָאוֹת
beverages
_____

_____
_____
_____
_____

☐	turkey	*(tar-nuh-gohl-hoh-doo)*	תַרְנְגוֹל הוֹדוּ ←
☐	cooked	*(muh-voo-shahl)*	מְבוּשָׁל
☐	roasted	*(tsah-loo-ee)*	צָלוּי
☐	fried	*(muh-too-gahn)*	מְטוּגָּן
☐	baked	*(ah-foo-ee)*	אָפוּי

89

אַתָּה will also get *(yuh-rah-koht)* יְרָקוֹת [vegetables] with your *(ah-roo-Hah)* אֲרוּחָה and perhaps a *(sah-laht)* סָלָט. One day at a *(shook)* שׁוּק [market] will

teach you *(hah-sheh-moht)* הַשֵׁמוֹת [names] ← for all the different kinds of *(yuh-rah-koht)* יְרָקוֹת [vegetables] and *(peh-roht)* פֵּרוֹת [fruit], plus it will be a

delightful experience for you. אַתָּה can always consult your menu guide at the back of this סֵפֶר

if אַתָּה forget the correct *(shem)* שֵׁם [name] ←. *(mah-gee-ah)* *(hah-mel-tsar)* הַמֶּלְצַר מַגִּיעַ [arrives]. עַכְשָׁו ← you are seated and

(boh-kair) *(ah-roo-Haht)* אֲרוּחַת בֹּקֶר [breakfast] ← is delicious. *(boh-kair)* *(ah-roo-Haht)* אֲרוּחַת בֹּקֶר [breakfast] ← includes yoghurt, cheese, eggs אוֹ herring,

ו bread אוֹ rolls. *(luh-mah-tah)* לְמַטָה [from below] ← is a sample of what אַתָּה can expect to greet you *(bah-boh-kair)* בַּבֹּקֶר [in the morning].

(leh-eh-Hohl) לֶאֱכֹל [to eat] ←

(leH-em) לֶחֶם

(gvee-nah) גְבִינָה [cheese]

(bay-tseem) בֵּיצִים [eggs]

(mah-loo-aH) *(dahg)* דָג מָלוּחַ [herring]

(muh-lahf-foh-nim) מְלָפְפוֹנִים [cucumbers]

(ahg-vah-n'yoht) עַגְבָנִיוֹת [tomatoes]

(ree-bah) רִיבָּה [jam]

(mahsh-kah-oht) מַשְׁקָאוֹת ←

(kah-feh) קָפֶה

(hah-fooH) קָפֶה הָפוּךְ [with foamed milk]

(tay) תֶה

(meets) מִיץ ←

(esh-kohl-yoht) מִיץ אֶשְׁכּוֹלִיוֹת [grapefruit]

(tah-poo-zeem) מִיץ תַפּוּזִים [orange]

(ah-nah-nahs) מִיץ אֲנָנָס [pineapple]

grilled	*(bee-gril)*	בְּגְרִיל ←	☐
stuffed	*(muh-moo-lah)*	מְמוּלָא	☐
rare	*(nah)*	נָא	☐
medium	*(bay-noh-nee)*	בֵּינוֹנִי	☐
well-done	*(muh-voo-shahl-hey-tev)*	מְבוּשָׁל הֵיטֵב	☐

הִנֵּה an example of what אַתָּה might select for your evening meal. Using your menu guide on pages 119 and 120, as well as what אַתָּה have learned in this Step, fill in the blanks *in English* with what אַתָּה believe your *(mel-tsar)* מֶלְצַר will bring you. *(hah-t'shoo-voht)* *(luh-mah-tah)* הַתְּשׁוּבוֹת לְמַטָּה.
the answers

מָנוֹת רִאשׁוֹנוֹת →

חוּמוּס, טְחִינָה וְזֵיתִים

_____

סָלָטִים

סָלַט מְלָפְפוֹנִים

_____

מָנוֹת עִיקָרִיוֹת →

שִׁישְׁלִיק עִם אוֹרֶז

_____

קִינוּחִים →

תּוּת שָׂדֶה בְּקַצֶּפֶת

_____

_____ (when)

_____ (how)

_____ (why)

הַתְּשׁוּבוֹת

Appetizers: Humus, tehina and olives
Salad: Cucumber salad
Entrees: Shashlik with rice
Desserts: Strawberries with cream

עַכְשָׁו it is a good time for a quick review. Draw lines between the עִבְרִית words ו their English equivalents.

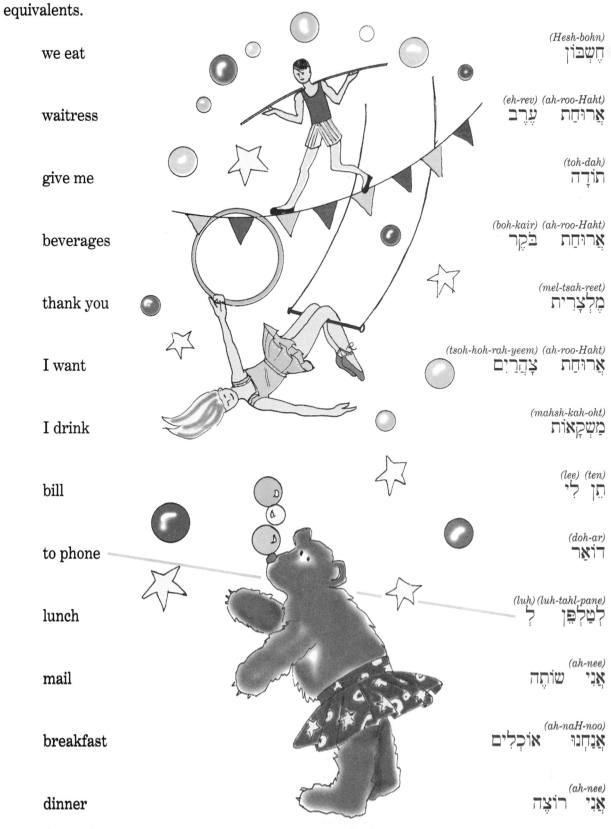

we eat

waitress

give me

beverages

thank you

I want

I drink

bill

to phone

lunch

mail

breakfast

dinner

(Hesh-bohn)
חֶשְׁבּוֹן

(eh-rev) (ah-roo-Haht)
אֲרוּחַת עֶרֶב

(toh-dah)
תּוֹדָה

(boh-kair) (ah-roo-Haht)
אֲרוּחַת בֹּקֶר

(mel-tsah-reet)
מֶלְצָרִית

(tsoh-hoh-rah-yeem) (ah-roo-Haht)
אֲרוּחַת צָהֳרַיִם

(mahsh-kah-oht)
מַשְׁקָאוֹת

(lee) (ten)
תֵּן לִי

(doh-ar)
דּוֹאַר

(luh) (luh-tahl-pane)
לְטַלְפֵּן לְ

(ah-nee)
אֲנִי שׁוֹתֶה

(ah-naH-noo)
אֲנַחְנוּ אוֹכְלִים

(ah-nee)
אֲנִי רוֹצֶה

Here are a few more holidays which you might experience during your visit.

_____ New Year . . . . *(rohsh-hah-shah-nah)* . . . רֹאשׁ הַשָּׁנָה ◄ ☐
_____ Day of Atonement . . . . *(yohm-kih-poor)* . . . . . . יוֹם כִּפּוּר ☐
_____ Feast of Tabernacles . . . . *(soo-koht)* . . . סוּכּוֹת ☐
_____ Festival of the Torah . . . . *(sim-Haht-toh-rah)* . . . שִׂמְחַת תּוֹרָה ☐

מַה is different about הַטֶּלֶפוֹן *(hah-teh-leh-fohn)* ← בְּיִשְׂרָאֵל? Well, אתה never notice such things until

אתה רוֹצֶה *(roht-seh)* ← to use them. הַטֶּלֶפוֹן *(hah-teh-leh-fohn)* ← allows you to reserve a חֶדֶר בְּמָלוֹן *(Hed-air)* *(buh-mah-lohn)* ← in
room

another city, call חֲבֵרִים *(Hah-vair-eem)*, reserve קוֹנְצֶרְט *(kohn-tsairt)* tickets, make emergency calls, check on הַשָּׁעוֹת *(hah-shah-oht)*
friends   concert   the hours

of a מוּזֵיאוֹן *(moo-zay-ohn)*, rent a מְכוֹנִית *(may-Hoh-neet)* and all those other דְּבָרִים *(dvah-rim)* which אֲנַחְנוּ *(ah-naH-noo)* do on a daily

basis. It also gives you a certain amount of freedom when אתה can phone on your own.

For many telephones אתה must לִקְנוֹת *(lik-noht)* ← an
buy

אֲסִימוֹן *(ah-see-mohn)*, or a telecard before אתה can use a
token

טֶלֶפוֹן צִיבּוּרִי *(tsih-boo-ree)* *(teh-leh-fohn)*. You can buy
public

אֲסִימוֹנִים *(ah-see-moh-neem)* and telecards at the post office.
tokens

So, let's learn how to operate הַטֶּלֶפוֹן.

Instructions can look complicated, but

remember, some of these מלים אתה ←

should be able to recognize already. Ready?

Well, before you turn the page it would be a

good idea to go back וֹ review all your numbers

one more time.

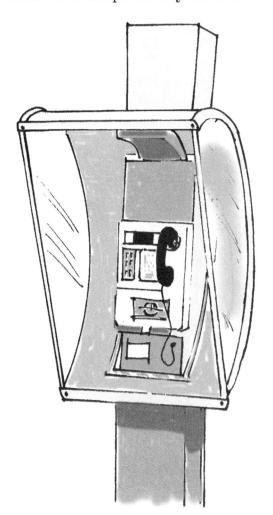

To dial from the United States to any other country אתה need that country's international

area code. Your סֵפֶר טֶלֶפוֹן ← at home should have a listing of international area codes. When

Here are some useful words built around the word "טֶלֶפוֹן."

_____	operator .... *(mair-kah-zahn)* .... מֶרְכָּזָן ← ☐
_____	public telephone .... *(teh-leh-fohn-tsih-boo-ree)* .. טֶלֶפוֹן צִיבּוּרִי ☐
_____	telephone book ...... *(sef-air-teh-leh-fohn)* ...... סֵפֶר טֶלֶפוֹן ☐
_____	telephone conversation ..... *(see-Haht-teh-leh-fohn)* ..... שִׂיחַת טֶלֶפוֹן ☐

אתה leave your contact numbers with friends, family אוֹ business colleagues, אתה should

include your destination country's area code וֹ city code whenever possible . For example,

	Country Codes		City Codes	
Israel	972	Haifa		(0) 4
Egypt	20	Tel Aviv		(0) 3
Turkey	90	Jerusalem		(0) 2

When calling from within Israel, you need to use the "0" with the city code. So אַתָּה יָכוֹל *(yah-Hohl)* / *can* ←

now use הַטֶּלֶפוֹן *(hah-teh-leh-fohn)* to make a call בְּיִשְׂרָאֵל *(buh-yiss-rah-el)* . יֵשׁ *(yesh)* / *there are* also more city codes called קִידוֹמֶת *(kee-doh-met)* ,

and these are listed in the סֵפֶר הַטֶּלֶפוֹן ←.

Do not be surprised if your first public telephone does not work. You may need to locate a

second one in order to make your call. This can be a common occurrence.

When answering הַטֶּלֶפוֹן ←, אַתָּה pick up the receiver וֹ say: ". _____ פֹּה *(poh)* / *here is* הַלוֹ *(hah-loh)* / *hello* "
_____ (your name)

When saying goodbye, אַתָּה say "שָׁלוֹם! *(shah-lohm)* " Your turn —

_____

(Hello, here is . . .)

_____

(goodbye)

Do not forget that אַתָּה יָכוֹל *(yah-Hohl)* / *can* ← ask . . .

_____ כַּמָה עוֹלָה שִׂיחָה לְאֵילַת ? *(oh-lah) (see-Hah) (luh-ay-laht)* / *costs / a call / to Eilat*

_____ כַּמָה עוֹלָה שִׂיחָה לַאֲמֵרִיקָה ? *(lah-ah-meh-ree-kah)*

These are free telephone calls.		
_____ 100	police . . . . *(mish-tah-rah)* . . . . מִשְׁטָרָה ← ☐
_____ 101	first aid . . . *(mah-gen-dah-veed-ah-dohm)* . . מָגֵן דָוִד אָדוֹם ☐
_____ 102	fire brigade . . . . . . *(muh-Hah-bay-esh)* . . . . מְכַבֵּי אֵשׁ ☐
Remember: you need a token or a telecard for the telephone!		

הִנֵּה some sample sentences for the telephone. Write them in the blanks לְמַטָּה *(luh-mah-tah)*.

_____ . אֲנִי רוֹצֶה לְטַלְפֵּן לְשִׁיקָגוֹ
(ah-nee) *(roht-seh)* *(luh-tahl-pane)* *(luh-shee-kah-goh)*
to telephone — to Chicago

_____ . אֲנִי רוֹצֶה לְדַבֵּר עִם "אֶל עַל" בִּשְׂדֵה הַתְּעוּפָה
(ah-nee) to speak *(luh-dah-bair)* El Al *(el)* *(ahl)* in airport *(bee-sday)* *(hah-too-fah)*

_____ . אֲנִי רוֹצֶה לְדַבֵּר עִם הַמּוֹדִיעִין
(ah-nee) *(luh-dah-bair)* information *(hah-moh-dee-een)*

_____ ? מַה מִסְפַּר הַטֶּלֶפוֹן שֶׁלְּךָ
what number telephone your
(mis-par) *(hah-teh-leh-fohn)* *(shel-Hah)*

_____ . 274 16 24 הַמִּסְפָּר שֶׁלִּי
number my
(hah-mis-par) *(sheh-lee)*

_____ ? מַה מִסְפַּר הַטֶּלֶפוֹן שֶׁל הַמָּלוֹן
of the hotel
(mis-par) *(hah-teh-leh-fohn)* *(shel)* *(hah-mah-lohn)*

← בֹּעַז : שָׁלוֹם . אֲנִי רוֹצֶה לְדַבֵּר עִם גְּבֶרֶת אַלוֹן, בְּבַקָּשָׁה.
Boaz *(boh-ahz)* *(shah-lohm)* *(luh-dah-bair)* Mrs. *(gveh-ret)* Alon *(ah-lohn)*

_____

מַזְכִּירָה : רַק רֶגַע . הַקַּו תָּפוּס .
secretary just a moment the line busy
(mahz-kee-rah) *(rahk)* *(reh-gah)* *(hah-kahv)* *(tah-foos)*

_____

בֹּעַז : עוֹד פַּעַם, בְּבַקָּשָׁה. בְּבַקָּשָׁה לְאַט יוֹתֵר .
more once slowly repeat
(ohd) *(pahm)* *(luh-aht)* *(yoh-tair)*

_____

מַזְכִּירָה : הַקַּו תָּפוּס .
the line busy
(hah-kahv) *(tah-foos)*

_____

בֹּעַז : תּוֹדָה רַבָּה, שָׁלוֹם .
(toh-dah) *(rah-bah)* *(shah-lohm)*

_____

עַכְשָׁו , you are ready to use any טֶלֶפוֹן in יִשְׂרָאֵל *(yiss-rah-el)* . Just take it slowly ו speak clearly.

There are two different kinds of calendars that are used in Israel. You will hear the months from the Gregorian calendar which you learned on pages 28 and 29. You will also encounter the months according to the Hebrew lunar calendar, which follows here and on the next two pages.

☐ ← תִּשְׁרֵי .... *(tish-ray)* .... September-October _____
☐ חֶשְׁוָן .... *(Hesh-vahn)* .... October-November _____

95

(tahk-see) *(shay-root)* *(oh-toh-boos)*

אוֹטוֹבּוּס, שֵׁירוּת, טָקְסִי

taxi   sherut   bus

Most   *(yiss-ruh-eh-leem)* יִשְׂרְאֵלִים   travel   *(bee-may-Hoh-neet)* בְּמְכוֹנִית or בָּאוֹטוֹבּוּסִים , but the buses can be very crowded. An

alternative to הָאוֹטוֹבּוּס is *(hah-shay-root)* הַשֵׁירוּת , or shared taxi. You can even take a *(shay-root)* שֵׁירוּת from

one town to another. The *(shay-root)* שֵׁירוּת leaves from a specific place and follows fixed routes.

(shay-root)
שֵׁירוּת
sherut

(oh-toh-boos)
אוֹטוֹבּוּס
bus

(tahk-see)
טָקְסִי
taxi

(hah-shay-root) *(tah-Hah-naht)*
הַשֵׁירוּת   תַּחֲנַת
sherut   stop

(tah-Hah-naht)
הָאוֹטוֹבּוּס   תַּחֲנַת
bus   stop

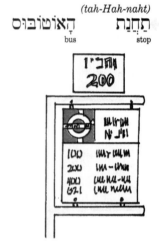

To ask for the *(shay-root)* שֵׁירוּת to your destination say, *(ah-veev)* *(luh-tel)* *(hah-shay-root)* "אֵיפֹה הַשֵׁירוּת לְתֵל אָבִיב?" When

(buh-shay-root) *(noh-seh-ah)* בְּשֵׁירוּת נוֹסֵעַ אַתָּה each person pays for his own seat and *(yoh-tseh)* *(hah-shay-root)* הַשֵׁירוּת יוֹצֵא when it
travel   leaves

is full — with *(shev-ah)* שִׁבְעָה people. You can always, hail a *(hah-ruh-Hohv)* טָקְסִי on הָרְחוֹב as well.
seven   the street

_____	November-December	(kis-lev)	כִּסְלֵו ← ☐
_____	December-January	(teh-vet)	טֵבֵת ☐☐
_____	January-February	(shvaht)	שְׁבָט ☐☐
_____	February-March	(ah-dar)	אֲדָר ☐☐
_____	March-April	(nee-sahn)	נִיסָן ☐☐

Other than having foreign words, the Israeli bus system functions just like those in San Francisco, New York אוֹ Boston. Locate your destination, select the correct line on your practice אוֹטוֹבּוּס and hop on board.

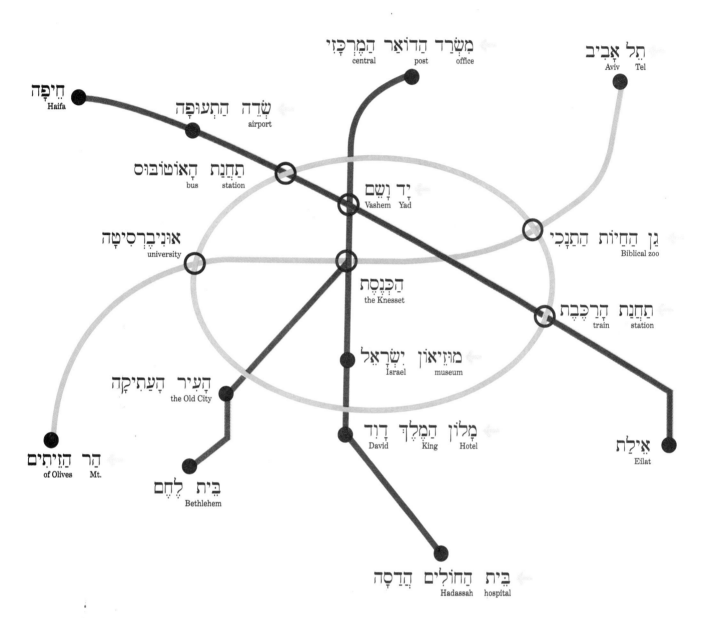

מִשְׂרַד הַדוֹאַר הַמֶּרְכָּזִי
central   post   office

תֵּל אָבִיב
Aviv   Tel

חֵיפָה
Haifa

שְׂדֵה הַתְּעוּפָה
airport

תַּחֲנַת הָאוֹטוֹבּוּס
bus   station

יָד וָשֵׁם
Vashem   Yad

אוּנִיבֶּרְסִיטָה
university

גַּן הַחַיּוֹת הַתַּנַּ"כִי
Biblical zoo

הַכְּנֶסֶת
the Knesset

תַּחֲנַת הָרַכֶּבֶת
train   station

מוּזֵיאוֹן יִשְׂרָאֵל
Israel   museum

הָעִיר הָעַתִּיקָה
the Old City

מָלוֹן הַמֶּלֶךְ דָּוִד
David   King   Hotel

אֵילַת
Eilat

הַר הַזֵּיתִים
of Olives   Mt.

בֵּית לֶחֶם
Bethlehem

בֵּית הַחוֹלִים הֲדַסָה
Hadassah   hospital

Say these questions aloud many times.

(hah-shay-root)
איפה הַשֵּׁירוּת ? ←

איפה הַטַקְסִי ? ←

(tah-Hah-naht)
איפֹה תַּחֲנַת הָאוֹטוֹבּוּס ? ←
(hah-shay-root)
איפה תַּחֲנַת הַשֵּׁירוּת ? ←

April-May .... (ih-yar) .... אִיָּיר ← ☐
May-June .... (sih-vahn) .... סִיוָן ☐
June-July .... (tah-mooz) .... תַּמּוּז ☐
July-August .... (ahv) .... אָב ☐
August-September .... (ay-lool) .... אֱלוּל ☐ 97

Practice the following basic *(shuh-eh-loht)* שְׁאֵלוֹת out loud וְ then write them in the blanks *(mee-smohl)* מִשְׂמֹאל.
to the left

1. _____ כֹּל כַּמָּה זְמַן בָּא הָאוֹטוֹבּוּס לִנְצֶרֶת ?
   (kohl) *(kah-mah)* *(zmahn)* *(bah)* *(luh-nahts-raht)*
   how often   comes   for Nazareth

_____ כֹּל כַּמָּה זְמַן בָּא הָאוֹטוֹבּוּס לַעֲרָד ?
   (lah-ah-rahd)
   for Arad

_____ כֹּל כַּמָּה זְמַן בָּא הָאוֹטוֹבּוּס לִשְׂדֵה הַתְּעוּפָה ?
   (zmahn)   *(lee-sday)* *(hah-too-fah)*
   for the airport

2. _____ מָתַי יוֹצֵאת הָרַכֶּבֶת ?
   (mah-tie) *(yoh-tset)* *(hah-rah-kev-et)*
   leaves

_____ מָתַי יוֹצֵא הָאוֹטוֹבּוּס ?
   (yoh-tseh)

_____ מָתַי יוֹצֵא הַשֵּׁירוּת ?
   (hah-shay-root)

3. _____ כַּמָּה עוֹלֶה כַּרְטִיס לָאוֹטוֹבּוּס ?
   (kah-mah) *(oh-leh)* *(kar-tees)*

_____ כַּמָּה עוֹלֶה כַּרְטִיס לַכְּנֶסֶת ?
   (lah-knes-set)
   for the Knesset

_____ כַּמָּה עוֹלֶה כַּרְטִיס לְתֵל אָבִיב ?
   (luh-tel) *(ah-veev)*

4. _____ אֵיפֹה אֲנִי קוֹנֶה כַּרְטִיס לָאוֹטוֹבּוּס ?
   (koh-neh)
   buy

_____ אֵיפֹה אֲנִי קוֹנֶה כַּרְטִיס לָרַכֶּבֶת ?
   (koh-neh)

Let's change directions וְ learn *(shtah-yeem)* שְׁתַּיִם new verbs. אַתָּה know the basic "plug-in" formula, so

write out your own sentences using these new verbs.

_____

(luh-Hah-bes)
לְכַבֵּס
to wash (clothes)

_____

(loh-kay-aH) *(zeh)*
זֶה לוֹקֵחַ
it takes

Here are a few more holidays to keep in mind.

_____ Festival of Lights .... *(Hah-noo-kah)* .... חֲנוּכָּה ← ☐
_____ Passover .... *(pay-saH)* .... פֶּסַח ☐
_____ Day of Independence ... *(yohm-hah-ahtz-mah-oot)* ... יוֹם הָעַצְמָאוּת ☐
_____ Pentecost .... *(shah-voo-oht)* .... שָׁבוּעוֹת ☐

Shopping abroad is exciting. The simple everyday task of buying a *(Hah-lahv)* חָלָב *(lee-tair)* לִיטֶר ← or a
milk · liter

(tah-poo-aH) תַּפּוּחַ becomes a challenge that אַתָּה should עַכְשָׁו be able to meet quickly וּ easily. Of course,
apple

אַתָּה will purchase *(oo-mahz-kah-roht)* וּמַזְכָּרוֹת *(boo-leem)* בּוּלִים, *(gloo-yoht)* גְּלוּיוֹת ← but don't forget those many other דְּבָרִים
and souvenirs · things

ranging from shoelaces to *(ahs-pee-reen)* אַסְפִּירִין that אַתָּה might need unexpectedly. Locate your store,
aspirin

draw a line to it וּ as always, write your new words in the blanks provided.

_____ *(kohl-boh)* כֹּל-בּוֹ *(Hah-noot)* חֲנוּת ←   _____ *(kohl-noh-ah)* קוֹלְנוֹעַ ←
department · store · cinema

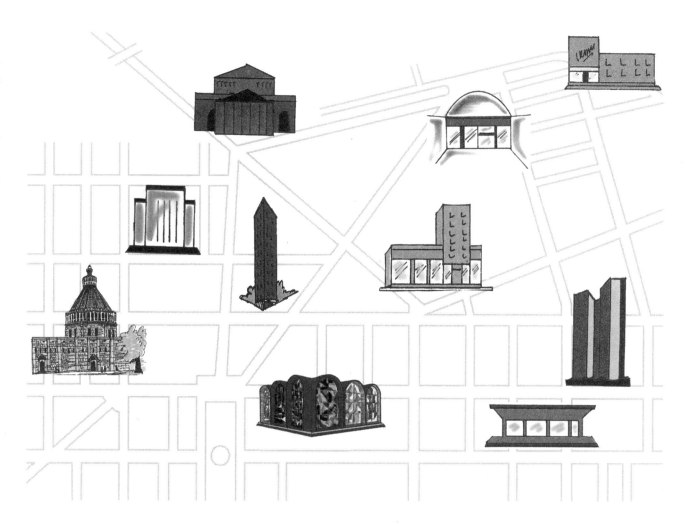

_____ *(hah-doh-ar)* הַדּוֹאַר *(mis-rahd)* מִשְׂרַד ←   _____ *(bahnk)* בַּנְק ←
post office · bank

_____ *(mah-lohn)* מָלוֹן ←   _____ *(del-ek)* דֶּלֶק *(tah-Hah-naht)* תַּחֲנַת ←
hotel · gas · station

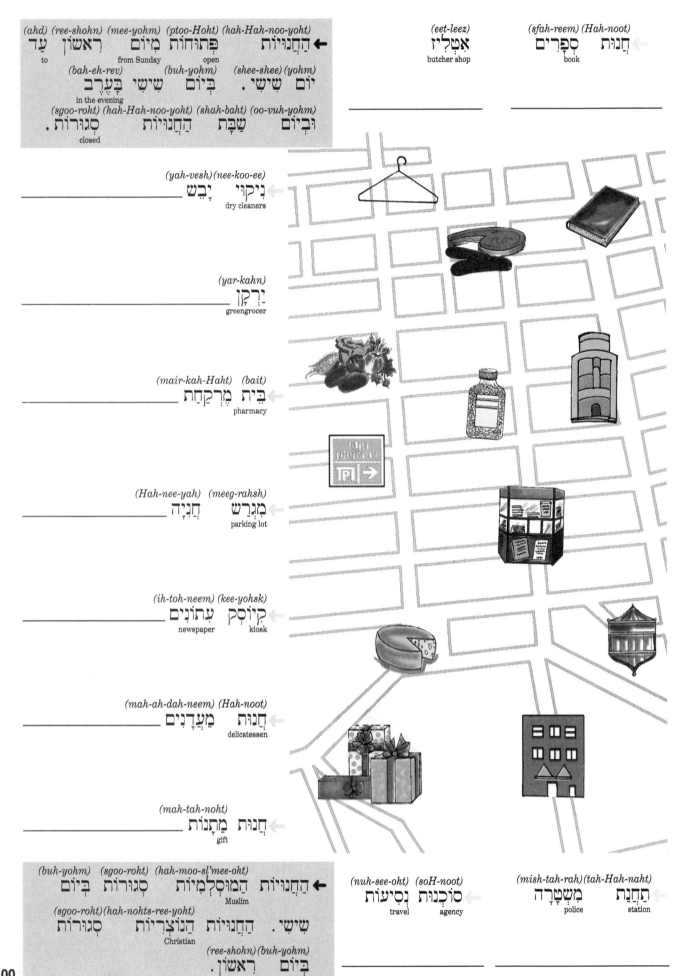

(eet-leez)
אַטְלִיז
butcher shop

_____

(sfah-reem) *(Hah-noot)*
← חֲנוּת סְפָרִים
book

_____

(yah-vesh) *(nee-koo-ee)*
← נִיקוּי יָבֵשׁ
dry cleaners

_____

(yar-kahn)
← יַרְקָן
greengrocer

_____

(mair-kah-Haht) *(bait)*
← בֵּית מֶרְקַחַת
pharmacy

_____

(Hah-nee-yah) *(meeg-rahsh)*
← מִגְרַשׁ חֲנִיָה
parking lot

_____

(ih-toh-neem) *(kee-yohsk)*
← קִיוֹסְק עִתּוֹנִים
newspaper   kiosk

_____

(mah-ah-dah-neem) *(Hah-noot)*
← חֲנוּת מַעֲדַנִים
delicatessen

_____

(mah-tah-noht)
← חֲנוּת מַתָּנוֹת
gift

_____

(nuh-see-oht) *(soH-noot)*
← סוֹכְנוּת נְסִיעוֹת
travel   agency

_____

(mish-tah-rah) *(tah-Hah-naht)*
מִשְׁטָרָה תַּחֲנַת
police   station

_____

חֲנוּת דָּגִים ➝
fish
(dah-geem)

חֲנוּת צִלּוּם ➝
photo
(tsee-loom)

שׁוּק ➝
open-air market
(shook)

חֲנוּת מַכֹּלֶת ➝
grocery
(mah-koh-let)

חֲנוּת תַּכְשִׁיטִים ➝
jewelry
(taH-shee-teem)

מַאֲפִיָּה ➝
bakery
(mah-ah-fee-yah)

בֵּית קָפֶה ➝
coffee house
(kah-feh) *(bait)*

מִכְבָּסָה ➝
laundry
(meeH-bah-sah)

(mahm-tah-keem) *(Hah-noot)*
חֲנוּת מַמְתַּקִים
candy

(prah-Heem) *(Hah-noot)*
חֲנוּת פְּרָחִים
flower

(Hah-noot)
חֲנוּת ➝
shop

(ktee-vah) *(klay)*
חֲנוּת כְּלֵי כְּתִיבָה ➝
stationery

(mees-pah-rah)
מִסְפָּרָה ➝
hairdresser

(ree-shoh-nah) *(koh-mah)*
קוֹמָה רִאשׁוֹנָה ➝ = ground floor

(shnee-yah)
קוֹמָה שְׁנִיָּה ➝ = second floor

(shlee-sheet)
קוֹמָה שְׁלִישִׁית ➝ = third floor

(kohl-boh) (Hah-noot)

← חֲנוּת כֹּל - בּוֹ

department · store

At this point, אתה *(nuh-see-ah)* should just about be ready for your נְסִיעָה ← אתה have gone shopping

trip

for those last-minute odds 'n ends. Most likely, the store directory at your local *(kohl-boh)(Hah-noot)* ← חֲנוּת כֹּל - בּוֹ

did not look like the one *(luh-mah-tah)* לְמַטָּה. *(yoh-day-ah)* אתה יוֹדֵעַ ← that "*(yel-ed)* יֶלֶד" is Hebrew for "child," so

know

if *(tsah-reeH)* אתה צָרִיך ← something for a *(yel-ed)* יֶלֶד you would probably look on *(hah-shlee-sheet)(hah-koh-mah)* הַקּוֹמָה הַשְּׁלִישִׁית ←

child · *third* · *floor*

wouldn't you?

5. קוֹמָה	חַרְסִינָה זְכוּכִית פֵּרוֹת	סַכִּינִים כְּלֵי מִטְבָּח יְרָקוֹת	מַפְתְּחוֹת ← קֵרָמִיקָה מַאֲפִיָּה	
4. קוֹמָה	סְפָרִים מַחְלֶקֶת צִלּוּם צַעֲצוּעִים	מִסְעָדָה תַּקְלִיטִים כְּלֵי כְּתִיבָה	טַבָּק ← עִתּוֹנִים שְׁבוּעוֹנִים	
3. קוֹמָה	מַחְלֶקֶת יְלָדִים נַעֲלֵי יְלָדִים רָהִיטֵי יְלָדִים	מַחְלֶקֶת גְּבָרִים בִּגְדֵי גְּבָרִים נַעֲלֵי גְּבָרִים	קוֹסְמֶטִיקָה ← כְּלֵי מִטָּה מִזְוָדוֹת	
2. קוֹמָה	שְׁטִיחִים לִבְנֵי נָשִׁים נַעֲלֵי נָשִׁים	מַחְלֶקֶת נָשִׁים בִּגְדֵי נָשִׁים כּוֹבְעֵי נָשִׁים	דִּבְרֵי סְפּוֹרְט ← צִיּוּד קֶמְפִּינְג בִּגְדֵי יָם	
1. קוֹמָה	מִטְרִיּוֹת מַפּוֹת כּוֹבָעִים	כְּפָפוֹת דִּבְרֵי עוֹר חֲגוֹרוֹת	שְׁעוֹנִים ← מִמְחָטוֹת בּוֹשֶׂם	

Let's start a checklist for your *(nuh-see-ah)* נְסִיעָה. Besides clothing, *(tsah-reeH)* *(mah)* מַה אתה צָרִיך? ← As you learn

these words, assemble these items in a *(pee-nah)* פִּנָה of your *(bite)* בַּיִת. Check ו make sure that they are

corner

clean ו ready for your *(nuh-see-ah)* נְסִיעָה. Be sure to do the same עִם the rest of הַדְּבָרִים that אתה pack.

trip

On the next pages, match each item to its picture, draw a line to it and write out the word many

times. As you organize these things, check them off on this list. Do not forget to take the next

group of sticky labels and label these things *(hah-yohm)* הַיּוֹם.

_____ □	**(dar-kohn)** **דַּרְכּוֹן** passport	
_____ □	**(kar-tees)** **כַּרְטִיס** ticket	
מְזוָדָה, מְזוָדָה, מְזוָדָה ☑	**(miz-vah-dah)** **מִזוָדָה** suitcase	
_____ □	**(teek)** **תִּיק** handbag	
_____ □	**(ar-nahk)** **אַרְנָק** wallet	
_____ □	**(kes-ef)** **כֶּסֶף** money	
_____ □	**(ahsh-rye) (kar-tees)** **כַּרְטִיס אַשְׁרַאי** credit card	
_____ □	**(noh-seem) (hahm-Hah-oht)** **הַמְחָאוֹת נוֹסְעִים** traveler's checks	
_____ □	**(mahts-leh-mah)** **מַצְלֵמָה** camera	
_____ □	**(film)** **פִילְם** film	
_____ □	**(yahm) (beg-ed)** **בֶּגֶד יָם** swimsuit	
_____ □	**(yahm) (beg-ed)** **בֶּגֶד יָם** swimsuit	
_____ □	**(sahn-dah-leem)** **סַנְדָלִים** sandals	
_____ □	**(mish-kah-fah-yeem)** **מִשְׁקָפַיִם** sunglasses	
_____ □	**(shee-nah-yeem) (meev-resh-et)** **מִבְרֶשֶׁת שִׁנַיִם** toothbrush	
_____ □	**(shee-nah-yeem) (mish-Haht)** **מִשְׁחַת שִׁנַיִם** toothpaste	
_____ □	**(sah-bohn)** **סַבּוֹן** soap	
_____ □	**(gee-loo-aH) (sah-keen)** **סַכִּין גִּלוּחַ** razor	
_____ □	**(day-oh-doh-rahnt)** **דֵיאוֹדוֹרַנְט** deodorant	

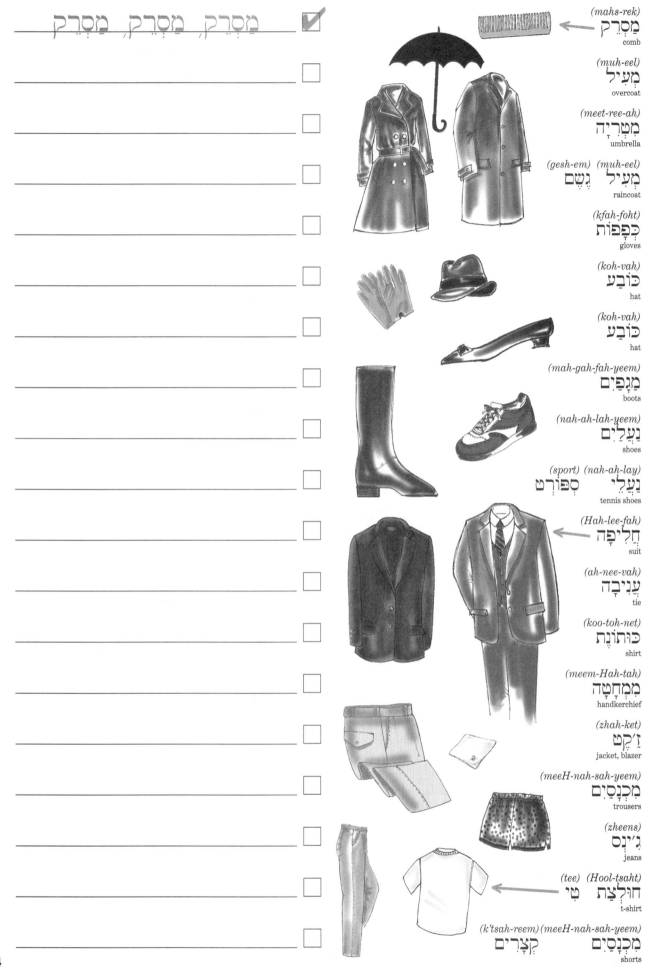

מַסְרֵק, מַסְרֵק, מַסְרֵק ✔

(mahs-rek)
מַסְרֵק
comb

(muh-eel)
מְעִיל
overcoat

(meet-ree-ah)
מִטְרִיָּה
umbrella

(gesh-em) (muh-eel)
מְעִיל גֶּשֶׁם
raincoat

(kfah-foht)
כְּפָפוֹת
gloves

(koh-vah)
כּוֹבַע
hat

(koh-vah)
כּוֹבַע
hat

(mah-gah-fah-yeem)
מַגָּפַיִם
boots

(nah-ah-lah-yeem)
נַעֲלַיִם
shoes

(sport) (nah-ah-lay)
נַעֲלֵי סְפּוֹרְט
tennis shoes

(Hah-lee-fah)
חֲלִיפָה
suit

(ah-nee-vah)
עֲנִיבָה
tie

(koo-toh-net)
כֻּתֹּנֶת
shirt

(meem-Hah-tah)
מִמְחָטָה
handkerchief

(zhah-ket)
זַ׳קֵט
jacket, blazer

(meeH-nah-sah-yeem)
מִכְנָסַיִם
trousers

(zheens)
גַ׳ינְס
jeans

(tee) (Hool-tsaht)
חֻלְצַת טִי
t-shirt

(k'tsah-reem) (meeH-nah-sah-yeem)
מִכְנָסַיִם קְצָרִים
shorts

☐	*(taH-toh-neem)* תַּחְתּוֹנִים underpants
☐	*(goo-fee-yah)* גּוּפִיָּה undershirt
☐	*(sim-lah)* שִׂמְלָה dress
☑ חוּלְצָה, חוּלְצָה, חוּלְצָה	*(Hool-tsah)* חוּלְצָה blouse
☐	*(Hah-tsah-eet)* חֲצָאִית skirt
☐	*(sved-air)* סְוֶדֶר sweater
☐	*(taH-toh-neet)* תַּחְתּוֹנִית slip
☐	*(Hah-zee-yah)* חֲזִיָּה brassiere
☐	*(taH-toh-neem)* תַּחְתּוֹנִים underpants
☐	*(gar-bah-yeem)* גַּרְבַּיִם socks
☐	*(gar-bee-oh-neem)* גַּרְבִּיּוֹנִים pantyhose
☐	*(pee-zhah-mah)* פִּיגָ׳מָה pajamas
☐	*(lie-lah)* *(koo-toh-net)* כֻּתֹּנֶת לַיְלָה nightshirt
☐	*(Hah-look)* חָלוּק bathrobe
☐	*(bite)* *(nah-aH-lay)* נַעֲלֵי בַּיִת slippers

From now on, אַתָּה have " *(sah-bohn)* סַבּוֹן " and not "soap." Having assembled these דְּבָרִים you are ready

for your *(nuh-see-ah)* נְסִיעָה . Let's add these important shopping phrases to your basic repertoire.

(mee-dah) *(ay-zoh)*
אֵיזוֹ מִידָה ?
size · which

(mah-tim) *(zeh)*
זֶה מַתְאִים .
fits · it

(mah-tim) *(loh)* *(zeh)*
זֶה לֹא מַתְאִים .
does not fit · it

105

Treat yourself to a final review. אַתָּה know הַשֵּׁמוֹת *(hah-sheh-moht)* for חֲנוּיוֹת *(Hah-noo-yoht)* בְּיִשְׂרָאֵל, so let's
the names

practice shopping. Just remember your basic שְׁאֵלוֹת *(shuh-eh-loht)* that you learned in Step 2. Whether

אַתָּה need to buy אַסְפִּירִין *(ahs-pee-reen)* or תַּפּוּחִים *(tah-poo-Heem)* the necessary מִלִּים are the same.
apples

1.   First step — אֵיפֹה ?

איפֹה יֵשׁ חֲנוּת צִילוּם ? *(tsee-loom) (Hah-noot)* • איפֹה יֵשׁ בַּנְק ? *(bahnk)* • איפֹה יֵשׁ קוֹלְנוֹעַ ? *(kohl-noh-ah)*
cinema

_____
(Where is the department store?)

_____
(Where is the grocery store?)

_____
(Where is the market?)

2.   Second step — tell them מַה אַתָּה רוֹצֶה אוֹ מַה אַתָּה צָרִיךְ . *(tsah-reeH) (mah) (roht-seh) (mah)*
need

אֲנִי צָרִיךְ... *(tsah-reeH)* • אֲנִי רוֹצֶה... *(roht-seh)* • יֵשׁ לְךָ ... ? *(luh-Hah) (yesh)* • יֵשׁ לָךְ ... ? *(lahH) (yesh)*
do you have (♂) do you have (♀)

_____
(Do you have postcards?)

_____
(I want four stamps, please.)

_____
(I need toothpaste.)

_____
(I want to buy film.)

_____
(Do you have coffee?)

Go through the glossary at the end of this סֵפֶר and select עֶשְׂרִים מִלִּים *(es-reem)* . Drill the above

patterns עִם these עֶשְׂרִים מִלִּים . Don't cheat. Drill them הַיּוֹם *(hah-yohm)* . Now, take עֶשְׂרִים more

מִלִּים from your glossary וּ do the same.

---

3.   Third step — find out כַּמָּה *(kah-mah)* זֶה *(zeh)* עוֹלֶה *(oh-leh)* ?

כַּמָּה עוֹלֶה הַבּוּל *(hah-bool)* ?   כַּמָּה עוֹלָה הַגְּלוּיָה *(hah-gloo-yah)* *(oh-lah)* ?   כַּמָּה עוֹלֶה קִילוֹ *(kee-loh)* תַּפּוּחִים *(tah-poo-Heem)* ?
                                                                                                          kilo   apples

_____

(How much does the toothpaste cost?)

_____

(How much does the soap cost?)

_____

(How much does a cup of tea cost?)

---

4.   Fourth step — success! I found it!

Once אַתָּה find what אַתָּה רוֹצֶה say,

_____   אֲנִי רוֹצֶה אֶת *(et)* זֶה *(zeh)* בְּבַקָּשָׁה.
                                                                           this

or

_____   בְּסֵדֶר *(beh-say-dair)*, אֶקַּח *(eh-kaH)* אֶת *(et)* זֶה.
                                                          okay   I'll take it

Or, if אַתָּה would not like it,

_____   אֲנִי לֹא *(loh)* רוֹצֶה אֶת *(et)* זֶה *(zeh)*, תּוֹדָה *(toh-dah)*.

or

_____   לֹא *(loh)* בְּבַקָּשָׁה *(bay-vah-kah-shah)*.
                                                          no   thank you

Congratulations! You have finished. By now you should have stuck your labels, flashed your

cards, cut out your menu guide and packed your suitcases. You should be very pleased with your

accomplishment. You have learned what it sometimes takes others years to achieve and you

hopefully had fun doing it.   נְסִיעָה *(nuh-see-ah)* טוֹבָה *(toh-vah)* !   **107**

Glossary

This glossary contains words used in this book only. It is not meant to be a dictionary. Consider purchasing a dictionary which best suits your needs - small for traveling, large for reference, or specialized for specific vocabulary needs.

Your glossary is organized in Hebrew alphabetical order starting with "א." Read each column from right to left. On the right is the Hebrew word, then the pronunciation and finally the English meaning.

א

father	(ah-bah)	אַבָּא
I lost the	(et) (ee-bah-deh-tee)	אִבַּדְתִּי אֶת
spring	(ah-veev)	אָבִיב
lake	(ah-gahm)	אֲגַם
red	(ah-dohm)	אָדֹם
sir	(ah-doh-nee)	אֲדוֹנִי
or	(oh)	אוֹ
August	(oh-goost)	אוֹגוּסְט
autograph	(oh-toh-grahf)	אוֹטוֹגְרַף
vending machine	(oh-toh-maht)	אוֹטוֹמָט
air	(ah-veer)	אֲוִיר
(we) say	(ohm-rim)	אוֹמְרִים
Australia	(oh-strahl-yah)	אוֹסְטְרַלְיָה
opera	(oh-peh-rah)	אוֹפֵּרָה
baker	(oh-feh)	אוֹפֶה
bicycle	(oh-fah-nah-yeem)	אוֹפַנַּיִם
motorcycle	(oh-fah-noh-ah)	אוֹפַנוֹעַ
October	(ohk-toh-bair)	אוֹקְטוֹבֶּר
brother	(aH)	אָח
nurse, sister	(ah-Hoht)	אָחוֹת
afternoon	(hah-tsoh-hoh-rah-yeem) (aH-ah-ray)	אַחֲרֵי הַצָּהֳרַיִם
one	(aH-aht)	אַחַת
eleven	(es-ray) (aH-aht)	אַחַת עֶשְׂרֵה
butcher shop	(eet-leez)	אִטְלִיז
aerograms	(ah-veer) (ee-gair-et)	אִגֶּרֶת אֲוִיר
which	(ay-zoh)	אֵיזוֹ
how	(ayH)	אֵיךְ
Italian	(ee-tahl-keet)	אִיטַלְקִית
Italy	(ee-tahl-yah)	אִיטַלְיָה
no exit	(yuh-tsee-ah) (ayn)	אֵין יְצִיאָה
no entrance, do not enter	(kuh-nee-sah) (ayn)	אֵין כְּנִיסָה
Europe	(ay-roh-pah)	אֵירוֹפָּה
European	(ay-roh-pee)	אֵירוֹפִּי
farmer	(ee-kar)	אִכָּר
infection	(in-fek-tsee-yah)	אִנְפֶקְצִיָה
where	(ay-foh)	אֵיפֹה
Ireland	(eer-lahnd)	אִירְלַנְד
man	(eesh)	אִישׁ
into, to	(el)	אֶל
photo album	(tmoo-noht) (ahl-bohm)	אַלְבּוֹם תְמוּנוֹת
El Al	(ahl) (el)	אֶל עַל
algebra	(ahl-geh-brah)	אַלְגֶבְּרָה
elegant	(eh-leh-gahn-tee)	אֶלֶגַנְטִי
alcohol	(ahl-koh-hohl)	אַלְכּוֹהוֹל
alphabet	(bait) (ah-lef)	אָלֶף בֵּית
one thousand	(el-ef)	אֶלֶף
electronic	(eh-lek-troh-nee)	אֶלֶקְטְרוֹנִי
mother	(ee-mah)	אִמָא
ambulance	(ahm-boo-lahns)	אַמְבּוּלַנְס
artist	(oh-mahn)	אָמָן
America	(ah-meh-ree-kah)	אֲמֶרִיקָה

Latin America	(hah-lah-tee-neet) (ah-meh-ree-kah)	אֲמֶרִיקָה הַלָטִינִית
American (man)	(ah-meh-ree-kahn-ee)	אֲמֶרִיקָנִי
American woman	(ah-meh-ree-kahn-eet)	אֲמֶרִיקָנִית
English man	(ahn-glee)	אַנְגְלִי
England	(ahn-glee-yah)	אַנְגְלִיָה
English woman	(ahn-glee-yah)	אַנְגְלִיָה
we	(ah-naH-noo)	אֲנַחְנוּ
I	(ah-nee)	אֲנִי
pineapple	(ah-nah-nahs)	אֲנָנָס
antibiotic	(ahn-tee-bee-oh-tee-kah)	אַנְטִיבִּיוֹטִיקָה
energy	(eh-nairg-yah)	אֶנֶרְגִיָה
people	(ah-nah-sheem)	אֲנָשִׁים
Asia	(ahs-yah)	אַסְיָה
token	(ah-see-mohn)	אַסִימוֹן
aspirin	(ahs-pee-reen)	אַסְפִּירִין
April	(ah-pril)	אַפְּרִיל
baked	(ah-foo-ee)	אָפוּי
gray	(ah-for)	אָפוֹר
zero	(ef-es)	אֶפֶס
Africa	(ah-free-kah)	אַפְרִיקָה
African	(ah-free-kahn-ee)	אַפְרִיקָנִי
(is it) possible	(ef-shar)	אֶפְשָׁר
I'll take it	(zeh)(et)(eh-kaH)	אֶקַח אֶת זֶה
academy	(ah-kah-deh-mee-yah)	אֲקַדְמִיָה
four	(ar-bah)	אַרְבַּע
fourty	(ar-bah-eem)	אַרְבָּעִים
fourteen	(es-ray) (ar-bah)	אַרְבַּע עֶשְׂרֵה
long	(ah-roH)	אָרֹךְ
meal	(ah-roo-Hah)	אֲרוּחָה
closet, wardrobe, cupboard	(ah-rohn)	אָרוֹן
breakfast	(boh-kair) (ah-roo-Haht)	אֲרוּחַת בֹּקֶר
dinner	(eh-rev) (ah-roo-Haht)	אֲרוּחַת עֶרֶב
lunch	(tsoh-hoh-rah-yeem) (ah-roo-Haht)	אֲרוּחַת צָהֳרַיִם
wallet	(ar-nahk)	אַרְנָק
grapefruit	(esh-kohl-yoht)	אֶשְׁכּוֹלִיוֹת
counter	(esh-nahv)	אֶשְׁנָב
you	(aht)	אַתְּ
indicator of a direct object, this	(et)	אֶת
you	(ah-tah)	אַתָה
Do you take.	(meh-kah-bleem) (ah-tem)	אַתֶם מְקַבְּלִים
yesterday	(et-mohl)	אֶתְמוֹל

ב

in, in the	(bah)	בַּ
on, in	(buh)	בְּ
in the morning	(bah-boh-kair)	בַּבֹּקֶר
please, you're welcome	(bay-vah-kah-shah)	בְּבַקָשָׁה
swimsuit	(yahm) (beg-ed)	בֶּגֶד יָם
Bedouin clothing	(bed-wee-yeem) (buh-gah-deem)	בְּגָדִים בֶּדְוִויִים
grilled	(bee-gril)	בִּגְרִיל
Bedouin	(bed-oo-ee)	בֶּדוּאִי

by airmail	(ah-veer) (buh-doh-ar)	בְּדוֹאַר אֲוִיר
good luck	(buh-hahts-lah-Hah)	בְּהַצְלָחָה
stamp	(bool)	בּוּל
Bulgaria	(bool-gah-ree-yah)	בּוּלְגַּרְיָה
boss	(bohs)	בּוֹס
between	(bane)	בֵּין
international	(lay-oo-mee) (bane)	בֵּין לְאוּמִי
medium	(bay-noh-nee)	בֵּינוֹנִי
in Israel	(buh-yiss-rah-el)	בְּיִשְׂרָאֵל
eggs	(bay-tseem)	בֵּיצִים
house	(bite)	בַּיִת
hospital	(Hoh-leem) (bait)	בֵּית חוֹלִים
factory	(Hah-roh-shet) (bait)	בֵּית חֲרֹשֶׁת
synagogue	(kness-et) (bait)	בֵּית כְּנֶסֶת
Bethlehem	(leh-Hem) (bait)	בֵּית לֶחֶם
workshop	(muh-lah-Hah) (bait)	בֵּית מְלָאכָה
pharmacy	(mair-kah-Haht) (bait)	בֵּית מִרְקַחַת
school	(sef-air) (bait)	בֵּית סֵפֶר
cafe	(kah-feh) (bait)	בֵּית קָפֶה
balloon	(bah-lon)	בַּלּוֹן
ballet	(bah-let)	בַּלֶּט
Belgium	(bel-gee-yah)	בֶּלְגִּיָה
son	(ben)	בֵּן
banana	(bah-nah-nah)	בָּנָנָה
bank	(bahnk)	בַּנְק
fine, okay	(beh-say-dair)	בְּסֵדֶר
in Hebrew	(beev-reet)	בְּעִבְרִית
in the evening	(bah-eh-rev)	בָּעֶרֶב
on the corner	(bah-pee-nah)	בַּפִּנָּה
morning	(boh-kair)	בֹּקֶר
good morning	(tohv) (boh-kair)	בֹּקֶר טוֹב
bar	(bar)	בַּר
healthy	(bah-ree)	בָּרִיא
meat	(bah-sar)	בָּשָׂר
beef	(bah-kar) (buh-sar)	בְּשַׂר בָּקָר
veal	(ay-gel) (buh-sar)	בְּשַׂר עֵגֶל
poultry	(ohf) (buh-sar)	בְּשַׂר עוֹף
mutton	(keh-ves) (buh-sar)	בְּשַׂר כֶּבֶשׂ
daughter	(baht)	בַּת
enjoy your meal	(buh-tay-ah-vohn)	בְּתֵאָבוֹן

ג

Mrs.	(gveh-ret)	גְּבֶרֶת
tall, high	(gah-voh-hah)	גָּבוֹהַּ
cheese	(gvee-nah)	גְּבִינָה
ladies	(gvah-roht)	גְּבָרוֹת
gentlemen	(gvah-reem)	גְּבָרִים
big	(gah-dohl)	גָּדוֹל
goulash	(goo-lahsh)	גּוּלָשׁ
undershirt	(goo-fee-yah)	גּוּפִיָּה
guitar	(gee-tah-rah)	גִּיטָרָה
jeans	(zheens)	גִּ'ינְס
postcard	(gloo-yah)	גְּלוּיָה
ice cream	(glee-doht)	גְּלִידוֹת
garden	(gahn)	גַּן
zoo	(Hah-yoht) (gahn)	גַּן חַיּוֹת
Garden of Eden	(ay-den) (gahn)	גַּן עֵדֶן
camel	(gah-mahl)	גָּמָל
pantyhose	(gar-bee-oh-neem)	גַּרְבִּיוֹנִים
socks	(gar-bah-yeem)	גַּרְבַּיִם
German	(gair-mah-neet)	גֶּרְמָנִית
Germany	(gair-mahn-yah)	גֶּרְמַנְיָה
rain	(gesh-em)	גֶּשֶׁם

bridge	(gesh-air)	גֶּשֶׁר
Gethsemane	(shmah-neem) (gaht)	גַּת שְׁמָנִים

ד

things	(dvah-rim)	דְּבָרִים
herring	(mah-loo-aH) (dahg)	דַּג מָלוּחַ
fish	(dah-geem)	דָּגִים
flag	(deg-el)	דֶּגֶל
mail	(doh-ar)	דּוֹאַר
uncle	(dohd)	דּוֹד
aunt	(doh-dah)	דּוֹדָה
felafel stand	(doo-Hahn)	דּוּכָן
mailman	(dah-var)	דַּוָּר
push	(duh-Hohf)	דְּחוֹף
deodorant	(day-oh-doh-rahnt)	דֵּיאוֹדוֹרַנְט
diet	(dee-eh-tah)	דִּיאֶטָה
dialogue	(dee-ah-lohg)	דִּיאָלוֹג
fisherman	(dah-yahg)	דַּיָּג
stewardess	(dah-yel-et)	דַּיֶּלֶת
gas	(del-ek)	דֶּלֶק
door	(deh-let)	דֶּלֶת
democracy	(deh-moh-krah-tee-yah)	דֶּמוֹקְרַטְיָה
service charge	(shay-root) (d'may)	דְּמֵי שֵׁירוּת
December	(deh-tsem-bair)	דֶּצֶמְבֶּר
minutes	(dah-koht)	דַּקּוֹת
south	(dah-rohm)	דָּרוֹם
road	(deh-reH)	דֶּרֶךְ
South America	(ah-meh-ree-kah) (d'rohm)	דָּרוֹם אֲמֶרִיקָה
South Africa	(ah-free-kah) (d'rohm)	דָּרוֹם אַפְרִיקָה
South Korea	(koh-ray-ah) (d'rohm)	דָּרוֹם קוֹרֵיאָה
passport	(dar-kohn)	דַּרְכּוֹן
religion	(daht)	דָּת

ה

reservation	(hahz-mah-nah)	הַזְמָנָה
room reservation*	(Heh-dair) (hiz-mahn-tee)	הִזְמַנְתִּי חֶדֶר
Holland	(hoh-lahnd)	הוֹלַנְד
Dutch	(hoh-lahn-dee)	הוֹלַנְדִי
hormone	(hor-mohn)	הוֹרְמוֹן
he	(hoo)	הוּא
she	(hee)	הִיא
today	(hah-yohm)	הַיּוֹם
historic	(hee-stoh-ree)	הִיסְטוֹרִי
history	(hee-stoh-ree-yah)	הִיסְטוֹרְיָה
parents	(hoh-reem)	הוֹרִים
everything	(hah-kohl)	הַכֹּל
hello	(hah-loh)	הַלּוֹ
round trip	(vah-shohv) (hah-loH)	הָלוֹךְ וָשׁוֹב
they	(hem)	הֵם
information	(moh-dee-een)	מוֹדִיעִין
traveler's checks	(noh-seem) (hahm-Hah-oht)	הַמְחָאוֹת נוֹסְעִים
(plane) departure	(hahm-rah-ah)	הַמְרָאָה
here (are)	(hin-ay)	הִנֵּה
help	(hah-tsee-loo)	הַצִּילוּ
the line	(hah-kahv)	הַקַּו
a lot	(har-bay)	הַרְבֵּה

Did you have fun learning your new language? We at Bilingual Books hope you enjoy your travels wherever they might take you.

109

ו

and	וְ (vuh)
dry river bed, wadi	וָאדִי (vah-dee)
Washington	וושינגטון (vah-sheeng-tohn)
half past	וָחֵצִי (vah-Hay-tsee)
viola	וִיוֹלָה (vee-oh-lah)
curtain	וִילוֹן (vee-lohn)
virus	וִירוּס (vee-roos)
virtuoso	וִירטוּאוֹזִי (veer-too-ohz)
a quarter after	וָרֶבַע (vah-rev-ah)
pink	וָרוֹד (vah-rohd)

ז

zebra	זֶבּרָה (zeb-rah)
it (is)	זֶה (zeh)
it takes	זֶה לוֹקֵחַ (zeh) (loh-kay-aH)
it fits	זֶה מַתאִים (zeh) (mah-tim)
zoology	זוֹאוֹלוֹגיָה (zoh-oh-lohg-yah)
memorial	זִיכָּרוֹן (zih-kah-rohn)
cheap	זוֹל (zohl)
time	זמַן (zeh-mahn)
singer	זַמָר (zah-mar)
old	זָקֵן (zah-ken)
jacket, blazer	ז'קֶט (zhah-ket)

ח

package	חֲבִילָה (Hah-vee-lah)
friends	חֲבֵרִים (Hah-vair-eem)
Happy Holiday	חַג שָׂמֵחַ (sah-may-aH) (Hahg)
dining room	חֲדַר אוֹכֶל (Hah-dar) (oh-Hel)
bathroom	חֲדַר אַמבַּטיָה (Hah-dar) (ahm-baht-yah)
office, study	חֲדַר עֲבוֹדָה (Hah-dar) (ah-voh-dah)
bedroom	חֲדַר שֵׁינָה (Hah-dar) (shay-nah)
room	חֶדֶר (Hed-air)
double room	חֶדֶר לְזוּג (Heh-dair) (lay-zoog)
single room	חֶדֶר לְיָחִיד (Heh-dair) (lay-yah-Heed)
new	חֲדָשׁוֹת (Hah-dah-shoht)
sick	חוֹלֶה (Hoh-leh)
blouse	חוּלצָה (Hool-tsah)
t-shirt	חוּלצַת טִי (Hool-tsaht) (tee)
brown	חוּם (Hoom)
brassiere	חֲזִיָה (Hah-zee-yah)
strong	חֲזָקָה (Hah-zah-kah)
humus	חוּמוּס (Hoo-moos)
milk	חָלָב (Hah-lahv)
window	חַלוֹן (Hah-lohn)
bathrobe	חָלוּק (Hah-look)
suit	חֲלִיפָה (Hah-lee-fah)
hot	חַם (Hahm)
butter	חֶמאָה (Hem-ah)
five	חָמֵשׁ (Hah-mesh)
five hundred	חֲמֵשׁ מֵאוֹת (Hah-mesh) (may-oht)
fifteen	חֲמֵשׁ עֶשׂרֵה (Hah-mesh) (es-ray)
fifty	חֲמִישִׁים (Hah-mee-sheem)
Festival of Lights	חֲנוּכָּה (Hah-noo-kah)
fish store	חֲנוּת דָגִים (Hah-noot) (dah-geem)
department store	חֲנוּת כֹּל - בּוֹ (Hah-noot) (kohl-boh)
stationery store	חֲנוּת כּלֵי כּתִיבָה (Hah-noot)(klay)(ktee-vah)
grocery store	חֲנוּת מַכֹּלֶת (Hah-noot) (mah-koh-let)
candy store	חֲנוּת מַמתַקִים (Hah-noot)(mahm-tah-keem)
delicatessen	חֲנוּת מַעֲדָנִים (Hah-noot) (mah-ah-dah-neem)
gift store	חֲנוּת מַתָנוֹת (Hah-noot) (mah-tah-noht)
book store	חֲנוּת סֹפָרִים (Hah-noot) (sfah-reem)
flower shop	חֲנוּת פּרָחִים (Hah-noot) (prah-Heem)
photo store	חֲנוּת צִילוּם (Hah-noot) (tsee-loom)
jewelry store	חֲנוּת תַכשִׁיטִים (Hah-noot)(taH-shee-teem)
skirt	חֲצָאִית (Hah-tsah-eet)
winter	חֹרֶף (Hoh-ref)
bill	חֶשׁבּוֹן (Hesh-bohn)
important	חָשׁוּב (Hah-shoov)
cat	חָתוּל (Hah-tool)

ט

chef	טַבָּח (tah-baH)
good	טוֹב (tohv)
tehina	טְחִינָה (tuh-Hee-nah)
windmill	טַחֲנַת רוּחַ (tah-Hah-naht) (roo-aH)
pilot	טַיָס (tah-yahs)
international flight	טִיסָה בֵּין לְאוּמִית (tee-sah) (bane) (luh-oo-meet)
domestic flight	טִיסָה פּנִים אַרצִית (tee-sah) (pnim) (ar-tseet)
technician	טֶכנַאי (teH-nah-ee)
technology	טֶכנוֹלוֹגיָה (teH-noh-lohg-yah)
(university) Technion	טֶכנִיוֹן (teH-nee-ohn)
television	טֶלֶוִיזיָה (tel-eh-vee-zee-yah)
telescope	טֶלֶסקוֹפ (teh-leh-skohp)
telephone	טֶלֶפוֹן (teh-leh-fohn)
public telephone	טֶלֶפוֹן צִיבּוּרִי (teh-leh-fohn) (tsih-boo-ree)
temperatures	טֶמפֶּרָטוּרוֹת (tem-peh-rah-too-roht)
tennis	טֶנִיס (teh-nis)
table tennis	טֶנִיס שׁוּלחָן (teh-nis) (shool-Hahn)
driver's license test	טֶסט (test)
I'm lost.	טָעִיתִי בַּדֶרֶך (tah-ee-tee) (bah-dair-eH)
taxi	טַקסִי (tahk-see)
text	טֶקסט (text)
textiles	טֶקסטִיל (teks-teel)
tragedy	טרָגֶדיָה (trah-geh-deh-yah)
tropical	טרוֹפִּי (troh-pee)
tractor	טרַקטוֹר (trahk-tor)

י

Jewish man	יְהוּדִי (yuh-hoo-dee)
Jewish woman	יְהוּדִיָה (yuh-hoo-dee-yah)
diamond	יַהֲלוֹם (yah-hah-lohm)
jubilee	יוֹבֵל (yoh-vel)
yoghurt	יוֹגוּרט (yoh-goort)
yoga	יוֹגָה (yoh-gah)
July	יוּלִי (yoo-lee)
day	יוֹם (yohm)
birthday	יוֹם הוֹלֶדֶת (yohm) (hoo-led-et)
Day of Independence	יוֹם הָעַצמָאוּת (yohm) (hah-ahtz-mah-oot)
Thursday	יוֹם חֲמִישִׁי (yohm) (Hah-mee-shee)
Day of Atonement	יוֹם כִּיפּוּר (yohm) (kih-poor)
Sunday	יוֹם רִאשׁוֹן (yohm) (ree-shohn)
Wednesday	יוֹם רְבִיעִי (yohm) (reh-veh-ee)
Saturday	יוֹם שַׁבָּת (yohm) (shah-baht)
Friday	יוֹם שִׁישִׁי (yohm) (shee-shee)
Tuesday	יוֹם שׁלִישִׁי (yohm) (shlee-shee)
Monday	יוֹם שֵׁנִי (yohm) (sheh-nee)

Greece	(yah-vahn)	יָוָן
June	(yoo-nee)	יוּנִי
comes down	(yoh-red)	יוֹרֵד
wine	(yah-yeen)	יַיִן
I can	(yah-Hohl)	יָכוֹל
child	(yel-ed)	יֶלֶד
children	(yuh-lah-deem)	יְלָדִים
sea	(yahm)	יָם
Dead Sea	(hah-mel-aH) (yahm)	יָם הַמֶּלַח
right	(yah-meen)	יָמִין
to the right	(yuh-mee-nah)	יָמִינָה
January	(yah-noo-ar)	יָנוּאָר
forest	(yah-ahr)	יַעַר
Japan	(yah-pahn)	יָפָן
Japanese	(yah-pah-nee)	יַפָּנִי
exit	(yuh-tsee-ah)	יְצִיאָה
(bus/train) departure	(yuh-tsee-ah)	יְצִיאָה
expensive	(yah-kar)	יָקָר
too expensive	(mee-die) (yah-kar)	יָקָר מִדַּי
Jordan	(yar-dane)	יַרְדֵּן
green	(yah-rok)	יָרוֹק
Jerusalem	(yuh-roo-shah-lah-yeem)	יְרוּשָׁלַיִם
vegetables	(yuh-rah-koht)	יְרָקוֹת
greengrocer	(yar-kahn)	יַרְקָן
there is	(yesh)	יֵשׁ
do you have? (♠)	(lahH) (yesh)	יֵשׁ לָךְ ?
I have	(lee) (yesh)	יֵשׁ לִי
we have	(lah-noo) (yesh)	יֵשׁ לָנוּ
straight ahead	(yah-shar)	יָשָׁר
Jesus	(yeh-shoo)	יֵשׁוּ
Israel	(yiss-rah-el)	יִשְׂרָאֵל

כ

fireman	(kah-by)	כַּבַּאי
freeway	(mah-heer) (k'veesh)	כְּבִישׁ מָהִיר
ball	(kah-door)	כַּדּוּר
baseball	(bah-sees) (kah-door)	כַּדּוּר בָּסִיס
basketball	(sahl) (kah-door)	כַּדּוּר סַל
soccer	(kah-doo-reg-el)	כַּדּוּרְגֶּל
priest	(koh-hen)	כֹּהֵן
glass	(kohs)	כּוֹס
the water glass	(hah-mah-yeem) (kohs)	כּוֹס הַמַּיִם
wine glass	(yah-yeen) (kohs)	כּוֹס יַיִן
shirt	(koo-toh-net)	כֻּתֹּנֶת
nightshirt	(lie-lah) (koo-toh-net)	כֻּתֹּנֶת לַיְלָה
blue	(kah-Hohl)	כָּחוֹל
one-way	(eh-Hahd) (kee-vuhn)	כִּוּוּן אֶחָד
chair	(kis-eh)	כִּסֵּא
cotton	(koot-nah)	כֻּתְנָה
washstand	(kee-yor)	כִּיּוֹר
yarmulke, dome	(kee-pah)	כִּפָּה
Dome of the Rock	(hah-sel-ah) (kee-paht)	כִּפַּת הַסֶּלַע
how often (time)	(zmahn)(kah-mah)(kohl)	כָּל כַּמָּה זְמָן
dog	(kel-ev)	כֶּלֶב
copper and brass goods	(neh-Hoh-shet) (klay)	כְּלֵי נְחֹשֶׁת
how much	(kah-mah)	כַּמָּה
yes	(ken)	כֵּן
entrance	(kuh-nee-sah)	כְּנִיסָה
churches	(kness-ee-yoht)	כְּנֵסִיּוֹת
Knesset	(kness-et)	כְּנֶסֶת
money	(kes-ef)	כֶּסֶף
spoon	(kah-peet)	כַּפִּית

village	(kfar)	כְּפָר
Capernaum	(nah-Hoom) (kfar)	כְּפַר נַחוּם
pillow	(kar)	כַּר
ticket	(kar-tees)	כַּרְטִיס
credit card	(ahsh-rye) (kar-tees)	כַּרְטִיס אַשְׁרַאי
ticket collector	(kar-tee-sahn)	כַּרְטִיסָן
Carmel	(kar-mel)	כַּרְמֶל
kosher	(kah-shair)	כָּשֵׁר
purity	(kahsh-root)	כַּשְׁרוּת
address	(k'toh-vet)	כְּתֹבֶת
orange	(kah-tohm)	כָּתֹם

ל

before, a quarter to, to	(luh)	לְ
no	(loh)	לֹא
slow, slowly	(luh-aht)	לְאַט
to eat	(leh-eh-Hohl)	לֶאֱכוֹל
to America	(lah-ah-meh-ree-kah)	לְאָמֶרִיקָה
to pack	(leh-ah-rohz)	לֶאֱרֹז
to come	(lah-voh)	לָבוֹא
Lebanon	(luh-vah-nohn)	לְבָנוֹן
linen, lingerie	(luh-vah-nim)	לְבָנִים
to order	(luh-vah-kesh)	לְבַקֵּשׁ
to speak	(luh-dah-bair)	לְדַבֵּר
to know	(lah-dah-aht)	לָדַעַת
to understand	(luh-hah-veen)	לְהָבִין
to arrive	(luh-hah-gee-ah)	לְהַגִּיעַ
to reserve, order	(luh-hahz-meen)	לְהַזְמִין
to enter	(luh-hih-kah-ness)	לְהִכָּנֵס
to stay	(luh-hish-ah-air)	לְהִשָׁאֵר
goodbye	(luh-hee-trah-oht)	לְהִתְרָאוֹת
timetable	(zmah-neem) (loo-aH)	לוּחַ זְמַנִּים
calendar	(shah-nah) (loo-aH)	לוּחַ שָׁנָה
go	(leH)	לֵךְ
to repeat	(ahl) (lah-Hah-zor)	לַחֲזוֹר עַל
to wait for	(luh) (luh-Hah-koht)	לְחַכּוֹת לְ
bread	(leh-Hem)	לֶחֶם
to say	(loh-mar)	לוֹמַר
London	(lohn-dohn)	לוֹנְדוֹן
luxury	(look-soos)	לוּקְסוּס
to look for	(luh-Hah-pes)	לְחַפֵּשׂ
to fly	(lah-toos)	לָטוּס
Latin	(lah-tee-neet)	לָטִינִית
to phone	(luh) (luh-tahl-pane)	לְטַלְפֵּן לְ
liberal	(lee-beh-rah-lee)	לִיבֶּרָלִי
league	(lee-gah)	לִיגָה
liter	(lee-tair)	לִיטֶר
night	(lie-lah)	לַיְלָה
good night	(tohv) (lie-lah)	לַיְלָה טוֹב
lemon	(lee-mohn)	לִימוֹן
lemonade	(lee-moh-nah-dah)	לִימוֹנָדָה
to sleep	(lee-shohn)	לִישׁוֹן
to wash (clothes)	(luh-Hah-bes)	לְכַבֵּס
to write	(liH-tohv)	לִכְתּוֹב
to learn	(lil-mohd)	לִלְמֹד
why	(lah-mah)	לָמָה
below, downstairs	(luh-mah-tah)	לְמַטָּה
to sell	(lim-kor)	לִמְכּוֹר
upstairs, above	(luh-mah-uh-lah)	לְמַעְלָה
to drive	(lin-hohg)	לִנְהוֹג
to travel	(lin-soh-ah)	לִנְסוֹעַ
to board	(ahl) (lah-ah-loht)	לַעֲלוֹת עַל
in front of	(lif-nay)	לִפְנֵי

to exit, leave, depart	(lah-tset) לָצֵאת
to buy	(lik-noht) לִקְנוֹת
to read	(lik-roh) לִקְרוֹא
to see	(luh-roht) לִרְאוֹת
to disembark, get off	(lah-red-et) לָרֶדֶת
to want	(leer-tsoht) לִרְצוֹת
to send	(lish-loh-aH) לִשְׁלוֹחַ
to pay	(luh-shah-lem) לְשַׁלֵם
to drink	(lish-toht) לִשְׁתּוֹת

מ

out of/from	(may) מ
out of/from	(me) מ
one hundred	(may-ah) מֵאָה
very	(may-ohd) מְאֹד
behind	(meh-ah-Hoh-ray) מֵאֲחוֹרֵי
May	(my) מַאי
from where	(may-ay-foh) מֵאֵיפֹה
bakery	(mah-ah-fee-yah) מַאֲפִיָה
cooked	(muh-voo-shahl) מְבוּשָׁל
well-done	(muh-voo-shahl-hey-tev) מְבוּשָׁל הֵיטֵב
telegram	(miv-rahk) מִבְרָק
toothbrush	(shee-nah-yeem) (meev-resh-et) מִבְרֶשֶׁת שִׁנַיִם
towels	(mah-gah-voht) מַגָבוֹת
tower	(mig-dahl) מִגְדָל
Tower of David	(dah-veed) (mig-dahl) מִגְדָל דָוִד
control tower	(pih-koo-aH) (mig-dahl) מִגְדָל פִיקוּחַ
scroll	(muh-gee-lah) מְגִילָה
Dead Sea Scrolls	(hah-mel-aH)(yahm)(muh-gee-loht) מְגִילוֹת יָם הַמֶלַח
arrives	(mah-gee-ah) מַגִיעַ
boots	(mah-gah-fah-yeem) מַגָפַיִם
parking lot	(Hah-nee-yah) (meeg-rahsh) מִגְרָשׁ חֲנָיָה
desert	(mid-bar) מִדְבָּר
sidewalk	(mid-rah-Hah) מִדְרָכָה
what	(mah) מָה
What time is it?	(hah-shah-ah) (mah) ? מָה הַשָׁעָה
how are you (♂)	(shlohm-Hah) (mah) מָה שְׁלוֹמְךָ
how are you (♀)	(shloh-mayH) (mah) מָה שְׁלוֹמֵךְ
What is your name?	(sheem-Hah) (mah) ? מָה שִׁמְךָ
fast	(mah-hair) מַהֵר
museum	(moo-zay-ohn) מוּזֵיאוֹן
Muhammed	(moo-Hah-mahd) מוּחֲמָד
taxi	(moh-neet) מוֹנִית
garage	(moo-saH) מוּסָךְ
music	(moo-see-kah) מוּסִיקָה
fork	(mahz-leg) מַזְלֵג
Muslim man	(moo-sluh-mee) מוּסְלְמִי
Muslim woman	(moo-sluh-meet) מוּסְלְמִית
teacher (♀)	(moh-rah) מוֹרָה
cooperative farm/moshav	(moh-shahv) מוֹשָׁב
weather	(hah-ah-veer) (meh-zeg) מֶזֶג הָאֲוִיר
suitcase	(miz-vah-dah) מִזְוָדָה
souvenirs	(mahz-kah-roht) מַזְכָּרוֹת
Congratulations	(tohv) (mah-zahl) מַזָל טוֹב
computer	(maH-shev) מַחְשֵׁב
tomorrow	(mah-Har) מָחָר
east	(miz-raH) מִזְרָח
East Africa	(ah-free-kah) (miz-rah) מִזְרָח אַפְרִיקָה
kitchen	(meet-baH) מִטְבָּח
fried	(muh-too-gahn) מְטוּגָן
orchard	(mah-tah) מַטָע
meter	(meh-tair) מֶטֶר
umbrella	(meet-ree-ah) מִטְרִיָה
who	(me) מִי
size	(mee-dah) מִידָה
bed	(mee-tah) מִטָּה
million	(meel-yohn) מִילְיוֹן
millionaire	(meel-yoh-nair) מִילְיוֹנֵר
milkshake	(milk-shake) מִילְק שֵׁייק
water	(mah-yim) מַיִם
on right	(mee-yah-meen) מִיָמִין
minimum	(mee-nee-moom) מִינִימוּם
missionary	(mees-yoh-nair) מִיסְיוֹנֵר
juice	(meets) מִיץ
laundry	(meeH-bah-sah) מִכְבָּסָה
mechanic	(muh-Hoh-nee) מְכוֹנַאי
car	(may-Hoh-neet) מְכוֹנִית
police car	(mish-tah-rah) (may-Hoh-neet) מְכוֹנִית מִשְׁטָרָה
sports car	(sport) (may-Hoh-neet) מְכוֹנִית סְפּוֹרְט
fuel tanker	(del-ek) (may-Hah-leet) מְכָלִית דֶלֶק
trousers	(meeH-nah-sah-yeem) מִכְנָסַיִם
shorts	(k'tsah-reem) (meeH-nah-sah-yeem) מִכְנָסַיִם קְצָרִים
letter	(miH-tahv) מִכְתָב
word	(mih-lah) מִלָה
dirty	(muh-looH-laH) מְלוּכְלָךְ
hotel	(mah-lohn) מָלוֹן
King David Hotel	(dah-veed)(hah-mel-eH)(mah-lohn) מָלוֹן הַמֶלֶךְ דָוִד
dictionary	(mih-lohn) מִלוֹן
salt	(mel-aH) מֶלַח
handkerchief	(meem-Hah-tah) מִמְחָטָה
king	(mel-eH) מֶלֶךְ
cucumbers	(muh-lahf-foh-nim) מְלָפְפוֹנִים
waiter	(mel-tsar) מֶלְצַר
waitress	(mel-tsah-reet) מֶלְצָרִית
stuffed	(muh-moo-lah) מְמוּלָא
lamp	(mnoh-rah) מְנוֹרָה
appetizers	(ree-shoh-noht) (mah-noht) מָנוֹת רִאשׁוֹנוֹת
(orchestra) conductor	(muh-nah-tsay-aH) מְנַצֵחַ
mosques	(mis-gah-deem) מִסְגָדִים
number	(mis-par) מִסְפָּר
restaurant	(mees-ah-dah) מִסְעָדָה
hairdresser	(mees-pah-rah) מִסְפָּרָה
numbers	(mis-pah-reem) מִסְפָּרִים
comb	(mahs-rek) מַסְרֵק
overcoat	(muh-eel) מְעִיל
raincoat	(gesh-em) (muh-eel) מְעִיל גֶשֶׁם
a little	(muh-aht) מְעַט
over	(lah) (may-ahl) מֵעַל לְ
degrees	(mah-ah-loht) מַעֲלוֹת
west	(mah-ah-rahv) מַעֲרָב
map	(mah-pah) מַפָּה
napkin	(mah-peet) מַפִּית
waterfall	(mah-yim) (mah-pahl) מַפַּל מַיִם
tablecloth	(shool-Hahn) (mah-paht) מַפַּת שׁוּלְחָן
key	(mahf-tay-aH) מַפְתֵחַ
camera	(mahts-leh-mah) מַצְלֵמָה
Egypt	(mits-rah-yim) מִצְרַיִם
seat	(mah-kohm) מָקוֹם
shower	(mik-lah-Haht) מִקְלַחַת
maximum	(mahk-see-moom) מַקְסִימוּם
refrigerator	(may-kah-reer) מְקָרֵר

Mr.	(mar)	מַר
margarine	(mar-gah-ree-nah)	מַרְגָּרִינָה
operator	(mair-kah-zahn)	מֶרְכָּזָן
soup	(mah-rahk)	מָרָק
March	(mairts)	מֶרְץ
marzipan	(mar-tsee-pahn)	מַרְצִיפָּן
basement	(mar-tef)	מַרְתֵּף
gas pump	(del-ek) (mah-sheh-vaht)	מַשְׁאֵבַת דֶּלֶק
Moses	(moh-sheh)	מֹשֶׁה
pull	(muh-shoH)	מָשׁוּךְ
toothpaste	(shee-nah-yeem) (mish-Haht)	מִשְׁחַת שִׁנַיִם
police	(mish-tah-rah)	מִשְׁטָרָה
Messiah	(mah-shee-aH)	מָשִׁיחַ
family	(mish-pah-Hah)	מִשְׁפָּחָה
beverages	(mahsh-kah-oht)	מַשְׁקָאוֹת
eyeglasses, sunglasses	(mish-kah-fah-yeem)	מִשְׁקָפַיִם
lost-and-found office	(hah-ah-veh-doht) (mis-rahd)	מִשְׂרַד הָאֲבֵידוֹת
truck	(mah-sah-eet)	מַשָּׂאִית
the post office	(hah-doh-ar) (mis-rahd)	מִשְׂרַד הַדֹּאַר
under	(lah) (mee-tah-Haht)	מִתַּחַת לְ
when	(mah-tie)	מָתַי
mathematics	(mah-tay-mah-tee-kah)	מָתֵמָטִיקָה
gift	(mah-tah-nah)	מַתָּנָה
olivewood presents	(zay-yit) (muh-etz) (mah-tah-noht)	מַתָּנוֹת מֵעֵץ זַיִת

נ

rare (cooked)	(nah)	נָא
prophet	(nah-vee)	נָבִיא
carpenter	(nah-gar)	נַגָּר
river	(nah-har)	נָהָר
Nahariya	(nah-hah-ree-yah)	נַהֲרִיָּה
November	(noh-vem-bair)	נוֹבֶמְבֶּר
traveler	(noh-say-ah)	נוֹסֵעַ
Christian man	(nohts-ree)	נוֹצְרִי
Christian woman	(nohts-ree-yah)	נוֹצְרִיָּה
Norway	(nor-veg-ee-yah)	נוֹרְבֶּגְיָה
arrival	(nuh-Hee-tah)	נְחִיתָה
stream	(nah-Hahl)	נַחַל
paper	(nyar)	נְיָר
New Zealand	(new-zee-lahnd)	נִיוּ - זִילַנְד
dry cleaners	(yah-vesh) (nee-koo-ee)	נִיקוּי יָבֵשׁ
short, low	(nah-mooH)	נָמוּךְ
harbor	(nah-mahl)	נָמָל
trip, journey	(nuh-see-ah)	נְסִיעָה
have a good trip	(toh-vah) (nuh-see-ah)	נְסִיעָה טוֹבָה
pleasant	(nah-eem)	נָעִים
slippers	(bite) (nah-ah-lay)	נַעֲלֵי בַּיִת
tennis shoes	(sport) (nah-ah-lay)	נַעֲלֵי סְפּוֹרְט
shoes	(nah-ah-lah-yeem)	נַעֲלַיִם
Nazareth	(nahts-raht)	נָצְרַת
candle	(nair)	נֵר
Netanya	(nuh-tahn-yah)	נְתַנְיָה

ס

grandfather	(sah-bah)	סַבָּא
grandmother	(sahv-tah)	סַבְתָּא
soap	(sah-bohn)	סַבּוֹן
closed	(sah-goor)	סָגוּר
closed	(sgoo-rah)	סְגוּרָה
soda water	(soh-dah)	סוֹדָה
sweater	(sved-air)	סְוֶדֶר

Feast of Tabernacles	(soo-koht)	סֻכּוֹת
sugar	(soo-kar)	סֻכָּר
travel agency	(nuh-see-oht) (soH-noot)	סוֹכְנוּת נְסִיעוֹת
Syria	(soo-ree-yah)	סוּרִיָּה
symphony	(seem-foh-nee-yah)	סִימְפוֹנְיָה
China	(seen)	סִין
Chinese	(see-nee)	סִינִי
boat	(see-rah)	סִירָה
fishing boat	(dah-yig) (see-raht)	סִירַת דַּיִג
knife	(sah-keen)	סַכִּין
wastepaper basket	(nyar-oht) (sahl)	סַל נְיָרוֹת
living room	(sah-lohn)	סָלוֹן
salad	(sah-laht)	סָלָט
excuse me	(slee-Hah)	סְלִיחָה
salmon	(sahl-mohn)	סַלְמוֹן
celery	(seh-leh-ree)	סֶלֶרִי
seminar	(seh-mee-nar)	סֶמִינָר
sandals	(sahn-dah-leem)	סַנְדָּלִים
razor	(gee-loo-aH) (sah-keen)	סַכִּין גִּילוּחַ
spaghetti	(spah-geh-tee)	סְפָּגֶטִי
sport	(sport)	סְפּוֹרְט
sofa	(sah-pah)	סַפָּה
September	(sep-tem-bair)	סֶפְּטֶמְבֶּר
cup	(sef-el)	סֵפֶל
book	(sef-air)	סֵפֶר
telephone book	(teh-leh-fohn) (sef-air)	סֵפֶר טֶלֶפוֹן
Spain	(sfah-rahd)	סְפָרַד
Spanish	(sfah-rah-dee)	סְפָרַדִי
ski	(skee)	סְקִי
Scandinavian	(skahn-dee-nah-vee)	סְקַנְדִּינָבִי
Scandinavia	(skahn-dee-nahv-yah)	סְקַנְדִּינָבְיָה
sardines	(sar-dee-neem)	סַרְדִּינִים
movie	(sair-et)	סֶרֶט
autumn	(stahv)	סְתָו

ע

Hebrew	(eev-reet)	עִבְרִית
tomatoes	(ahg-vah-n'yoht)	עַגְבָנִיּוֹת
cart	(ah-gah-lah)	עֲגָלָה
cake	(oo-gah)	עוּגָה
once more	(pahm) (ohd)	עוֹד פַּעַם
costs	(oh-leh)	עוֹלֶה
poultry	(ohf)	עוֹף
pencil	(ip-ah-rohn)	עִפָּרוֹן
pen	(et)	עֵט
on, above	(ahl)	עַל
next to	(yahd) (ahl)	עַל יַד
with	(eem)	עִם
page	(ah-mood)	עַמּוּד
tie	(ah-nee-vah)	עֲנִיבָה
poor	(ah-nee)	עָנִי
cloud	(ah-nahn)	עָנָן
tree	(ehts)	עֵץ
evening	(eh-rev)	עֶרֶב
good evening	(tohv) (eh-rev)	עֶרֶב טוֹב
Arab	(ah-rah-vee)	עֲרָבִי
Arabic	(ah-rah-veet)	עֲרָבִית
fog	(ah-rah-fel)	עֲרָפֶל
rich	(ah-sheer)	עָשִׁיר
ten	(es-air)	עֶשֶׂר

Don't forget your *Language Map*®!

twenty . . . . (es-reem) עֶשְׂרִים
newspaper . . . . (ih-tohn) עִתּוֹן
antique . . . . (ah-teek) עַתִּיק

פ

puzzle . . . . (pah-zel) פָּאזֶל
pie . . . . (pie) פַּאי
here is . . . . (poh) פֹּה
political . . . . (poh-lee-tee) פּוֹלִיטִי
politics . . . . (poh-lee-tee-kah) פּוֹלִיטִיקָה
policy . . . . (poh-lee-sah) פּוֹלִיסָה
popcorn . . . . (korn) (pohp) פּוֹפּ קוֹרְן
poker . . . . (poh-kair) פּוֹקֶר
pajamas . . . . (pee-zhah-mah) פִּיגָ'מָה
corner . . . . (pee-nah) פִּינָה
picnic . . . . (peek-neek) פִּיקְנִיק
pita . . . . (pee-tah) פִּיתָה
pepper . . . . (pil-pel) פִּלְפֵּל
turn . . . . (pneh) פְּנֵה
free . . . . (pah-noo-ee) פָּנוּי
domestic (internal) . . . . (pneem) פְּנִים
lantern . . . . (pah-nahs) פָּנָס
lamppost . . . . (pah-nahs-ruh-Hohv) פָּנָס רְחוֹב
Passover . . . . (pes-aH) פֶּסַח
statue . . . . (pes-el) פֶּסֶל
project . . . . (proh-yekt) פְּרוֹיֶקְט
fruit . . . . (peh-roht) פֵּרוֹת
flowers . . . . (prah-Heem) פְּרָחִים
permanent (hair) . . . . (pair-mah-nent) פֶּרְמָנֶנְט
park . . . . (park) פָּרְק
open . . . . (pah-too-aH) פָּתוּחַ
open . . . . (ptoo-Hah) פְּתוּחָה

פ

February . . . . (feb-roo-ar) פֶבְּרוּאָר
physical . . . . (fee-zee) פִיזִי
physicist . . . . (fee-zee-kah-ee) פִיזִיקָאי
physics . . . . (fee-zee-kah) פִיזִיקָה
film . . . . (film) פִילְם
Arab coffee set . . . . (feen-zhahn) פִינְגָ'ן
falafel . . . . (fah-lah-fel) פָלָפֵל
fantastic . . . . (fahn-tahs-tee) פַנְטַסְטִי
festival . . . . (fes-tee-vahl) פֶסְטִיבָל
fax . . . . (fahks) פַקְס
Fahrenheit . . . . (far-en-hite) פַרֶנְהַייְט

צ

painter . . . . (tsah-bah) צַבָּע
paint . . . . (tseh-vah) צֶבַע
colorful . . . . (tsiv-oh-nee) צִבְעוֹנִי
colors . . . . (ts'vah-eem) צְבָעִים
yellow . . . . (tsah-hohv) צָהוֹב
diver . . . . (tsoh-luh-lahn) צוֹלְלָן
civilization . . . . (tsee-vee-lee-zah-tsee-yah) צִיוִילִיזַצְיָה
painting . . . . (tsee-yoor) צִיּוּר
cynical . . . . (tsee-nee) צִינִי
bird . . . . (tsih-por) צִיפּוֹר
roasted . . . . (tsah-loo-ee) צָלוּי
plate . . . . (tsah-lah-Haht) צַלַּחַת
Celsius . . . . (tsel-see-oos) צֶלְסִיוּס
thirsty . . . . (tsah-may) צָמֵא
plant . . . . (tseh-maH) צֶמַח

I must, have to . . . . (tsah-reeH) צָרִיךְ
to need . . . . (tsah-reeH) צָרִיךְ
France . . . . (tsar-faht) צָרְפַת
French . . . . (tsar-fah-tee) צָרְפָתִי
young . . . . (tsah-eer) צָעִיר
north . . . . (tsah-fohn) צָפוֹן
North America . . . (ah-meh-ree-kah) (ts'fohn) צְפוֹן אַמֶרִיקָה
North Korea . . . . . . (koh-ray-ah) (ts'fohn) צְפוֹן קוֹרֵיאָה

ק

receipt . . . . (kah-bah-lah) קַבָּלָה
kibbutz . . . . (kee-boots) קִיבּוּץ
cinema . . . . (kohl-noh-ah) קוֹלְנוֹעַ
comedy . . . . (koh-meh-dee-ah) קוֹמֶדְיָה
ground floor . . . (ree-shoh-nah) (koh-mah) קוֹמָה רִאשׁוֹנָה
congress . . . . (kohn-gres) קוֹנְגְרֶס
conflict . . . . (kohn-fleekt) קוֹנְפְלִיקְט
concert . . . . (kohn-tsairt) קוֹנְצֶרְט
cashier . . . . (koo-pah-ee) קוּפַּאי
cocktail . . . . (kohk-tail) קוֹקְטֵייל
small . . . . (kah-tahn) קָטָן
kibbutz . . . . (kee-boots) קִיבּוּץ
city codes . . . . (kee-doh-met) קִידוֹמֶת
kiosk . . . . (kee-yohsk) קִיוֹסְק
dessert . . . . (kee-noo-aH) קִינוּחַ
summer . . . . (kah-yits) קַיִץ
easy . . . . (kahl) קַל
client . . . . (klee-ent) קְלַיְינְט
campus . . . . (kahm-poos) קַמְפּוּס
Canada . . . . (kah-nah-dah) קָנָדָה
coffee . . . . (kah-feh) קָפֶה
butcher . . . . (kah-tsahv) קַצָב
short . . . . (kah-tsar) קָצָר
little . . . . (k'tsaht) קְצָת
cold . . . . (kar) קַר
relatives . . . . (kroh-veem) קְרוֹבִים
motor home . . . . (kah-rah-vahn) קַרָוָון
ceramics . . . . (keh-rah-mee-kah) קֶרָמִיקָה
carp . . . . (kar-pee-ohn) קַרְפִּיוֹן
circus . . . . (keer-kahs) קִרְקָס
hard, difficult . . . . (kah-sheh) קָשֶה

ר

mirror . . . . (ruh-ee) רְאִי
New Year . . . . (hah-shah-nah) (rohsh) רֹאשׁ הַשָּׁנָה
very much . . . . (rah-bah) רַבָּה
rabbi . . . . (rahv) רַב
a quarter . . . . (rev-ah) רֶבַע
a quarter to . . . . (lif-nay) (rev-ah) רֶבַע לִפְנֵי
radio . . . . (rahd-yoh) רַדְיוֹ
radical . . . . (rah-dee-kahl-ee) רַדִיקָלִי
wind . . . . (roo-aH) רוּחַ
zipper . . . . (roH-sahn) רוֹכְסָן
romantic . . . . (roh-mahn-tee) רוֹמַנְטִי
Russian . . . . (roo-see) רוּסִי
Russia . . . . (roos-yah) רוּסְיָה
doctor . . . . (roh-fay) רוֹפֵא
dentist . . . . (roh-fay-shih-nah-yim) רוֹפֵא שִׁינַיים
want . . . . (roht-seh) רוֹצֶה
street . . . . (ruh-Hohv) רְחוֹב
wet . . . . (rah-tohv) רָטוֹב
jam . . . . (ree-bah) רִיבָּה

empty	(rake)	רֵיק
train	(rah-kev-et)	רַכֶּבֶת
Ramadan	(rah-mah-dahn)	רַמַדָן
traffic lights	(rahm-zoh-reem)	רַמְזוֹרִים
bad	(rah)	רַע
hungry	(rah-ev)	רָעֵב
rational	(rah-tsee-oh-nah-lee)	רַצִיוֹנָלִי
only	(rahk)	רַק
just a minute	(reh-gah) (rahk)	רַק רֶגַע
dancer	(rahk-dahn)	רַקְדָן

ש

question	(shuh-eh-lah)	שְׁאֵלָה
questions	(shuh-eh-laht)	שְׁאֵלוֹת
Sabbath	(shah-baht)	שַׁבָּת
Good Sabbath	(shah-lohm) (shah-baht)	שַׁבָּת שָׁלוֹם
Swedish	(shveh-dee)	שְׁבֵדִי
Sweden	(shved-ee-yah)	שְׁבֵדִיָה
path	(shveel)	שְׁבִיל
week	(shah-voo-ah)	שָׁבוּעַ
magazine	(shuh-voo-ohn)	שְׁבוּעוֹן
Pentecost	(shah-voo-oht)	שָׁבוּעוֹת
seven	(sheh-vah)	שֶׁבַע
seventeen	(es-ray) (shvah)	שְׁבַע עֶשְׂרֵה
seventy	(sheev-eem)	שִׁבְעִים
Switzerland	(shvit-zah-ree-yah)	שְׁוֵיצַרְיָה
policeman	(shoh-tair)	שׁוֹטֵר
table	(shool-Hahn)	שֻׁלְחָן
desk	(ktee-vah) (shool-Hahn)	שֻׁלְחָן כְּתִיבָה
judge	(shoh-fet)	שׁוֹפֵט
market	(shook)	שׁוּק
carpet	(shah-tee-aH)	שָׁטִיחַ
black	(shah-Hor)	שָׁחוֹר
shared taxi	(sheh-root)	שֵׁירוּת
toilet	(shay-roo-teem)	שֵׁירוּתִים
sixty	(shih-sheem)	שִׁשִׁים
of	(shel)	שֶׁל
snow	(shel-eg)	שֶׁלֶג
good day/hello/peace	(shah-lohm)	שָׁלוֹם
three	(shah-lohsh)	שָׁלוֹשׁ
thirteen	(es-ray) (shlohsh)	שְׁלוֹשׁ עֶשְׂרֵה
thirty	(shloh-sheem)	שְׁלוֹשִׁים
my	(sheh-lee)	שֶׁלִי
your	(shel-Hah)	שֶׁלְךָ
there	(shahm)	שָׁם
there is... over there	(yesh) (shahm)	שָׁם יֵשׁ
name	(shem)	שֵׁם
to the left	(smoh-lah)	שְׂמֹאלָה
her name is	(shmah)	שְׁמָה
his name is	(shmoh)	שְׁמוֹ
eighty	(shmoh-neem)	שְׁמוֹנִים
eight	(shmoh-neh)	שְׁמוֹנֶה
eighteen	(es-ray) (shmoh-neh)	שְׁמוֹנֶה עֶשְׂרֵה
names	(sheh-moht)	שֵׁמוֹת
my name (is)	(shmee)	שְׁמִי
your name is (♀)	(shim-Hah)	שְׁמֵךְ
your name is (♂)	(sh'meyH)	שְׁמֵךְ
my name is	(shmee)	שְׁמִי
sun	(sheh-mesh)	שֶׁמֶשׁ
year	(shah-nah)	שָׁנָה
Happy New Year	(toh-vah) (shah-nah)	שָׁנָה טוֹבָה
clock	(shah-ohn)	שָׁעוֹן

wristwatch	(yahd) (shuh-ohn)	שְׁעוֹן יָד
alarm clock	(muh-oh-reer) (shah-ohn)	שְׁעוֹן מְעוֹרֵר
gate	(shah-ar)	שַׁעַר
shekel, unit of Israeli money	(shek-el)	שֶׁקֶל
six	(shesh)	שֵׁשׁ
sixteen	(es-ray) (shesh)	שֵׁשׁ עֶשְׂרֵה
two	(shtah-yeem)	שְׁתַּיִם
twelve	(es-ray) (shtem)	שְׁתֵּים עֶשְׂרֵה

ש

field	(sah-deh)	שָׂדֶה
airport	(too-fah) (sday)	שְׂדֵה תְעוּפָה
bush	(see-aH)	שִׂיחַ
a call	(see-Hah)	שִׂיחָה
conversations	(see-Hoht)	שִׂיחוֹת
telephone conversation	(teh-leh-fohn) (see-Haht)	שִׂיחַת טֶלֶפוֹן
left	(smohl)	שְׂמֹאל
Festival of the Torah	(toh-rah) (sim-Haht)	שִׂמְחַת תוֹרָה
blanket	(smee-Hah)	שְׂמִיכָה
dress	(sim-lah)	שִׂמְלָה
language	(sah-fah)	שָׂפָה
seaside	(hah-yahm) (s'faht)	שְׂפַת הַיָם

ת

tea	(tay)	תֵה
thank you	(toh-dah)	תוֹדָה
Torah	(toh-rah)	תוֹרָה
Turkish	(toor-kee)	תוּרְכִּי
Turkey	(toor-kee-yah)	תוּרְכִּיָה
strawberries, field berries	(sah-deh) (toot)	תוּת שָׂדֶה
station	(tah-Hah-naht)	תַחֲנָה
bus station	(oh-toh-boos) (tah-Hah-naht)	תַחֲנַת אוֹטוֹבּוּס
gas station	(del-ek) (tah-Hah-naht)	תַחֲנַת דֶלֶק
sherut stop	(shay-root) (tah-Hah-naht)	תַחֲנַת שֵׁירוּת
police station	(mish-tah-rah) (tah-Hah-naht)	תַחֲנַת מִשְׁטָרָה
train station	(rah-kev-et) (tah-Hah-naht)	תַחֲנַת רַכֶּבֶת
underpants	(taH-toh-neem)	תַחְתוֹנִים
slip	(taH-toh-neet)	תַחְתוֹנִית
theater	(tay-ah-trohn)	תִיאַטְרוֹן
mailbox	(doh-ar) (tay-vaht)	תֵיבַת דוֹאַר
handbag	(teek)	תִיק
tourist	(tah-yar)	תַיָר
jewelry	(taH-shee-teem)	תַכְשִׁיטִים
Tel Aviv	(ah-veev) (tel)	תֵל אָבִיב
picture	(tmoo-nah)	תְמוּנָה
date, palm tree	(tah-mar)	תָמָר
signpost	(tahm-roor)	תַמְרוּר
give me	(lee) (ten)	תֵן לִי
stove	(tah-noor)	תַנוּר
orange	(tah-poo-zeem)	תַפּוּזִים
apple	(tah-poo-aH)	תַפּוּחַ
occupied, busy	(tah-foos)	תָפוּס
menu	(tahf-reet)	תַפְרִיט
photograph	(tahts-loom)	תַצְלוּם
medicine	(troo-fah)	תְרוּפָה
turkey	(hoh-doo) (tar-nuh-gohl)	תַרְנְגוֹל הוֹדוּ
answers	(t'shoo-voht)	תְשׁוּבוֹת
nine	(tay-shah)	תֵשַׁע
nineteen	(es-ray) (tay-shah)	תְשַׁע עֶשְׂרֵה
ninety	(tee-sheem)	תִשְׁעִים

This beverage guide is intended to explain the variety of beverages available to you while בְּיִשְׂרָאֵל . It is by no means complete. Some of the experimenting has been left up to you, but this should get you started.

◄מַשְׁקָאוֹת חַמִּים (hot beverages)

coffee	קָפֶּה►
coffee with cream	קָפֶּה הָפוּךְ
iced coffee	קָפֶּה קַר
black coffee	קָפֶּה שָׁחוֹר
Turkish coffee	קָפֶּה טוּרְקִי
espresso	אֶסְפְּרֶסוֹ

The coffee house is an institution in Israel. Sit outside at one of the sidewalk cafes and sample one of the many varieties of coffee.

tea	תֶּה►
tea with milk	תֶּה עִם חָלָב
tea with lemon	תֶּה עִם לִימוֹן
hot chocolate	קָקָאוֹ

◄מַשְׁקָאוֹת חֲרִיפִים (alcohol)

A variety of liqueurs and brandies is available in Israel, including local brands.

brandy, cognac	קוֹנְיָאק►
Carmel Mizrahi 777	שֶׁבַע - שֶׁבַע - שֶׁבַע

Israel produces a delicious orange and chocolate-flavored liqueur called סַבְּרָה. The name "sabra" also refers to a person born and raised in Israel.

gin	גִ׳ין►
gin and tonic	גִ׳ין וְטוֹנִיק
whiskey	וִיסְקִי
whiskey soda	וִיסְקִי עִם סוֹדָה
vodka	וֹדְקָה
neat	נָקִי
on the rocks	עִם קֶרַח
double	כָּפוּל

◄מַשְׁקָאוֹת קָרִים (cold beverages)

mineral water	מַיִם מִינֶרָלִיִּים►
soda water	סוֹדָה
lemonade	לִימוֹנָדָה
orangeade	אוֹרַנְגְ׳דָה
fruit syrup with soda water	גָּזוֹז
sweet fruit syrup	גָּזוֹז מָתוֹק
sour fruit syrup	גָּזוֹז חָמוּץ
milk	חָלָב
milk shake	מִילְק שֵׁיק

◄מַשְׁקָאוֹת חֲרִיפִים (fruit juice)

Israel is famous for its oranges. You can buy a glass of freshly-squeezed orange juice from street vendors. It's delicious!

orange juice	מִיץ תַּפּוּזִים►
pineapple juice	מִיץ אֲנָנָס
grapefruit juice	מִיץ אֶשְׁכּוֹלִיּוֹת
lemon juice	מִיץ לִימוֹן
apricot juice	מִיץ מִשְׁמֵשִׁים
tomato juice	מִיץ עַגְבָנִיּוֹת

◄יַיִן (wine)

Israel has several wine-growing regions, which produce a variety of excellent white, rosé and red wines.

red	אָדוֹם►
white	לָבָן
rosé	רוֹזֶה
dry	יָבֵשׁ
sweet	מָתוֹק
sparkling	תּוֹסֵס

◄בִּירָה (beer)

If you are visiting during the summer, you'll want to visit the street-side beer stalls.

beer	בִּירָה►
malt beer	בִּירָה שְׁחוֹרָה

הַתַּפְרִיט
the menu

כְּלָלִי
general

רִבָּה	jam
גֶ'לִי	jelly
דְּבַשׁ	honey
מֶלַח	salt
פִּלְפֵּל	pepper
חֹמֶץ	vinegar
חַרְדָּל	mustard
שֶׁמֶן	oil
קֶטְשׁוּפ	ketchup
גְּבִינָה	cheese
זֵיתִים	olives
שֶׁמֶן זַיִת	olive oil
נַקְנִיק	sausage
עוּגָה	cake
גְּלִידָה	ice cream
קֶצֶפֶת	whipped cream
סֶנְדְוִיצִ'ים	sandwiches
פַּנְקֵיקִים	pancakes
הַמְבּוּרְגֶּר	hamburger
צִ'יפְּס	french fries (chips)
פּוֹפְּקוֹרְן	popcorn
אִטְרִיּוֹת	noodles
אֹרֶז	rice

יְרָקוֹת
vegetables

קִישׁוּאִים	zucchini
כְּרוּבִית	cauliflower
כְּרוּב	cabbage
אַסְפָּרָגוּס	asparagus
קוֹלְרַבִּי	kohlrabi
מְלָפְפוֹנִים	cucumber
עַגְבָנִיּוֹת	tomatoes
חֲצִילִים	eggplant
שְׁעוּעִית	beans
תֶּרֶד	spinach
אֲבוֹקָדוֹ	avocado

בְּתֵאָבוֹן!
(buh-tay-ah-vohn)
enjoy your meal

עוֹף
poultry

עוֹף	chicken
עוֹף מְמֻלָּא	stuffed chicken
כָּבֵד עוֹף	chicken liver
תַּרְנְגוֹל הֹדוּ	turkey
שְׁנִיצֶל הֹדוּ	turkey schnitzel
אַוָּז	goose

קִנּוּחִים
desserts

שְׁטְרוּדֶל	strudel
גְּלִידָה	ice-cream
פּוּדִינְג	pudding
מוּס מוֹקָה	mocha mousse
מוּס שׁוֹקוֹלָד	chocolate mousse
קְרֶם בָּוַורְיָה	Bavarian cream
קְרֶם קָרָמֶל	creme caramel
תּוּתִים וְקֶצֶפֶת	strawberries and cream
טוֹרְט	torte
עוּגַת פֵּרוֹת	fruit cake
בַּקְלָוָה	baklava
עוּגִיּוֹת	cookies

Israeli/Middle Eastern Specialties

חוּמוּס	humus
טְחִינָה	tehina
עֲלֵי גֶּפֶן	stuffed vine leaves
קוּסְקוּס	couscous
פָלָאפֶל	falafel
לֶבֶּן	sour milk, assorted flavors
יוֹגוּרְט	yoghurt

מְנוֹת רֹאשׁוֹנוֹת — appetizers

mushrooms in sour cream	פִּטְרִיּוֹת בְּשַׁמֶּנֶת
olives	זֵיתִים
stuffed tomatoes	עַגְבָנִיּוֹת מְמֻלָּאוֹת
eggs in mayonnaise	בֵּיצִים בְּמָיוֹנֶז
herring	דָּג מָלוּחַ
sardines	סַרְדִּינִים

מְרָקים — soups

clear broth	מָרָק צַח
vegetable soup	מְרַק יְרָקוֹת
onion soup	מְרַק בָּצָל
meat soup	מְרַק בָּשָׂר
chicken soup	מְרַק עוֹף
cream of chicken soup	מְרַק עוֹף מְרֻסָּק
tomato soup	מְרַק עַגְבָנִיּוֹת
bean soup	מְרַק שְׁעוּעִית
pea soup	מְרַק אֲפוּנָה
lentil soup	מְרַק עֲדָשִׁים
mushroom soup	מְרַק פִּטְרִיּוֹת
borscht	בּוֹרְשְׁט

דָּגים — fish dishes

carp	קַרְפְּיוֹן
trout	פּוֹרֵל
hake	בָּקָלָה
filet	פִילֶה
gefilte fish	דָּג מְמֻלָּא
tuna	טוּנָה
sardines	סַרְדִּינִים

FOLD HERE

לֶחֶם — bread

white bread	לֶחֶם לָבָן
rye bread	לֶחֶם שִׁיפוֹן
grain bread	לֶחֶם דָּגָן
black bread	לֶחֶם שָׁחוֹר
baguette	בָּגֵט
rolls	לַחְמָנִיּוֹת
challah (braided egg bread)	חַלָּה
pita (flat pocket bread)	פִּיתָה

בֵּיצים — eggs

soft egg	בֵּיצָה רַכָּה
hard egg	בֵּיצָה קָשָׁה
fried egg	בֵּיצַת עַיִן
omelette	חֲבִיתָה
scrambled eggs	בֵּיצִים מְקֻשְׁקָשׁוֹת

בָּשָׂר — meat dishes

veal schnitzel	שְׁנִיצֶל עֵגֶל
shashlik	שַׁשְׁלִיק
kebab	קֵבָּב
shawarmah	שַׁוַּארְמָה
lamb ribs	צַלְעוֹת כֶּבֶשׂ
tongue	לָשׁוֹן
liver	כָּבֵד
goulash	גּוּלָאשׁ
meatballs	קְצִיצוֹת
sausages	נַקְנִיקִיּוֹת
steak	סְטֵייק

FOLD HERE

סָלָטים — salads

cucumber salad	סְלַט מְלָפְפוֹנִים
eggplant salad	סְלַט חֲצִילִים
green salad	סְלַט יָרוֹק
tomato salad	סְלַט עַגְבָנִיּוֹת
beetroot salad	סְלַט סֶלֶק
coleslaw	סְלַט כְּרוּב
carrot salad	סְלַט גֶּזֶר
potato salad	סְלַט תַּפּוּחֵי אֲדָמָה

פֵּירוֹת — fruit

apples	תַּפּוּחִים
pears	אַגָּסִים
apricots	מִשְׁמְשִׁים
peaches	אֲפַרְסְקִים
bananas	בָּנָנוֹת
strawberries	תּוּתִים
kumquats	קֻמְקְוָטִים
guavas	גּוּיָבוֹת
figs	תְּאֵנִים
pomegranates	רִמּוֹנִים
grapes	עֲנָבִים
plums	שְׁזִיפִים
oranges	תַּפּוּזִים
grapefruit	אֶשְׁכּוֹלִיּוֹת
mandarin oranges	מַנְדָּרִינוֹת
dates	תְּמָרִים
nuts	אֱגוֹזִים
cantaloupe	מֶלוֹן
watermelon	אֲבַטִּיחִים

(ah-nee) אֲנִי	*(hoo)* הוּא
(hee) הִיא	*(ah-naH-noo)* אֲנַחְנוּ
(ah-tah) 🧍 אַתָּה *(aht)* 🧍‍♀️ אַתְּ	*(hem)* הֵם
🧍 *(muh-vah-kesh)* מְבַקֵשׁ 🧍‍♀️ *(muh-vah-kesh-et)* מְבַקֶשֶׁת } *(ah-nee)* אֲנִי	🧍 *(koh-neh)* קוֹנֶה 🧍‍♀️ *(koh-nah)* קוֹנָה } *(ah-nee)* אֲנִי
🧍 *(loh-med)* לוֹמֵד 🧍‍♀️ *(loh-med-et)* לוֹמֶדֶת } *(ah-nee)* אֲנִי	🧍 *(Hoh-zair)* *(ahl)* חוֹזֵר עַל 🧍‍♀️ *(Hoh-zair-et)* *(ahl)* חוֹזֶרֶת עַל } *(ah-nee)* אֲנִי
🧍 *(may-veen)* מֵבִין 🧍‍♀️ *(muh-vee-nah)* מְבִינָה } *(ah-nee)* אֲנִי	🧍 *(muh-dah-bair)* מְדַבֵּר 🧍‍♀️ *(muh-dah-bair-et)* מְדַבֶּרֶת } *(ah-nee)* אֲנִי

he	I
we	she
they	you
I buy	I order
I repeat	I learn
I speak	I understand

(ah-nee) אֲנִי	(nish-ar) נִשְׁאָר ♂ (nish-air-et) נִשְׁאֶרֶת ♀	(ah-nee) אֲנִי	(mah-gee-ah) מַגִּיעַ ♂ (mah-gee-ah) מַגִּיעָה ♀
(ah-nee) אֲנִי	(roh-eh) רוֹאֶה ♂ (roh-ah) רוֹאָה ♀	(ah-nee) אֲנִי	(oh-mair) אוֹמֵר ♂ (oh-mair-et) אוֹמֶרֶת ♀
(ah-nee) אֲנִי	(lah) (muh-Hah-keh) מְחַכֶּה לְ ♂ (leh) (muh-Hah-kaht) מְחַכָּה לְ ♀	(ah-nee) אֲנִי	(muh-Hah-pes) מְחַפֵּשׂ ♂ (muh-Hah-pes-et) מְחַפֶּשֶׂת ♀
(ah-nee) אֲנִי	(oh-Hel) אוֹכֵל ♂ (oh-Hel-et) אוֹכֶלֶת ♀	(ah-nee) אֲנִי	(shoh-teh) שׁוֹתֶה ♂ (shoh-tah) שׁוֹתָה ♀
(ah-nee) אֲנִי	(roht-seh) רוֹצֶה ♂ (roht-sah) רוֹצָה ♀	(ah-nee) אֲנִי	(tsah-reeH) צָרִיךְ ♂ (ts'reH-ah) צְרִיכָה ♀
	(shmee) שְׁמִי ...		(yesh) (lee) יֵשׁ לִי

I arrive	I stay
I say	I see
I look for	I wait for
I drink	I eat
I need	I want
I have . . .	my name is . . .

Hebrew (male/female)	Pronoun
(moh-Hair) מוֹכֵר 👨 / *(moh-Her-et)* מוֹכֶרֶת 👩	אֲנִי *(ah-nee)*
(shoh-lay-aH) שׁוֹלֵחַ 👨 / *(shoh-laH-aht)* שׁוֹלַחַת 👩	אֲנִי *(ah-nee)*
(yah-shen) יָשֵׁן 👨 / *(yuh-shen-ah)* יְשֵׁנָה 👩	אֲנִי *(ah-nee)*
(muh-tahl-pane) מְטַלְפֵּן לְ *(luh)* 👨 / *(muh-tahl-pen-et)* מְטַלְפֶּנֶת לְ *(luh)* 👩	אֲנִי *(ah-nee)*
תֵּן *(ten)* לִי *(lee)*	
(koh-tev) כּוֹתֵב 👨 / *(koh-tev-et)* כּוֹתֶבֶת 👩	אֲנִי *(ah-nee)*
(bah) בָּא 👨 / *(bah-ah)* בָּאָה 👩	אֲנִי *(ah-nee)*
(muh-shah-lem) מְשַׁלֵם 👨 / *(muh-shah-lem-et)* מְשַׁלֶמֶת 👩	אֲנִי *(ah-nee)*
(yoh-day-ah) יוֹדֵעַ 👨 / *(yoh-dah-aht)* יוֹדַעַת 👩	אֲנִי *(ah-nee)*
(yah-Hohl) יָכוֹל 👨 / *(yuh-Hoh-lah)* יְכוֹלָה 👩	אֲנִי *(ah-nee)*
(koh-ray) קוֹרֵא 👨 / *(koh-ret)* קוֹרֵאת 👩	אֲנִי *(ah-nee)*
(noh-seh-ah) נוֹסֵעַ 👨 / *(noh-sah-aht)* נוֹסַעַת 👩	אֲנִי *(ah-nee)*

I send	I sell
I phone	I sleep
I write	give me . . .
I pay	I come
I am able to/I can	I know
I travel	I read

♂ טָס *(tahs)* ♀ טָסָה *(tah-sah)* } אֲנִי *(ah-nee)*	♂ יוֹצֵא *(yoh-tseh)* ♀ יוֹצֵאת *(yoh-tset)* } אֲנִי *(ah-nee)*
♂ יוֹרֵד *(yoh-red)* ♀ יוֹרֶדֶת *(yoh-red-et)* } אֲנִי *(ah-nee)*	♂ עוֹלֶה *(oh-leh)* ♀ עוֹלָה *(oh-lah)* } אֲנִי *(ah-nee)*
♂ אוֹרֵז *(oh-rez)* ♀ אוֹרֶזֶת *(oh-rez-et)* } אֲנִי *(ah-nee)*	*(mah-gee-ah)* *(hah-oh-toh-boos)* הָאוֹטוֹבּוּס מַגִּיעַ
(yoh-tseh) *(hah-oh-toh-boos)* הָאוֹטוֹבּוּס יוֹצֵא	♂ מַזְמִין *(mahz-meen)* ♀ מַזְמִינָה *(mahz-mee-nah)* } אֲנִי *(ah-nee)*
♂ נוֹהֵג *(noh-heg)* ♀ נוֹהֶגֶת *(noh-heg-et)* } אֲנִי *(ah-nee)*	♂ מְכַבֵּס *(muh-Hah-bes)* ♀ מְכַבֶּסֶת *(muh-Hah-bes-et)* } אֲנִי *(ah-nee)*
♂ צָרִיךְ *(tsah-reeH)* ♀ צְרִיכָה *(ts'reH-ah)* } אֲנִי *(ah-nee)*	*(loh-kay-aH)* *(zeh)* זֶה לוֹקֵחַ...

I leave	I fly
I board	I get off/disembark
the bus arrives	I pack
I reserve/order	the bus departs
I wash (clothes)	I drive
it takes	I must

(mah) *(shlohm-Hah)* ♂ ? מַה שְׁלוֹמְךָ *(shloh-mayH)* ♀ ? מַה שְׁלוֹמֵךְ	*(shah-lohm)* שָׁלוֹם
(bay-vah-kah-shah) בְּבַקָשָׁה	*(slee-Hah)* סְלִיחָה
(toh-dah) תּוֹדָה	*(hah-yohm)* הַיוֹם
(mah-Har) מָחָר	*(et-mohl)* אֶתְמוֹל
(kah-mah) *(zeh)* *(oh-leh)* ? כַּמָה זֶה עוֹלֶה	*(yesh)* *(luh-Hah)* ♂ ? ... יֵשׁ לְךָ *(lahH)* ♀ ? ... יֵשׁ לָךְ
(pah-too-aH) *(sah-goor)* → פָּתוּחַ - סָגוּר	*(gah-dohl)* *(kah-tahn)* → גָּדוֹל - קָטָן

hello/goodbye	How are you?
excuse me	please/ you're welcome
today	thank-you
yesterday	tomorrow
Do you have . . .?	How much does this cost?
big - small	open - closed

(Hoh-leh) ... *(bah-ree)* חוֹלֶה - בָּרִיא ←	*(rah)* ... *(tohv)* טוֹב - רָע ←
(kar) ... *(Hahm)* חַם - קַר ←	*(ah-roH)* ... *(kah-tsar)* קָצָר - אָרוֹךְ ←
(nah-mooH) ... *(gah-voh-hah)* גָבוֹהַ ← - נָמוּךְ	*(lah)* ... *(mee-tah-Haht)* ... *(lah)* ... *(may-ahl)* מֵעַל ל - מִתַחַת ל ←
(yah-meen) ... *(smohl)* שְׂמֹאל - יָמִין ←	*(mah-hair)* ... *(luh-aht)* לְאַט - מַהֵר
(tsah-eer) ... *(zah-ken)* זָקֵן - צָעִיר ←	*(zohl)* ... *(yah-kar)* יָקָר - זוֹל
(ah-nee) ... *(ah-sheer)* עָשִׁיר - עָנִי ←	*(muh-aht)* ... *(har-bay)* הַרְבֵּה - מְעַט ←

good - bad	healthy - sick
short - long	hot - cold
above - below	tall - short
slow - fast	left - right
expensive - inexpensive	old - young
a lot - a little	rich - poor

Now that
you've finished...

You've done it!

You've completed all the Steps, stuck your labels, flashed your cards and cut out your menu guide. Do you realize how far you've come and how much you've learned?

You can now confidently

- ask questions,
- understand directions,
- make reservations,
- order food and
- shop anywhere.

And you can do it all in a foreign language! You can now go anywhere — from a large cosmopolitan restaurant to a small, out-of-the-way village where no one speaks English. Your experiences will be much more enjoyable and worry-free now that you speak the language.

Yes, learning a foreign language can be fun.

Kristine Kershul

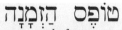

טוֹפֶס הַזְמָנָה
order form

10 minutes a day® Series	QTY.	PRICE	TOTAL
ARABIC in 10 minutes a day®		$19.95	
CHINESE in 10 minutes a day®		$19.95	
FRENCH in 10 minutes a day®		$19.95	
GERMAN in 10 minutes a day®		$19.95	
HEBREW in 10 minutes a day®		$19.95	
INGLÉS en 10 minutos al día®		$19.95	
ITALIAN in 10 minutes a day®		$19.95	
JAPANESE in 10 minutes a day®		$19.95	
NORWEGIAN in 10 minutes a day®		$19.95	
PORTUGUESE in 10 minutes a day®		$18.95	
RUSSIAN in 10 minutes a day®		$19.95	
SPANISH in 10 minutes a day®		$18.95	
10 minutes a day® AUDIO CD	**QTY.**	**PRICE**	**TOTAL**
FRENCH in 10 minutes a day® AUDIO CD		$59.95	
FRENCH AUDIO CDs only (no book)		$42.95	
GERMAN in 10 minutes a day® AUDIO CD		$59.95	Available
GERMAN AUDIO CDs only (no book)		$42.95	Fall 2006
ITALIAN in 10 minutes a day® AUDIO CD		$59.95	
ITALIAN AUDIO CDs only (no book)		$42.95	
SPANISH in 10 minutes a day® AUDIO CD		$59.95	
SPANISH AUDIO CDs only (no book)		$42.95	
Language Map® Series	**QTY.**	**PRICE**	**TOTAL**
ARABIC a language map®		$7.95	
CHINESE a language map®		$7.95	
FRENCH a language map®		$7.95	
GERMAN a language map®		$7.95	
GREEK a language map®		$7.95	
HAWAIIAN a language map®		$7.95	
HEBREW a language map®		$7.95	
INGLÉS un mapa del lenguaje®		$7.95	
ITALIAN a language map®		$7.95	
JAPANESE a language map®		$7.95	
NORWEGIAN a language map®		$7.95	
POLISH a language map®		$7.95	
PORTUGUESE a language map®		$7.95	
RUSSIAN a language map®		$7.95	
SPANISH a language map®		$7.95	
VIETNAMESE a language map®		$7.95	

Item Total	
** Shipping	+
Total	
† Sales Tax	+
ORDER TOTAL	

† For delivery to individuals in Washington State, you must add 8.8% sales tax on the item total and the shipping costs combined. If your order is being delivered outside Washington State, you do not need to add sales tax.

Name _____

Address _____

City _____ State _____ Zip _____

Day Phone (_____)_____

❏ My check or money order for $_____ is enclosed.
   Please make checks and money orders payable to Bilingual Books, Inc.

❏ Bill my credit card ❏ VISA ❏ MC ❏ AMEX

   No. _____ Exp. date ____/____

   Signature _____

Bilingual Books, Inc. • 1719 West Nickerson Street
Seattle, WA 98119 USA

10 minutes a day® AUDIO CD Series

by Kristine K. Kershul

The *10 minutes a day*® **AUDIO CD Series** is based on the immensely successful *10 minutes a day*® Series. Millions of people around the world have used the *10 minutes a day*® Series for over two decades.

• Eight hours of personal instruction on six CDs.

• Use the CDs in combination with the companion book, and maximize your progress as you see AND hear the language.

• Listen to native speakers and practice right along with them.

• Suitable for the classroom, the homeschooler, as well as business and leisure travelers.

• The CDs in the *10 minutes a day*® **AUDIO CD Series** may also be purchased separately from the *10 minutes a day*® books.

Language Map® Series

by Kristine K. Kershul

These handy *Language Maps*® provide the essential words and phrases to cover the basics for any trip.

• Over 1,000 essential words and phrases divided into convenient categories.

• Laminated , folding design allows for quicker reference while resisting spills, tearing, and damage from frequent use.

• Durable, to hold up to being sat on, dropped, and stuffed into backpacks, pockets, and purses.

• An absolute must for anyone traveling abroad or studying at home.

For a list of available languages and ordering information, please see the order form on the previous page.